Operating Systems

OPERATING SYSTEMS

Ritu Choudhary

CENTRUM PRESS
NEW DELHI-110002 (INDIA)

CENTRUM PRESS

H.O.: 4360/4, Ansari Road, Daryaganj,
New Delhi-110002 (India)
Tel: 23278000, 23261597, 23255577, 23286875

B.O.: No. 1015, Ist Main Road, BSK IIIrd Stage,
IIIrd Phase, IIIrd Block, Bangalore-560085 (INDIA)
Tel: 080-41723429

Email: centrumpress@gmail.com
Visit us at: www.centrumpress.com

Operating Systems

First Edition, 2011

PRINTED IN INDIA

Printed at Tarun Offset Printers, Delhi-110053

Contents

Preface

Operating Systems are resource managers. The main resource is computer hardware in the form of processors, storage, input/output devices, communication devices, and data. Some of the operating system functions are: implementing the user interface, sharing hardware among users, allowing users to share data among themselves, preventing users from interfering with one another, scheduling resources among users, facilitating input/output, recovering from errors, accounting for resource usage, facilitating parallel operations, organizing data for secure and rapid access, and handling network communications.

Controlling the computer involves software at several levels. We will differentiate kernel services, library services, and application-level services, all of which are part of the operating system. Processes run Applications, which are linked together with libraries that perform standard services. The kernel supports the processes by providing a path to the peripheral devices. The kernel responds to service calls from the processes and interrupts from the devices. The core of the operating system is the kernel, a control program that functions in privileged state (an execution context that allows all hardware instructions to be executed), reacting to interrupts from external devices and to service requests and traps from processes. Generally, the kernel is a permanent resident of the computer. It creates and terminates processes and responds to their request for service.

Author

1

Introduction

COMPUTER SYSTEM

OVERVIEW

A computer is a device that accepts information (in the form of digitalized data) and manipulates it for some result based on a programme or sequence of instructions on how the data is to be processed. Complex computers also include the means for storing data (including the programme, which is also a form of data) for some necessary duration. A programme may be invariable and built into the computer (and called *logic circuitry* as it is on microprocessors) or different programs may be provided to the computer (loaded into its storage and then started by an administrator or user). Today's computers have both kinds of programming.

Most histories of the modern computer begin with the Analytical Engineen visioned by Charles Babbage following the mathematical ideas of George Boole, the mathematician who first stated the principles of logic inherent in today's digital computer. Babbage's assistant and collaborator, Ada Lovelace, is said to have introduced the ideas of programme loops and subroutines and is sometimes considered the first programmer. Apart from mechanical calculators, the first really useable computers began with the vacuum tube, accelerated with the invention of the transistor, which then became embedded in large numbers in integrated circuits, ultimately making possible the relatively low-cost personal computer.

Modern computers inherently follow the ideas of the stored programme laid out byJohn von Neumann in 1945. Essentially, the programme is read by the computer one instruction at a time, an operation is performed, and the computer then reads in the next instruction, and so on. Recently, computers and programs have been devised that allow multiple programs (and computers) to work on the same problem at the same time in parallel. With the advent of the Internet and higher bandwidth data transmission, programs and data that are part of the same overall project can be distributed over a network and embody the Sun Microsystems slogan: "The network is the computer."

Technically, a computer is a programmable machine. This means it can execute a programmed list of instructions and respond to new instructions that it is given. Today, however, the term is most often used to refer to the desktop and laptop computers that most people use. When referring to a desktop model, the term "computer" technically only refers to the computer itself—not the monitor, keyboard, and mouse. Still, it is acceptable to refer to everything together as the computer. If you want to be really technical, the box that holds the computer is called the "system unit."

Some of the major parts of a personal computer (or PC) include the motherboard, CPU, memory (or RAM), hard drive, and video card. While personal computers are by far the most common type of computers today, there are several other types of computers. For example, a "minicomputer" is a powerful computer that can support many users at once. A "mainframe" is a large, high-powered computer that can perform billions of calculations from multiple sources at one time. Finally, a "supercomputer" is a machine that can process billions of instructions a second and is used to calculate extremely complex calculations.

Computers are not very intelligent devices, but they handle instructions flawlessly and fast. They must follow explicit directions from both the user and computer programmer. Computers are really nothing more than a very powerful calculator with some great accessories. Applications like word processing and games are just a very complex math problem. What a computer is in a specific, contemporary sense.Personal computers are found in most aspects of daily life, and for some it is hard to even imagine a world without them. But the term *computer* means more than simply the Macs and PCs we are familiar with. A computer is, at its most basic, a machine which can take instructions, and perform computations based on those instructions.

It is the ability to take instructions — often known as programs in the parlance of computers — and execute them, that distinguishes a computer from a mechanical calculator. While both are able to make computations, a calculator responds simply to immediate input. In fact, most modern calculators are actually computers, with a number of pre-installed programs to help aid in complex tasks.

Computers range from the very small to the very large. Some are capable of doing millions of calculations in a single second, while others may take long periods of time to do even the most simple calculations. But theoretically, anything one computer is capable of doing, another computer will also be able to do. Given the right instructions, and sufficient memory, a computer found in a wristwatch should be able to accomplish anything a supercomputer can — although it might take thousands of years for the wristwatch to complete the operation.

PERSONAL COMPUTERS

Personal computers are computers that are meant to be used by individuals in homes or offices. Their retail prices, size, and capabilities make them practical for use in almost every home and office in the United States and other developed countries. The operation of personal computers relies on a small computer chip known as a microprocessor, which governs the functioning of the computer.

All personal computers have several basic components which allow the computer to function and be used. The microprocessor already mentioned oversees everything the computer does, and every process has to go through it first.

Personal computers also have memory, usually in the form of random-access memory (RAM). This type of memory is used to store information that the computer is currently working with, such as open programs.

The microprocessor and memory are contained as part of a large circuit board called the motherboard. The motherboard also acts as an intermediary between the microprocessor and other systems on the computer, such as drives and ports. The hard drive or hard disk is where programs and files are stored. As opposed to the RAM, the hard drive has a large capacity and is meant for long-term storage. This is where the majority of data in personal computers are located.

Another important part which is common to all personal computers is the power supply, which regulates the amount of electricity that the PC is using at a given time. Most personal computers also have sound cards and graphics cards as well. These are small circuit boards which connect to the motherboard to process audio and video data, respectively. More modern PCs also include a CD-ROM drive, where a compact disk containing programs or files can be inserted. Programs can be run directly from the CD-ROM, which acts as a form of external data storage for a PC.

Personal computers were first introduced on the market in the late 1970s. Their capabilities and speed left much to be desired in comparison with modern PCs, but because of the advancement they represented, their popularity grew quickly. PCs began to be developed for everyday household use. Computer games and programs were developed which could be used on household computers, further opening up the market for these devices. By the year 2002, one billion PCs had been sold worldwide, since they were first introduced.

PCS

PCS, or a personal communications service, is the designation for a portion of theradio frequency band that is devoted to the use of wireless phone service in the United States, Canada, and Mexico. Here is some background on the development of the concept of the PCS, and how PCS continues to function today.

Early in the development of cell phone technology, the need to assign particular bandwidths to the signals that would be used for cellular services was evident. To this end, the need to carve out a radio band that would be for the exclusive use of cellular wireless networks was studied. Ultimately, the conclusions of the FCC in the United States and Industry Canada was that the designation of the 1850-1990 MHz range for use with cellular telephone service would ensure there was no interference with frequencies that were used for public broadcast or governmental functions. During 1994, both countries established the 1900 MHz band as the standard for use in any wireless network based for service in the United States or Canada. This effectively created the first unified PCS on the market.

While this helped to ensure that the new technology did not interfere with other bandwidth uses, and also helped to make the process of interacting with a wired network easier, this did not address the issue of cellular phone interaction with European and Asian locations and services. Over time, the development of dual band phones that allowed for signals to be processed that would accommodate both North American standards and other worldwide standards to be compatible. Sometimes referred to as multi-band GSMsystems, many parts of the world now use PCS as a term to describe GSM services that operate in the 1900 MHz range.

SUPERCOMPUTER

A supercomputer is a computer which performs at a rate of speed which is far above that of other computers. Given the constantly changing world of computing, it should come as no surprise to learn that most supercomputers bear their superlative titles for a few years, at best. Computer programmers are fond of saying that today's supercomputer will become tomorrow's computer; the computer you are reading this article on is probably more powerful than most historic supercomputers, for example. The term "supercomputer" was coined in 1929 by the New York World, referring to tabulators manufactured by IBM. To modern computer users, these tabulators would probably appear awkward, slow, and cumbersome to use, but at the time, they represented the cutting edge of technology. This continues to be true of supercomputers today, which harness immense processing power so that they are incredibly fast, sophisticated, and powerful.

The primary use for supercomputers is in scientific computing, which requires high-powered computers to perform complex calculations. Scientific organizations like NASAboast supercomputers the size of rooms for the purpose of performing calculations, rendering complex formulas, and performing other tasks which require a formidable amount of computer power. Some supercomputers have also been designed for very specific functions like cracking codes and playing chess; Deep Blue is a famous chess-playing supercomputer.

In many cases, a supercomputer is custom-assembled, utilizing elements from a range of computer manufacturers and tailored for its intended use. Most supercomputers run on a Linux or Unix operating system, as these operating systems are extremely flexible, stable, and efficient. Supercomputers typically have multiple processors and a variety of other technological tricks to ensure that they run smoothly.

SOFTWARE AND HARDWARE

DESCRIPTION

Hardware and software work together in digital devices and systems to provide computerized functionality. Hardware includes the physical components, such as the motherboard, chips, memory, and hard drives, while software includes the programs that run on the hardware. Ergo, a computer is hardware, while anoperating system such as Microsoft XP is the software that makes the hardware functional. Though hardware and software are most often associated with computers, software also runs on other hardware, such as cellular phones, personal digital assistants (PDAs), Global Positioning Satellite (GPS) units,medical equipment, and air traffic control systems. Modern cash registers are also computerized with software to better organize sales-related issues likeinventory, tax, and coupon discounts.

Computer technology is employed in nearly every facet of modern society. Many software programs used in industry are proprietary, which means they are designed for a specific function. This differs from computers that are generally multi-purpose, with many different kinds of software programs for various tasks. Hardware and software are constantly improving in a kind of leapfrog fashion. Hardware is most often the bottleneck when it comes to data transfer speeds, or how fast a software programme can work. Therefore, as hardware improves, it becomes capable of running more robust software programs. Old hardware from just ten years ago may not run current software, as the software might be designed to take advantage of hardware in ways that older hardware cannot support.

INDUSTRY

The Computer Hardware and Software industry of Bangalore is regarded as the focal point of advanced technology that acts as the prime catalyst in the economic growth of the city. Housing the biggest international names of Information Technology, Bangalore is referred as the Silicon Valley of India.

With the widening of the global business horizon, Bangalore has emerged as the key player in the field of Information Technology and Information Technology enabled services. From proposed plans of Hardware Park to a thriving Business Process Outsourcing sector, Bangalore is progressing beyond leaps and bounds.

The city deals with the latest models of Hardware tools Computer parts, Software programmes and accessories. The newest developments in the Software programming domain enable Bangalore to compete with the best IT brands of the world. The major IT and ITes organizations of global repute that add credibility to the Computer Hardware and Software contours of Bangalore are:

- Microsoft Corporation
- IBM Global Services Ltd.
- Infosys Technologies Ltd.
- Intel Asia Electronics Inc.
- ITC Ltd. – Information Systems Div.
- Oracle Software (I) Ltd.
- SAP India Pvt. Ltd.
- Satyam Computer Services Ltd.
- Tata Consultancy Services
- Wipro Infotech Group
- Dell Asia Pacific SDN
- Citicorp
- CMC Ltd.
- Aptech Ltd.
- Compaq India
- Tata Infotech Ltd.
- Verifone
- TVS Electronics South Asia (P) Ltd.

The software a series of very simple computer instructions carefully organized to complete complex tasks. These instructions are written in programming languages (like BASIC, PASCAL, C.) to help simplify the development of applications. The hardware is what sits on your desk and executes the software instructions. The player piano is useless unless the roll of music has been written correctly.

HARDWARE COMPONENTS

Input Devices

A keyboard and mouse are the standard way to interact with the computer. Other devices include joysticks and game pads used primarily for games. A hardware device that sends information into the CPU. Without any input devices a computer would simply be a display device and not allow users to interact with it, much like a TV. Below is a listing of different types of computer input devices.

Digital Camera

A type of camera that stores the pictures or video it takes in electronic format instead of to film. There are several features that make digital cameras a popular choice when compared to film cameras. First, the feature often enjoyed the most is the LCD display on the digital camera. This display allows users to view photos or video after the picture or video has been taken, which means if you take a picture and don't like the results, you can delete it; or if you do like the picture, you can easily show it to other people. Another nice feature with digital cameras is the ability to take dozens, sometimes hundreds of different pictures.

Digital cameras have quickly become the camera solution for most users today as the quality of picture they take has greatly improved and as the price has decreased. Many users however are hesitant in buying a digital camera because of the inability of getting their pictures developed. However, there are several solutions in getting your digital pictures developed. For example, there are numerous Internet companies capable of developing your pictures and send you your pictures in the mail. In addition, many of the places that develop your standard cameras film now have the ability to develop digital pictures

Joystick

A peripheral input device that looks similar to a control

device you would find on an arcade game at your local arcades.

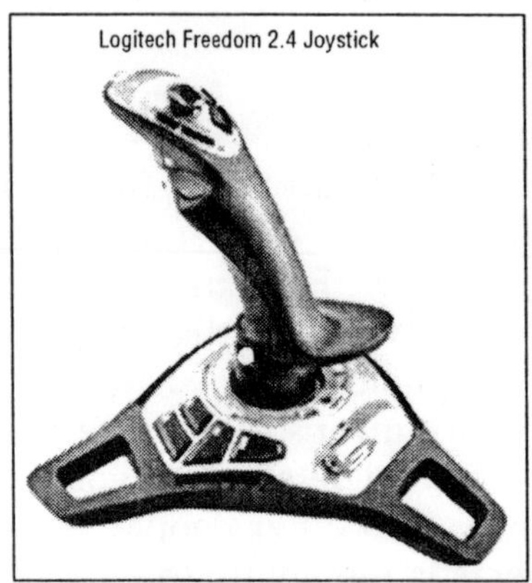
Logitech Freedom 2.4 Joystick

A computer joystick allows an individual to easily navigate an object in a game such as navigating a plane in a flight simulator. The image is of the Logitech Freedom 2.4 joystick and is an example of what you would expect most computer joysticks to look like.

Keyboard

One of the main input devices used on a computer, a PC's keyboard looks very similar to the keyboards of electric typewriters, with some additional keys. Below is a graphic of the Saitek Gamers' keyboard with indicators pointing to each of the major portions of the keyboard.

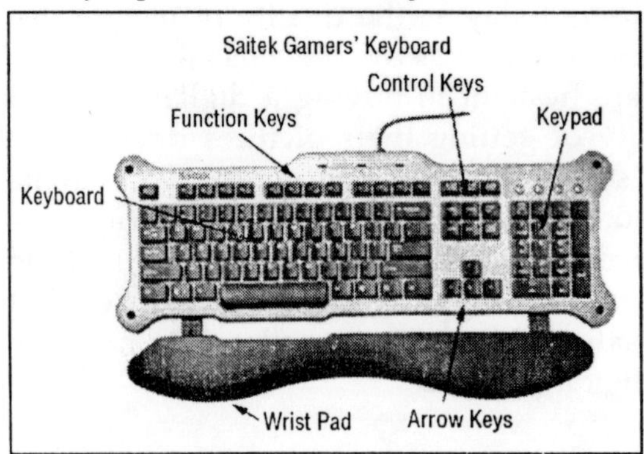

Saitek Gamers' Keyboard

Finally, today most users use the QWERTY style

keyboards. Below is a graphic illustration of where each of the keys are on a QWERTY style keyboard.

~ ` | ! 1 | @ 2 | # 3 | $ 4 | % 5 | ^ 6 | & 7 | * 8 | (9 |) 0 | _ - | + = | Delete
Tab | Q | W | E | R | T | Y | U | I | O | P | { [| }] | | \
Caps | A | S | D | F | G | H | J | K | L | : ; | " ' | Enter
Shift | Z | X | C | V | B | N | M | < , | > . | ? / | Shift
Ctrl | | Alt | | Alt | | Ctrl

Microphone

Sometimes abbreviated as mic, a microphone is a hardware peripheral that allows computer users to input audio into their computers. To the right is a visual example of a USB headset from Logitech with a microphone. A popular solution for computer gaming.

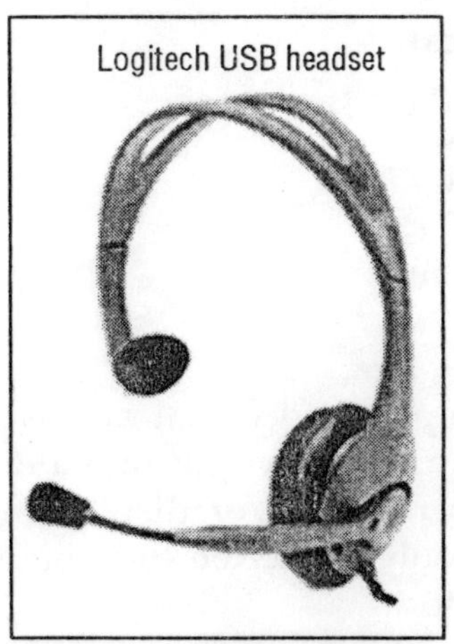
Logitech USB headset

Mouse

A hardware input device that was invented by Douglas Engelbart in 1963, who at the time was working at the Stanford Research Institute, which was a think tank sponsored by University. The mouse allows an individual to control a pointer in a graphical user interface (GUI). Utilizing a mouse a user has the ability to perform various functions such as opening a programme or file and does not require the user to memorize commands, like those used in a text-based command line environment such as MS-DOS.

The Mouse was originally referred to as an X-Y Position Indicator for a Display System. Xerox later applied the mouse to its revolutionary Alto computer system in 1973. However, because of Alto's unfortunate success, it was first widely used in the Apple Lisa computer. Today, the mouse is now found on virtually every computer.

Types of computer mouse:

- Cordless
- Footmouse
- Glidepoint
- IntelliMouse
- J mouse
- Joystick
- Mechanical
- Optical
- Touchpad
- Trackball
- TrackPoint
- Wheel mouse

Scanner

Hardware input device that allows a user to take an image and/or text and convert it into a digital file, allowing the computer to read and/or display the scanned object. A scanner commonly connected to a computer USB Firewire Parallel or SCSI port.

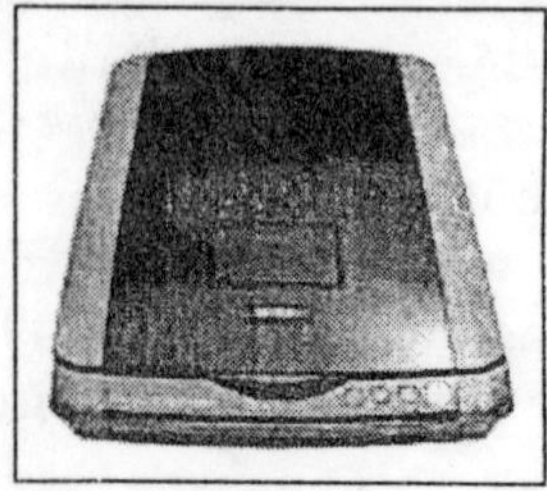

Web Cam

A camera connected to a computer or server that allows anyone connected to the Internet to view still pictures or motion video of a user. The majority of webcam web sites are still pictures that are frequently refreshed every few seconds, minutes, hours, or days. However, there are some sites and personal pages that can supply streaming video for users with broadband.

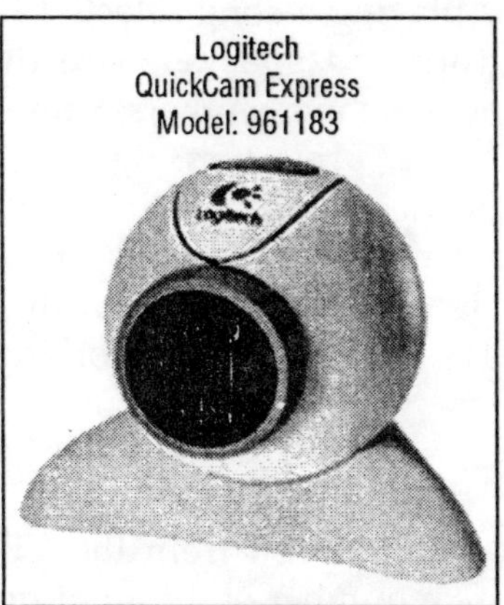

The image of the Logitech QuickCam Express and an example of what a webcam may look like. Today, most webcams are connected to the USB or Firewire port on a computer.

- There are millions of webcams around the world that allow you to view other people, places, and even events. If you're interested in looking at webcams.
- If you're looking to chat with other webcam users live a great site with millions of other webcam users is Stickam.
- Parents with children should be aware of the potential dangers of children and webcams. Additional information about protecting children from harmful material on the Internet can be found on document CH000526.
- Document CH000890 for additional information about users without webcams viewing users with webcams.

Output Devices

Any device that outputs information from a computer is called, not surprisingly, an output device. Since most information from a computer is output in either a visual or auditory format, the most common output devices are the monitor and speakers. These two devices provide instant feedback to the user's input, such as displaying characters as they are typed or playing a song selected from a playlist.

While monitors and speakers are the most common output devices, there are many others. Some examples include headphones, printers, projectors, lighting control systems, audio recording devices, and robotic machines. A computer without an output device connected to it is pretty useless, since the output is what we interact with. Anyone who has ever had a monitor or printer stop working knows just how true this is.

Printer

Printers take information from the CPU and transfer it to paper. There are a number of different printer technologies available.

Dot Matrix

Dot Matrix printers are inexpensive and reliable, but they are loud and slow. They do not have nearly the print quality of some of the other types of printers.

Ink Jet

Ink Jet printers squirt small streams of ink onto the paper. They tend to be slightly more expensive than dot matrix printers, but the quiet operation and improved print quality make them very popular with buyers of home computers. Some ink jet printers can make colour prints. These can be very entertaining, but the ink becomes expensive.

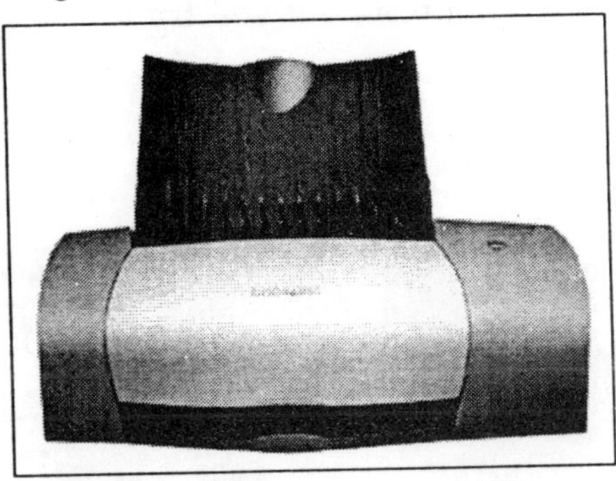

Laser Printers

Laser Printers use a combination of laser and copying technology to make very clear copies. Laser printers tend to make clearer copies than the other types of printers, and operate much more quickly, but they can be quite expensive to purchase and maintain.

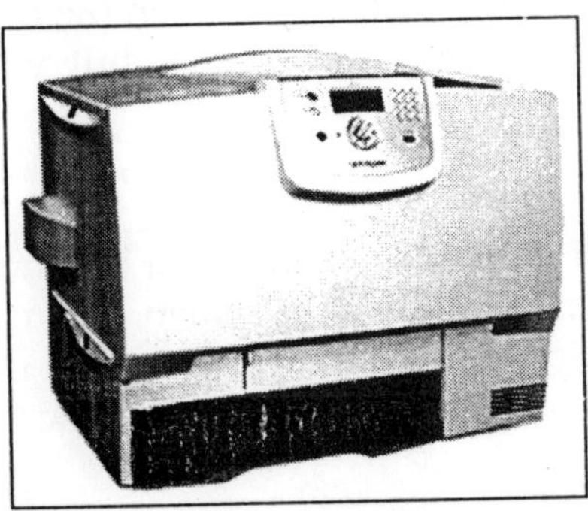

Many people try to save money on a printer purchase and are disappointed. If the main reason you will use your computer is to type letters, remember that the people you write to will not see your monitor. What they will see is only what comes out of your printer. If printed documents are an important part of what you will use a computer for, consider a higher quality printer. Ink Jets are probably most appropriate for home use, and laser printers are more popular in an office setting. A dot matrix machine is fine for test printing or use on a kid's computer, but you will be disappointed with the results if you try to use it for business correspondence.

Monitors

Desktop Monitor

Liquid Crystal Display

The monitor is the part of the system that you look at most of the time. Monitors resemble televisions. Most computer monitors use the same technology as televisions, but with much higher resolution. Often the monitor will come packaged with a computer system, but you may wish to upgrade.

Size

The size of a monitor can make a big impact. You might get a headache squinting at a screen that is too small. The size of a monitor is measured in diagonal inches. a 15 inch monitor is 15 inches diagonally from corner to corner of the screen.

Dot Pitch and DPI

Monitors are also measured by their precision. There are two main measures, Dot Pitch, and DPI. Dot pitch is a measure of the size of each tiny dot the monitor can display. The smaller each dot is, the nicer the picture will look, but the more expensive the monitor will be. When discussing Dot

Pitch, SMALLER IS BETTER!! DPI stands for Dots Per Inch. As you can guess, the smaller the dot pitch rating for a monitor is, the more of those tiny dots you could squeeze into a square inch. If you are considering DPI, LARGER IS BETTER.

Video Controller Card

Dealing with graphics takes a lot of work. Modern computers usually have a separate computer built in just to help with controlling the monitor. This little computer has its own cpu and memory! The power and speed of this little computer, as well as its memory capacity, have a huge effect on how graphics are drawn to your screen. This little computer is referred to as a graphics controller card. The most common cards now are called SVGA. Of course it gets way more complicated than this, but all you have to know is that there are fancier cards that do more and cost more, but you may not need the fanciest one out there for your first computer.

Projectors

A hardware device that enables an image, such as a computer screen, to be projected onto a flat surface. These devices are commonly used in meetings and presentations as they allow for a large image to be shown so everyone in a room can see. A general diagram of projector as an example image of what a projector may look like is shown below. As can be seen in this image the projector is a small device often a little bigger than a toaster and typically weighs a few pounds.

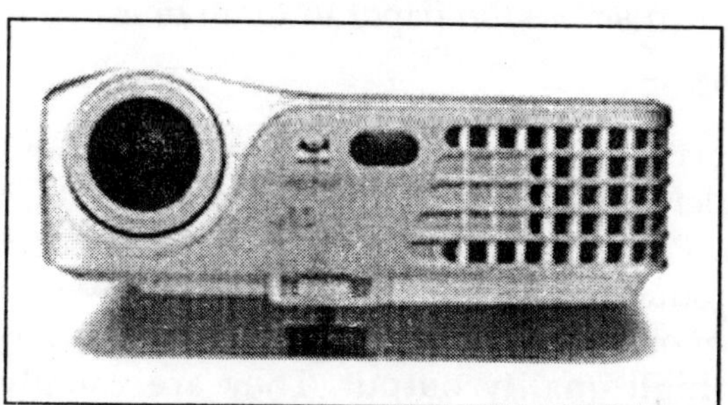

Speakers

A hardware device connected to a computer's sound card that outputs sounds generated by the card. Below is a graphic image example of the general speakers with subwoofer; speakers like the ones shown below are an example of what most computer speakers resemble.

Plotters

A plotter can be used to produce very large drawings on paper sizes up to A0 (16 times as big as A4). A plotter draws onto the paper using very fine pens. There are two types of plotter. They differ in the way that the pen can be moved about on the piece of paper to draw lines:

Flatbed Plotter

The paper is fixed and the pen moves left and right and up and down across the paper to draw lines.

Drum Plotter

The pen moves up and down on the paper and the paper is moved left and right by rotating a drum on which the paper is placed. Plotters can automatically change their pens and so can produce colour output. The lines drawn by a plotter are continuous and very accurate. Plotters are very slow but produce high quality output. They are usually used for

Computer Aided Design (CAD) and Computer Aided Manufacturing (CAM) applications such as printing out plans for houses or car parts.

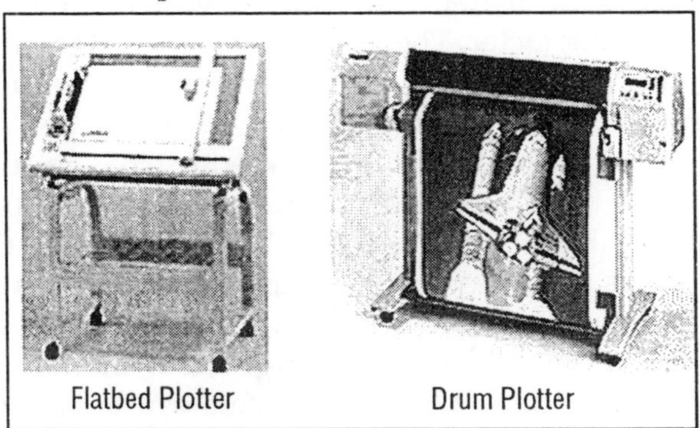

Flatbed Plotter Drum Plotter

The quality of the output produced by ink jet printers is now very good and large format (big) ink-jet printers are steadily replacing plotters for most tasks.

Common Input Output Devices

RAM

RAM is perhaps the most important of the input/output devices. When we talk about computer memory, we are mainly talking about RAM. In this class, when we think about the banks of light switches that can be manipulated, we are thinking of RAM memory. The term Random Access is pretty unfortunate. There is nothing random about how memory is accessed. The programme running will determine what is in memory. (of course, the programme itself is in memory too!) RAM can be read from by the CPU. This means that the CPU can 'look' at any address in RAM and get the contents of that address. It can also be written to by the CPU, meaning that the CPU can change the value of memory cells on the fly.

One VERY important aspect of RAM memory is that it requires power. RAM can only hold values while power is going through it. If the power is interrupted, the RAM will lose ALL the values in it. This is why it is so important to save your work frequently when working on a computer. RAM memory is volatile. When the room you are working on is hit by a tsunami and the power goes out of your computer, you lose everything that was in RAM. This could be bad.

The amount of RAM in your computer is obviously a pretty important factor. The more memory you have, the more 'room' there is in your computer for information and programs. Modern programs have gotten HUGE, and the kinds of information you can work with have gotten much larger. Some early home computers had 4 or 16 K of RAM. The original IBM PC had 640 K of RAM. In its day, this was thought of as an extravagant amount of memory that would never be fully used. Modern computers with less than 16 Megabytes (16,000 K) are considered a bit lame. (pun completely intended.) Older computers can be quite happy with much less RAM, but they will not be able to run the newer programs.

Disk Drives

Disk drives are special devices that allow us to make copies of parts of RAM and store them magnetically. If RAM memory is electronic, think of disk drives as a special kind of magnetic memory. When you save something to a disk, the electronic impulses in RAM are copied and stored to the disk as a series of magnetic impulses. All a disk drive does is translate electronic impulses and magnetic impulses back and forth.

Disk drives are handy because magnetic impulses are more permanent than electronic ones. The disk drive does not require electricity to keep values in memory, so if you store something to a disk, the information will be there when the tidal wave knocks the power out to your computer. (Assuming, of course, that the disk stayed dry and clean) Disks are sometimes thought of as secondary storage for this reason.

Floppy Drives

A floppy drive is a machine that is designed to read floppy disks. Floppy disks are the removable devices that you stick in slots in the front of the machine. I know, they look square, not disk-shaped, and they don't look floppy at all, but they are indeed floppy disks. Floppy disks come in hard plastic cases to make them a little more sturdy and easier to handle, but inside the plastic case, there is an actual disk. It is made of a plastic-like substance called mylar which really is floppy. Floppy disks come in two main sizes; 5 1/4 inch, and 3 1/2 inch. The 5 1/4 disks are becoming obsolete, but you still see them from time to time. The 3 1/2 inch disks, although physically smaller, can usually hold more information!

There are different flavours of floppy disks. In a modern computer, the only kind of floppy you need to purchase is High Density 1.44 MB. As you can guess, they hold 1.44 MegaBytes of information, which is a pretty good amount. (You could hold several hundred pages of text or about a dozen full colour pictures on a 1.44 MB disk) This type of disk may carry some other markings as well, such as DSHD or HD. The HD is the important part. That tells you it can handle 1.44 MB.

Hard Drives

A hard drive is a special disk that is usually mounted permanently inside your computer's cabinet. You rarely see the hard drive, and almost never take it out. Hard drives are made of different material than floppies, and they are physically hard (although if you touched the actual hard surface, you would destroy it!) They spin much more quickly than floppies, and require much more precision. They are sealed inside a special case, and that is sealed inside the computer case. A hard drive has a much larger capacity than a floppy, and is much faster at saving and retrieving information. Modern computers frequently have hard drives with 500 MB or more of capacity. As this capacity grows, people are beginning to measure it in terms of gigabytes. Software programs are always becoming larger and taking more room on hard drives. It never takes long to completely fill up the capacity of a drive. If you can afford a large drive when you buy the computer, you won't be sorry, but you can usually add another drive or upgrade later.

Fancier kinds of Drives

There are a number of other types of drives you may encounter when buying or upgrading a computer. You may encounter such things as Bernoulli tape drives, WORM (write once, read many) drives, optical floppies, and removable hard drives. All these things are really cool, but you may want to stick with the basics until you are a little more comfortable with the technology. Any computer system ought to have at least one 3.5 inch floppy drive, as large a hard drive as possible, and a CD-ROM drive.

Drive Controller Cards

Most computers come with a small card installed that helps control all your disk drives. It is called the Drive Controller Card. There are two major kinds, IDE and SCSI. The only time you will ever care about this is when you buy a hard drive. Just know that the terms IDE and SCSI are terms that describe the drive controller card.

Network Card

In a home computer, you will generally not have a network card, but these devices are very common for computers in office settings. A network card is a special card which allows your computer to talk to other computers that are physically attached via cables. Depending on how the network is set up, you can send messages from computer to computer, run programs that are stored on different computers, and share devices like hard drives and printers. In many offices, the network also gives you access to the Internet. Network connections are generally faster than modem connections.

Modem

Modems were once thought of as somewhat extravagant, but with the advent of the Internet, they are becoming a necessity for home computers. They allow you to connect your computer to the Internet or other computer systems through a telephone connection. The term Modem stands for Modulator/Demodulator. It is a device that converts back and forth from the digital signals that computers understand to analog signals (sounds) that can be transferred over telephone lines. Modems can be internal or external. The external ones have their own little case and power supply, and are generally a little more expensive than the internal ones, which are little cards that fit inside the computer. Modems are rated by their transmission speed, which is measured in BAUD (Bits of Audio Data/Second).

If you want to do any Internet connections, you need a baud rate of 1440 BAUD (also sometimes called 14400 BPS or 14.4 KBPS) You can also purchase faster modems, but they are of course more expensive. In the near future, something will happen in this arena. It is likely that we will be switching to a completely new kind of communication technology for home computers, but nobody knows exactly what that will be just yet. Some modems also include faxing and voice mail capabilities. These features can be very convenient for people with home offices.

2

Organisation of Computer

COMPUTER HARDWARE

INTRODUCTION

The Personal Computer is a system, which consist of many components like Windows, CPU, Keyboard, Mouse, UPS and Printer. The programs are called as software and the parts what you can see and touch is hardware.

The *system unit* is the actual computer; everything else is called a *peripheral* device. The computer's system unit probably has at least one floppy disk drive, and one CD or DVD drive, into which you can insert floppy disks and CDs.

The floppy drive and CD drive are often referred to as *drives with removable media* or *removable drives* for short, because you can remove whatever disk is currently in the drive, and replace it with another. The computer's hard disk can store as much information as tens of thousands of floppy disks, so don't worry about running out of space on your hard disk any time soon. As a rule, you want to store everything you create or download on your hard disk. Use the floppy disks and CDs to send copies of files through the mail, or to make backup copies of important items.

PC CASE

The PC case is a thin sheet metal enclosure that houses the motherboard, power supply and various drives (HDD, FDD, CD, DVD).

- Cases are offered in two styles, desktop and tower.

Today the tower type is predominant. It stands upright and is much taller than it is wide. It is usually placed on the floor next to, or under a desk. The desktop has a pizza box profile and usually sits on the desktop.

- Tower cases are offered in two basic sizes, one that can fit ATX (12" wide) motherboards and one that can accommodate ATX mini (8.5" wide) motherboards. The number of drive bays offered also varies depending on manufacturer.
- The motherboard and power supply mount to the floor at the rear of the case. The drives (hard, floppy and CD/DVD) mount in enclosures called drive bays at the front of the case.
- Cases run from $20 to $70 depending on size (ATX or ATX mini), number of drive bays and the wattage of the power supply.

MOTHERBOARD

The motherboard is the main circuit board in a PC. It contains all the circuits and components that run the PC.

Major Components found on the motherboard are:

- *CPU*: The Central Processing Unit is often an Intel Pentium or Celeron processor. It is the heart of every *PC*: All scheduling, computation and control occurs here.
- *BIOS*: Basic Input Output System is a non-volatile memory that contains configuration information about the PC. It contains all the code required for the CPU to communicate with the keyboard, mouse video display, disk drives and communications devices.

When a PC is powered on it uses the BIOS 'boot code' to set up many required functions that bring the PC to a point where it is ready to work.

- *RTC*: The Real Time Clock chip keeps date, day and time in a 24 hour format just like your watch. The PC uses this clock to 'time stamp' files as they are created and modified. When you print a file it time stamps the pages as they are printed.

- *Chip set*: These are large chip(s) that integrate many functions that used to be found in separate smaller chips on the motherboard. They save space and cost.

The functions performed by these chip sets often broken into two devices with one providing an interface from the CPU to the memory and the other providing controllers for IDE, ISA, PCI and USB devices.

Primary Connectors found on the motherboard are:

- *Power*: A 20 pin connector accepts a plug from the power supply. This plug carry DC power to all the circuits on the motherboard.
- *Keyboard*: A Mini-din 6-pin (round) connector found at the back of the motherboard is where the keyboard plugs in.
- *Mouse*: A Mini-din 6-pin connector found next to the keyboard connector is where the where the mouse plugs in.
- *Display*: This connector is not integrated into the motherboard but is included in this list since its function is absolutely necessary. It is a 15-pin, D-shell type connector found on a video card that plugs into the AGP connector of the motherboard.
- *IDE*: Stands for Integrated Drive Electronics. These are 40 pin connectors that provide a place to connect the ribbon cables from the drives (hard and CD/ DVD). All data between the motherboard and the drives is carried in these cables. They are not accessible unless the PC cover is removed.
- *FDD connector*: It is similar in function to the IDE connector. It is a 34 pin ribbon connector that carries data between the motherboard and any floppy drive installed in the PC. Not accessible with PC cover on.
- *Dram*: Dynamic Random Access Memory connectors for SIMM and DIMM type memory modules. Not accessible with chassis cover on.
- Serial Connectors
  - *Standard serial connector*: This connector has been

around in PCs since they first appeared. It was originally located on ISA expansion type cards. Today it is an integral part of newer motherboards. It is a 9- pin, D-shell connector that allows you to connect external devices with serial ports to your PC. The maximum data rate is 115 KB/s.

  - *USB*: Universal Serial Bus This is a relatively new serial bus. Originally specified as low speed, 1.2 Mb/s, it was enhanced to full speed, 12Mb/s. The latest version 2.0 is specified as high speed, 400 MB/s.

Unlike serial and parallel ports, the USB port is designed to power devices connected to it. The devices must be low power devices and must be able to reduce their current draw to less than 0.5uAmps when commanded to do so by the PC.

- Parallel Connectors
  - *Centronix or standard parallel*: This connector has been around in PCs since they first appeared. It has 37-pins and is now integrated on new motherboards. It is usually used to connect your printer to the PC and moves data at about 1MB/s.
  - *SCSI*: Small Computer System Interface moves data at a maximum of up to 80Mb/s. It not integrated into most PC motherboards. It can be added to a PC as an Expansion card. Some printers and hard disk drives use SCSI interfaces.
- Expansion Card Connectors - The CPU connects to expansion card connectors through one of the chip set ICs mentioned above. They are located on the motherboard near the rear of the PC. These connectors allow special function cards to plug into and work with the PC.

POWER SUPPLY

- A power supply is installed in the back corner of the PC case, next to the motherboard.
- It converts 120vac (standard house power) into DC

voltages that are used by other components in the PC.

- A 20 conductor cable carries +5vdc, -5vdc +12vdc, -12vdc and ground to the motherboard.
- Another pair of cables, each with four conductors and two 4-pin connectors daisy-chained along it, carry +5vdc, +12vdc and ground to the drives (hard, floppy and CD/DVD).
- Typical PC power supplies are rated at 200-250 watts and sell for about $50-$75. Higher wattage supplies are available.

RANDOM ACCESS MEMORY (RAM)

There's too much "stuff" on your computer's hard disk to use it all at the same time. During the average session sitting at the computer, you'll probably use only a small amount of all that's available. The stuff you're working with at any given moment is stored in random access memory (often abbreviated RAM, and often called simply "memory"). The advantage using RAM to store whatever you're working on at the moment is that RAM is very fast. Much faster than any disk. So if RAM is so fast, why not put everything in it? Why have a hard disk at all? The answer to that lies in the fact that RAM is volatile. As soon as the computer is shut off, whether intentionally or by an accidental power outage, every thing in RAM disappears, just as quickly as a light bulb goes out when the plug is pulled. So you don't want to rely on RAM to hold everything. A disk, on the other hand, holds its information whether the power is on or off.

HARD DISK

All of the information that's "in your computer", so to speak, is stored on your computer's *hard disk.* Unlike RAM, which is volatile, the hard disk can hold information forever—with or without electricity. Most modern hard disks have tens of billions of *bytes* of storage space on them. Which, in English, means that you can create, save, and download files for months or years without using up all the storage space it provides. In the unlikely event that you do manage to fill up your hard disk, Windows will start showing a little message on the screen that reads "You are running low on disk space" well in advance of any problems. In fact, if that message appears, it won't until you're down to about 800 MB of free space. And 800 MB of empty space is equal to about 600 blank floppy disks.

That's still plenty of room!

- The HDD installs in one of the 3-1/2 inch internal drive bays in the PC. It is secured by machine screws.
- It is powered by a 4 conductor cable coming from the power supply.
- Data to and from the motherboard is carried on a 40-pin IDE (Integrated Drive Electronics) cable.
- Data is stored magnetically on multiple rigid disks that are stacked up like pancakes. Small arms with magnetic pickups move rapidly back and forth across the top and bottom surface of each disk in the drive. The sensors float just a few microns above the rotating disk surface and can read and write data at very high rates.
- Most commercially available hard drives rotate at 5400 or 7200 RPM (revolutions per minute) which translates to 90 or 120 revolutions per second respectively. The data transfer rate from the drive to the motherboard is 33 Mbytes/second in bursts. Newer drives are capable of higher speeds up to 66 Mbytes/sec. To use this faster drive, the PC must have an ATA/66 interface that is capable of keeping up with it.

FLOPPY DISK DRIVE

- The FDD installs in one of the external drive bays at the front of the PC case and is secured by machine screws. External means you can access the drive from the outside.
- It is powered by a cable with a 4-pin connector that comes from the power supply.

- It transfers data to and from the motherboard by means of a 34 pin ribbon cable.
- It stores data magnetically on a removable floppy disk. A pickup arm in the drive floats above the disk surface. The arm moves rapidly back and forth across the disk surface as a small magnetic sensor at the end of the arm reads and writes data on the rotating disk surface.
- Floppy disks hold 1.44 Mbytes, which at one time was a large amount of data. Today many programs and files are much larger than this. In spite of being surpassed in size by CD and DVD, floppy drives are still found on many newer PCs.

COMPACT DISK DRIVE

- The CDD installs in one of the external 5-1/4 inch drive bays in the front of the PC case. It is secured by machine screws. Some manufacturers offer special rail-like systems that mount on the CDD. These allow the drive to be removed from the PC without having to remove any screws.
- Data is stored optically on the surface of the disk. A laser attached to an arm that moves back and forth across near the disk surface and sends light towards the disk surface which is coated with of a thin layer of aluminum.
- Smooth areas called a lands reflect the light back to a photo diode located near the laser. The reflected light is read as a 1. Areas called pits are where the aluminum has been removed. When the laser light hits these, it is scattered and very little is picked up by the photo diode. The absence of light is read as a 0.
- CDD have become the predominant removable storage media for PCs and can store 700 Mbytes of data.
- A 4-pin cable from the power supply plugs into the CDD and provides power to it.
- Data to and from the motherboard is carried on a 40-pin IDE (Integrated Drive Electronics) cable.

- There are two types of Compact Disk drives available for PCs.
  - CD-ROM (read only memory) is the older type. As the title implies it can only read CDs. It can read any standard CD and most CD-R type disks. It may be able to read some types of CD-RW disks too. A 24x CD-ROM unit costs about $30.
  - CD-RW (ReWritable)units can read and write CD-R and CD-RW type disks. It can also read standard CD type disks.

A 24x10x40 CD-RW unit costs about $115. The 24x10x 40 means the unit can write at 24x, re-write at 10x and read at 40x, where x is 150Kbytes/sec.

DIGITAL VIDEO DISK DRIVE

- DVD also known as the Digital Versatile Disk drive, installs in one of the external 5 1/4 inch drive bays in the PC. It is secured by machine screws. Some manufacturers offer special rail-like systems that mount on the DVD. These allow the drive to be removed from the PC without having to remove screws.
- It is designed to optically access data stored on a DVD. A laser moves back and forth near the disk surface and accesses data at a very fast rate.
- A 4-pin cable from the power supply plugs into the CDD and provides power to it.
- Data between the DVD drive and the motherboard is carried on a 40-pin IDE (Integrated Drive Electronics) cable.
- There are two types of DVD drives that typically go into PCs.
  - DVD-ROM (Read Only Memory) can read DVDs and CDs and costs about $75.
  - DVD-RAM (Random Access Memory) units can read and write DVDs. They can also read CDs and cost about $500.
- A standard DVD stores up to 4.7 Gbytes on one side

of the disk. Digitally formatted movies can be stored on a standard DVD in MPEG-2 format.

MONITOR

CRT Monitors

- Up until recently, CRTs (Cathode RayTubes) were the only type of displays for use with desktop PCs. They are relatively big (14" to 16" deep) and heavy (over 15 lbs).
- They are available in screen sizes from 14" to 21". A 17" display means that it is 17" measured diagonally from one corner of the tube to the other. The actual viewing area is smaller than 17" (about 16") since the electron gun can't sweep completely to the tube edge.
- CRTs send a stream of electrons at the screen, which is charged to about 25,000 volts. As they strike it they cause phosphor on the backside of the screen to glow creating light which you see. The electron stream is sweep back and forth and up and down at about 60 sweeps per second and turned off and on at the right time to make text and graphics images appear.
- They are powered by standard 120Vac wall power.
- Data is transferred to the display on a cable with a 15-pin D-shell connector that plugs into a connector on the video card which in turn plugs into one of the PC's expansion slots.
- A 17" monitor with 1280 x 1024 resolution and.27mm dot pitch sells for around $150.

LCD Monitors

- Liquid Crystal Display (LCD) technology has been used in laptops for some time. It has recently been made commercially available as monitors for desktop PCs.
- LCDs have no electron gun and are therefore not very deep like CRTs. The text and images you see are

created by a back light behind the panel, that shines through pixels (picture elements). Each pixel is made up of three chambers red, green and blue. The chambers in each pixel must be opened enough and in the proper proportion to produce the correct brightness and colour.

- For an LCD to provide a screen resolution 1024 x 768 pixels (SVGA), it must have 786,432 (1024 x 768) pixels. In TFT (Thin Film Transistor) type LCDs, each pixel is controlled by a tiny transistor that opens and closes the chambers in each pixel.
- Desk top LCD displays are powered by standard 120Vac wall power.
- Data is transferred to the display on a cable with a 15-pin connector that plugs into a mating connector on the video card seated in an expansion slot in the PC.
- A 17" LCD monitor with 1280 x 1024 resolution and.27mm dot pitch sells for around $500.

MOUSE \ MICE

Obviously you know how to use your mouse, since you must have used it to get here. But let's take a look at the facts and buzzwords anyway. Your mouse probably has at least two buttons on it.

The button on the left is called the *primary mouse button,* the button on the right is called the *secondary mouse button* or just the *right mouse button.* The idea is to rest your hand comfortably on the mouse, with your index finger touching (but not pressing on) the left mouse button. Then, as you move the mouse, the *mouse pointer* (the little arrow on the screen) moves in the same direction. When moving the mouse, try to keep the buttons aimed towards the monitor—don't "twist" the mouse as that just makes it all the harder to control the position of the mouse pointer.

If you find yourself reaching too far to get the mouse pointer where you want it to be on the screen, just pick up the mouse, move it to where it's comfortable to hold it, and place it back down on the mousepad or desk.

The buzzwords that describe how you use the mouse are as follows:

- *Point*: To point to an item means to move the mouse pointer so that it's touching the item.
- *Click*: Point to the item, then tap (press and release) the left mouse button.
- *Double-click*: Point to the item, and tap the left mouse button twice in rapid succession-click-click as fast as you can.
- *Right-click*: Point to the item, then tap the mouse button on the right.
- *Drag*: Point to an item, then hold down the left mouse button as you move the mouse. To *drop* the item, release the left mouse button.
- *Right-drag*: Point to an item, then hold down the right mouse button as you move the mouse. To *drop* the item, release the right mouse button.

The mouse is the most common 'pointing device' used in PCs. Every mouse has two buttons and most have one or two scroll wheels.

- By default the left button is used to select items. The right button is assigned as a context or alternate menu. A single wheel is normally set to scroll up and down on the active page. If a second wheel is present, it is usually assigned to scroll left and right on the page.
- The button functions can be reassigned by going to Control Panel > Mouse > Buttons tab.
- Data is transferred to the PC over a short cable with a circular 6-pin Mini-din connector that plugs into the back of the motherboard.
- Some versions of the mouse are wireless. They communicate with a receiver pod that is plugs into the mouse port. Radio Frequency (RF) or InfraRed (IR) technology is used for communication between the mouse and the pod.

Track Ball

This type of mouse uses a rolling (track) ball. As the mouse moves the ball rolls. The rolling motion is converted electronically into matching movements of the mouse pointer that moves across your video display. The track ball mouse is rapidly becoming another casualty of rapidly changing technology. The optical mouse has pretty much replaced it. The track ball mouse is already becoming a thing of the past.

Optical

This mouse uses an InfraRed transmitter/receiver pair to optically detect the motion of the mouse.

It has a number of advantages over the track ball mouse:

- No mouse pad is required.
- Can work on any flat surface
- No rolling track ball that collects and transfers dirt to the internal rollers, making them slip. When they do, your mouse pointer jumps around in an unpredictable and annoying way!
- See the Easy Tips section of this web site for an explanation on how to clean a track ball mouse.

KEYBOARD

Like the mouse, the keyboard is a means of interacting with your computer. You really only need to use the keyboard when you're typing text. Most of the keys on the keyboard are laid out like the keys on a typewriter. But there are some special keys like Esc (Escape), Ctrl (Control), and Alt (Alternate). There are also some keys across the top of the keyboard labeled F1, F2, F3, and so forth. Those are called the *function keys,* and the exact role they play depends on which programme you happen to be using at the moment.

Most keyboards also have a *numeric keypad* with the keys laid out like the keys on a typical adding machine. It doesn't really matter which keys you use. The numeric keypad is just there as a convenience to people who are accustomed to adding machines. Most keyboards also contain a set of *navigation keys.* You can use the navigation keys to move around around through text on the screen. The navigation keys won't move the mouse pointer. Only the mouse moves the mouse pointer. On smaller keyboards where space is limited, such as on a notebook computer, the navigation keys and numeric keypad might be one in the same. There will be a Num Lock key on the keypad. When the Num Lock key is "on", the numeric keypad keys type numbers. When the Num Lock key is "off", the navigation keys come into play. The Num Lock key acts as a toggle. Which is to say, when you tap it, it switches to the opposite state. For example, if Num Lock is on, tapping that key turns it off. If Num Lock is off, tapping that key turns Num Lock on.

SPEAKERS AND HEADPHONES

- Speakers and headphones are the primary audio output devices for a PC.
- Some monitors have speakers built into their sides. Other speakers are free standing.
- Passive speakers plug into and are powered directly from the output signal provided by the 'speaker out' port on the sound card.
- Active speakers amplify the sound signal from the sound card using battery or rectified AC house power.

CABLES AND WIRES

- Although these are not the most sophisticated part of the system, they are just as important as any other component.
- All the components in a PC are connected together and to power with wires and cables.
- Ninety per cent of all electronics problems (including PCs) are the result of poor connections.
- If you have a PC problem, it is always a good idea to first check that all the cables on your PC are plugged in and properly seated.

COMPUTER SYSTEM

INTRODUCTION

To understand digital signal processing systems, we must understand a little about how computers compute. The modern definition of a *computer* is an electronic device that performs calculations on data, presenting the results to humans or other computers in a variety of (hopefully useful) ways. The generic computer contains *input* devices (keyboard, mouse, A/D (analog-to-digital) converter, etc.), a *computational unit*, and output devices (monitors, printers, D/A converters). The computational unit is the computer's heart, and usually consists of a *central processing unit* (CPU), a *memory*, and an input/output (I/O) interface. What I/O devices might be present on a given computer vary greatly.

- *A simple computer operates fundamentally in discrete time.* Computers are *clocked* devices, in which computational steps occur periodically according to ticks of a clock. This description belies clock speed: When you say "I have a 1 GHz computer," you mean that your computer takes 1 nanosecond to perform each step. That is incredibly fast! A "step" does not, unfortunately, necessarily mean a computation like an addition; computers break such computations down into several stages, which means that the clock speed need not express the computational speed. Computational speed is expressed in units of millions of instructions/second (Mips). Your 1 GHz computer (clock speed) may have a computational speed of 200 Mips.
- *Computers perform integer (discrete-valued) computations.* Computer calculations can be numeric (obeying the laws of arithmetic), logical (obeying the laws of an algebra), or symbolic (obeying any law you like).1 Each computer instruction that performs an elementary numeric calculation—an addition, a multiplication, or a division—does so only for integers. The sum or product of two integers is also an integer, but the quotient of two integers is likely to not be an integer.

FIXED-POINT NUMBERS

ABOUT FIXED-POINT NUMBERS

Fixed-point numbers and their data types are characterized by their word size in bits, binary point, and whether they are signed or unsigned. The Simulink Fixed Point software supports integers, fixed-point numbers. The main difference among these data types is their binary point.

SIGNED FIXED-POINT NUMBERS

Computer hardware typically represents the negation of a binary fixed-point number in three different ways: sign/ magnitude, one's complement, and two's complement. Two's complement is the preferred representation of signed fixed-point numbers and supported by the Simulink Fixed Point software.

Negation using two's complement consists of a bit inversion (translation into one's complement) followed by the addition of a one. For example, the two's complement of 000101 is 111011. Whether a fixed-point value is signed or unsigned is usually not encoded explicitly within the binary word; that is, there is no sign bit. Instead, the sign information is implicitly defined within the computer architecture.

BINARY POINT INTERPRETATION

The binary point is the means by which fixed-point numbers are scaled. It is usually the software that determines the binary point. When performing basic math functions such as addition or subtraction, the hardware uses the same logic circuits regardless of the value of the scale factor. In essence, the logic circuits have no knowledge of a scale factor. They are performing signed or unsigned fixed-point binary algebra as if the binary point is to the right of b_0.

SCALING

The dynamic range of fixed-point numbers is much less than floating-point numbers with equivalent word sizes. To avoid overflow conditions and minimize quantization errors, fixed-point numbers must be scaled. With the Simulink Fixed Point software, you can select a fixed-point data type whose scaling is defined by its binary point, or you can select an arbitrary linear scaling that suits your needs. This section presents the scaling choices available for fixed-point data types. You can represent a fixed-point number by a general slope and bias encoding scheme,

$$V \approx \tilde{V} = SQ + B$$

where,

- V is an arbitrarily precise real-world value
- $\tilde{V}$ is the approximate real-world value
- *Q*, the stored value, is an integer that encodes *V*
- $S = F\,2^E$ is the slope
- *B* is the bias

The slope is partitioned into two components:

- 2^E specifies the binary point. *E* is the fixed power-of-two exponent.
- *F* is the slope adjustment factor. It is normalized such that

Note *S* and *B* are constants and do not show up in the computer hardware directly. Only the quantization value *Q* is stored in computer memory.

Binary-Point-Only Scaling

Binary-point-only or power-of-two scaling involves moving the binary point within the fixed-point word. The advantage of this scaling mode is to minimize the number of processor arithmetic operations.

With binary-point-only scaling, the components of the general slope and bias formula have the following values:

- $F = 1$
- $S = F2^E = 2^E$
- $B = 0$

The scaling of a quantized real-world number is defined by the slope *S*, which is restricted to a power of two. The negative of the power-of-two exponent is called the fraction length. The fraction length is the number of bits to the right of the binary point.

For Binary-Point-Only scaling, specify fixed-point data types as:

- *Signed types*: Fixdt(1, Word Length, Fraction Length)
- *Unsigned types*: Fixdt(0, Word Length, Fraction Length)

Integers are a special case of fixed-point data types. Integers have a trivial scaling with slope 1 and bias 0, or equivalently with fraction length 0.

Specify integers as:

- *Signed integer*: Fixdt(1, WordLength, 0)
- *Unsigned integer for Binary-Point-Only scaling, specify fixed-point data types as*: Fixdt(0, WordLength, 0)

Slope and Bias Scaling

When you scale by slope and bias, the slope *S* and bias *B* of the quantized real-world number can take on any value. The slope must be a positive number.

Using slope and bias, specify fixed-point data types as:

- Fixdt(Signed, WordLength, Slope, Bias)

Unspecified Scaling

Specify fixed-point data types with an unspecified scaling as,

- Fixdt (Signed, Word Length)

Simulink signals, parameters, and states must never have unspecified scaling. When scaling is unspecified, you must use some other mechanism such as automatic best precision scaling to determine the scaling that the Simulink software uses.

QUANTIZATION

The quantization *Q* of a real-world value *V* is represented by a weighted sum of bits. Within the context of the general slope and bias encoding scheme, the value of an unsigned fixed-point quantity is given by,

$$\tilde{V} = S \cdot \left[\sum_{i=0}^{ws-1} b_i 2^i \right] + B$$

while the value of a signed fixed-point quantity is given by,

$$\tilde{V} = S \cdot \left[-b_{ws-1} 2^{ws-1} + \sum_{i=0}^{ws-2} b_i 2^i \right] + B$$

where,

- b_i are binary digits, with $b_i = 1, 0$.

- The word size in bits is given by *ws*, with *ws* = 1, 2, 3., 128.
- *S* is given by $F\,2^E$, where the scaling is unrestricted because the binary point does not have to be contiguous with the word. b_i are called *bit multipliers* and 2^i are called the *weights*.

RANGE AND PRECISION

The *range* of a number gives the limits of the representation, while the *precision* gives the distance between successive numbers in the representation. The range and precision of a fixed-point number depends on the length of the word and the scaling.

Range

The range of representable numbers for an unsigned and two's complement fixed-point number of size *ws*, scaling *S*, and bias *B*. For both the signed and unsigned fixed-point numbers of any data type, the number of different bit patterns is 2^{ws}.

For example, if the fixed-point data type is an integer with scaling defined as *S* = 1 and *B* = 0, then the maximum unsigned value is $2^{ws} - 1$, because zero must be represented. In two's complement, negative numbers must be represented as well as zero, so the maximum value is $2^{ws-1} - 1$.

Additionally, since there is only one representation for zero, there must be an unequal number of positive and negative numbers.

This means there is a representation for -2^{ws-1} but not for 2^{ws-1}.

Precision

The precision of a data type is given by the slope. In this usage, precision means the difference between neighbouring representable values.

FIXED-POINT DATA TYPE PARAMETERS

The low limit, high limit, and default binary-point-only

scaling for the supported fixed-point data types discussed in Binary Point Interpretation are given in the following table.

Fixed-Point Data Type Range and Default Scaling

Name	Data Type	Low Limit	High Limit	Default Scaling (~Precision)
Unsigned Integer	fixdt(0,ws,0)	0	$2^{ws} - 1$	1
Signed Integer	fixdt(1,ws,0)	-2^{ws-1}	$2^{ws-1} - 1$	1
Unsigned Binary Point	fixdt(0,ws,fl)	0	$(2^{ws} - 1)2^{-fl}$	2^{-fl}
Signed Binary Point	fixdt(1,ws,fl)	$-2^{ws-1-fl}$	$(2^{ws-1} - 1)2^{-fl}$	2^{-fl}
Unsigned Slope Bias	fixdt(0,ws,s,b)	0	$s(2^{ws} - 1) + b$	s
Signed Slope Bias	fixdt(1,ws,s,b)	$-s(2^{ws-1}) + b$	$s(2^{ws-1} - 1) + b$	s

s = Slope, b = Bias, ws = WordLength, fl = Fraction Length

Binary-Point-Only Scaling

The precisions, range of signed values, and range of unsigned values for an 8-bit generalized fixed-point data type with binary-point-only scaling are listed in the follow table. Note that the first scaling value (2^1) represents a binary point that is not contiguous with the word.

Scaling	Precision	Range of Signed Values (Low, High)	Range of Unsigned Values (Low, High)
2^1	2.0	–256, 254	0, 510
2^0	1.0	–128, 127	0, 255
2^{-1}	0.5	–64, 63.5	0, 127.5
2^{-2}	0.25	–32, 31.75	0, 63.75
2^{-3}	0.125	–16, 15.875	0, 31.875
2^{-4}	0.0625	–8, 7.9375	0, 15.9375
2^{-5}	0.03125	–4, 3.96875	0, 7.96875
2^{-6}	0.015625	–2, 1.984375	0, 3.984375
2^{-7}	0.0078125	–1, 0.9921875	0, 1.9921875
2^{-8}	0.00390625	–0.5, 0.49609375	0, 0.99609375

Range of an 8-Bit Fixed-Point Data Type — Slope and Bias Scaling

The precision and ranges of signed and unsigned values for an 8-bit fixed-point data type using slope and bias scaling are listed in the following table. The slope starts at a value of 1.25 with a bias of 1.0 for all slopes. Note that the slope is the same as the precision.

Bias	Slope/Precision	Range of Signed Values (low, high)	Range of Unsigned Values (low, high)
1	1.25	-159, 159.75	1, 319.75
1	0.625	-79, 80.375	1, 160.375
1	0.3125	-39, 40.6875	1, 80.6875
1	0.15625	-19, 20.84375	1, 40.84375
1	0.078125	-9, 10.921875	1, 20.921875
1	0.0390625	-4, 5.9609375	1, 10.9609375
1	0.01953125	-1.5, 3.48046875	1, 5.98046875
1	0.009765625	-0.25, 2.240234375	1, 3.490234375
1	0.0048828125	0.375, 1.6201171875	1, 2.2451171875

FLOATING POINT NUMBER

There are several ways to represent real numbers on computers. Fixed point places a radix point somewhere in the middle of the digits, and is equivalent to using integers that represent portions of some unit. For example, one might represent 1/100ths of a unit; if you have four decimal digits, you could represent 10.82, or 00.01. Another approach is to use rationals, and represent every number as the ratio of two integers.

Floating-point representation-the most common solution basically represents reals in scientific notation. Scientific notation represents numbers as a base number and an exponent. For example, 123.456 could be represented as 1.23456×10^2. In hexadecimal, the number 123.abc might be represented as $1.23abc \times 16^2$.

Floating-point solves a number of representation problems. Fixed-point has a fixed window of representation, which limits it from representing very large or very small numbers. Also, fixed-point is prone to a loss of precision when two large numbers are divided. Floating-point, on the other hand, employs a sort of "sliding window" of precision appropriate to the scale of the number. This allows it to represent numbers from 1,000,000,000,000 to 0.0000000000000001 with ease.

STORAGE LAYOUT

IEEE floating point numbers have three basic components: the sign, the exponent, and the mantissa. The mantissa is composed of the *fraction*and an implicit leading digit (explained below). The exponent base (2) is implicit and need not be stored. The following will show the layout for single (32-bit) and double (64-bit) precision floating-point values.

The number of bits for each field are shown (bit ranges are in square brackets):

	Sign	Exponent	Fraction	Bias
Single Precision	1 [31]	8 [30-23]	23 [22-00]	127
Double Precision	1 [63]	11 [62-52]	52 [51-00]	1023

THE SIGN BIT

The sign bit is as simple as it gets. 0 denotes a positive number; 1 denotes a negative number. Flipping the value of this bit flips the sign of the number.

THE EXPONENT

The exponent field needs to represent both positive and negative exponents. To do this, a *bias* is added to the actual exponent in order to get the stored exponent. For IEEE single-precision floats, this value is 127.

Thus, an exponent of zero means that 127 is stored in the exponent field. A stored value of 200 indicates an exponent of (200-127), or 73. For reasons discussed later, exponents of -127 (all 0s) and +128 (all 1s) are reserved for special numbers. For double precision, the exponent field is 11 bits, and has a bias of 1023.

THE MANTISSA

The *mantissa,* also known as the *significand,* represents the precision bits of the number. It is composed of an implicit leading bit and the fraction bits. To find out the value of the implicit leading bit, consider that any number can be expressed in scientific notation in many different ways.

For example, the number five can be represented as any of these:

5.00×10^0

0.05×10^2

5000×10^{-3}

In order to maximize the quantity of representable numbers, floating-point numbers are typically stored in *normalized* form. This basically puts the radix point after the first non-zero digit. In normalized form, five is represented as 5.0×10^0.

A nice little optimization is available to us in base two, since the only possible non-zero digit is 1. Thus, we can just assume a leading digit of 1, and don't need to represent it explicitly. As a result, the mantissa has effectively 24 bits of resolution, by way of 23 fraction bits.

PUTTING IT ALL TOGETHER

So, to sum up:

- The sign bit is 0 for positive, 1 for negative.
- The exponent's base is two.
- The exponent field contains 127 plus the true exponent for single-precision, or 1023 plus the true exponent for double precision.
- The first bit of the mantissa is typically assumed to be 1.*f*, where *f* is the field of fraction bits.

RANGES OF FLOATING-POINT NUMBERS

Let's consider single-precision floats for a second. Note that we're taking essentially a 32-bit number and re-jiggering the fields to cover a much broader range. Something has to give, and it's precision. For example, regular 32-bit integers, with all precision centered around zero, can precisely store integers with 32-bits of resolution. Single-precision floating-point, on the other hand, is unable to match this resolution with its 24 bits. It does, however, approximate this value by effectively truncating from the lower end. The approximates the 32-bit value, but doesn't yield an exact representation. On the other hand, besides the ability to represent fractional components (which integers lack completely), the floating-point value can represent numbers around 2^{127}, compared to 32-bit integers maximum value around 2^{32}.

The range of positive floating point numbers can be split into normalized numbers (which preserve the full precision of the mantissa), and*denormalized* numbers.

Since the sign of floating point numbers is given by a special leading bit, the range for negative numbers is given by the negation of the above values.

There are five distinct numerical ranges that single-precision floating-point numbers are not able to represent:

- Negative numbers less than $-(2-2^{-23}) \times 2^{127}$ (*negative overflow*)
- Negative numbers greater than -2^{-149} (*negative underflow*)
- Zero
- Positive numbers less than 2^{-149} (*positive underflow*)
- Positive numbers greater than $(2-2^{-23}) \times 2^{127}$ (*positive overflow*)

Overflow means that values have grown too large for the representation, much in the same way that you can overflow integers. Underflow is a less serious problem because is just denotes a loss of precision, which is guaranteed to be closely approximated by zero.

Here's a table of the effective range (excluding infinite values) of IEEE floating-point numbers:

	Binary	**Decimal**
Single	$\pm (2-2^{-23}) \times 2^{127}$	$\sim \pm 10^{38.53}$
Double	$\pm (2-2^{-52}) \times 2^{1023}$	$\sim \pm 10^{308.25}$

Note that the extreme values occur (regardless of sign) when the exponent is at the maximum value for finite numbers (2^{127} for single-precision, 2^{1023} for double), and the mantissa is filled with 1s (including the normalizing 1 bit).

COMPUTER ARCHITECTURE

OVERVIEW

In describing computer system, a distinction is often made between computer architecture and computer organization. Computer architecture refers to those attributes of a system visible to a programmer, or put another way, those attributes that have a direct impact on the logical execution of a programme. Computer organization refers to the operational units and their interconnection that realise the architecture specification. Examples of architecture attributes include the instruction set, the number of bit to represent various data types (*e.g.*, numbers, and characters), I/O mechanisms, and technique for addressing memory.

Examples of organization attributes include those hardware details transparent to the programmer, such as control signals, interfaces between the computer and peripherals, and the memory technology used. As an example, it is an architectural design issue whether a computer will have a multiply instruction. It is an organizational issue whether that instruction will be implemented by a special multiply unit or by a mechanism that makes repeated use of the add unit of the system. The organization decision may be bases on the anticipated frequency of use of the multiply instruction, the relative speed of the two approaches, and the cost and physical size of a special multiply unit.

Historically, and still today, the distinction between architecture and organization has been an important one. Many computer manufacturers offer a family of computer model, all with the same architecture but with differences in organization. Consequently, the different models in the family have different price and performance characteristics. Furthermore, an architecture may survive many years, but its organization changes with changing technology.

STRUCTURE AND FUNCTION

A computer is a complex system; contemporary computers contain million of elementary electronic components. How, then, can one clearly describe them? The key is to recognize the hierarchical nature of most complex system. A hierarchical system is a set of interrelated subsystem, each of the later, in turn, hierarchical in structure until we reach some lowest level of elementary subsystem.

The hierarchical nature of complex systems is essential to both their design and their description. The designer need only deal with a particular level of the system at a time. At each level, the system consists of a set of components and their interrelationships. The behaviour at each level depends only on a simplified, abstracted characterization of the system at the next lower level.

At each level, the designer is concerned with structure and function:

- *Structure*: The way in which the components are interrelated.
- *Function*: The operation of each individual component as part of the structure.

In term of description, we have two choices: starting at the bottom and building up to a complete description, or beginning with a top view and decomposing the system, describing their structure and function, and proceed to successively lower layer of the hierarchy. The approach taken in this course follows the latter.

Function

In general terms, there are four main functions of a computer:

- Data processing
- Data storage
- Data movement
- Control

The computer, of course, must be able to process data. The data may take a wide variety of forms, and the range of processing requirements is broad. However, we shall see that there are only a few fundamental methods or types of data processing.

It is also essential that a computer store data. Even if the computer is processing data on the fly (*i.e.*, data come in and get processed, and the results go out immediately), the computer must temporarily store at least those pieces of data that are being worked on at any given moment. Thus, there is at least a short-term data storage function. Files of data are stored on the computer for subsequent retrieval and update.

The computer must be able to move data between itself and the outside world. The computer's operating environment consists of devices that serve as either sources or destinations of data. When data are received from or delivered to a device that is directly connected to the computer, the process is known as input-output (I/O), and the device is referred to as a peripheral. When data are moved over longer distances, to or from a remote device, the process is known as data communications. The computer can function as a data movement device that simply transferring data from one peripheral or communications line to another.

Structure

The computer is an entity that interacts in some fashion with its external environment. In general, all of its linkages to the external environment can be classified as peripheral devices or communication lines. We will have something to say about both types of linkages.

- *Central processing unit (CPU)*: Controls the operation of the computer and performs its data processing functions. Often simply referred to as processor.
- *Main memory*: Stores data.
- *I/O*: Moves data between the computer and its external environment.
- *System interconnection*: Some mechanism that provides for communication among CPU, main memory, and I/O.

Traditionally, there has been just a single CPU. In recent years, there has been increasing use of multiple processors, in a single system. Each of these components will be examined in some detail in later lectures. However, for our purpose, the most interesting and in some ways the most complex component is the CPU.

Its major structural components are:

- *Control unit (CU)*: Controls the operation of the CPU and hence the computer.
- *Arithmetic and logic unit (ALU)*: Performs computer's data processing functions.
- *Register*: Provides storage internal to the CPU.
- CPU Interconnection: Some mechanism that provides for communication among the control unit, ALU, and register.

COMPUTER TYPES

Since the invention of computers from first generation and fourth generation computers, they have been classified according to their types and how they operate that is input, process and output information. Below you will get a brief discussion on various types of Computers we have. Computer types can be divided into 3 categories according to electronic nature. Types of computers are classified according to how a particular Computer functions.

These computer types are:

- Analogue Computers
- Digital Computers
- Hybrid Computers

ANALOGUE COMPUTERS

Analogue types of Computer uses what is known as analogue signals that are represented by a continuous set of varying voltages and are used in scientific research centers?, hospitals and flight centers.

The analog computer is almost an extinct type of computer these days. It is different from a digital computer in respect that it can perform numerous mathematical operations simultaneously. It is also unique in terms of operation as it utilizes continuous variables for the purpose of mathematical computation. It utilizes mechanical, hydraulic, or electrical energy or operation. With analogue types of computer no values are represented by physical measurable quantities *e.g.* voltages. Analogue computer types programme arithmetic and logical operations by measuring physical changes *i.e.* temperatures or pressure.

DIGITAL COMPUTER

With these types of computers operation are on electrical input that can attain two inputs, states of ON=1 and state of OFF = 0. With digital type of computers data is represented by digital of 0 and 1 or off state and on state. Digital computer type recognizes data by counting discrete signal of (0 0r 1), they are high speed programmable; they compute values and stores results. After looking at the Digital computer type and how it functions will move to the third computer type as mentioned above.

HYBRID COMPUTER

Hybrid computer types are very unique, in the sense that they combined both analogue and digital features and operations. These types of computers are, as the name suggests, a combination of both Analog and Digital computers. The Digital computers which work on the principle of binary digit system of "0" and "1" can give very precise results. But the problem is that they are too slow and incapable of large scale mathematical operation. In the hybrid types of computers the Digital counterparts convert the analog signals to perform Robotics and Process control.

With Hybrid computers operate by using digital to analogue convertor and analogue to digital convertor. By linking the two types of computer above you come up with this new computer type called Hybrid.

OTHER TYPES

Supercomputer and Mainframe

Supercomputer is a broad term for one of the fastest computers currently available. Supercomputers are very expensive and are employed for specialized applications that require immense amounts of mathematical calculations (number crunching). For example, weather forecasting requires a supercomputer. Other uses of supercomputers scientific simulations, (animated) graphics, fluid dynamic calculations, nuclear energy research, electronic design, and analysis of geological data (*e.g.* in petrochemical prospecting). Perhaps the best known supercomputer manufacturer is Cray Research.

Mainframe was a term originally referring to the cabinet containing the central processor unit or "main frame" of a room-filling Stone Age batch machine. After the emergence of smaller "minicomputer" designs in the early 1970s, the traditional big iron machines were described as "mainframe computers" and eventually just as mainframes. Nowadays a Mainframe is a very large and expensive computer capable of supporting hundreds, or even thousands, of users simultaneously.

The chief difference between a supercomputer and a mainframe is that a supercomputer channels all its power into executing a few programs as fast as possible, whereas a mainframe uses its power to execute many programs concurrently. In some ways, mainframes are more powerful than supercomputers because they support more simultaneous programs. But supercomputers can execute a single programme faster than a mainframe. The distinction between small mainframes and minicomputers is vague, depending really on how the manufacturer wants to market its machines.

Minicomputer

It is a midsize computer. In the past decade, the distinction between large minicomputers and small mainframes has blurred, however, as has the distinction between small minicomputers and workstations. But in general, a minicomputer is a multiprocessing system capable of supporting from up to 200 users simultaneously.

Workstation

It is a type of computer used for engineering applications (CAD/CAM), desktop publishing, software development, and other types of applications that require a moderate amount of computing power and relatively high quality graphics capabilities. Workstations generally come with a large, high-resolution graphics screen, at large amount of RAM, built-in network support, and a graphical user interface. Most workstations also have a mass storage device such as a disk drive, but a special type of workstation, called a diskless workstation, comes without a disk drive. The most common operating systems for workstations are UNIX and Windows NT. Like personal computers, most workstations are single-user computers. However, workstations are typically linked together to form a local-area network, although they can also be used as stand-alone systems.

Personal Computer

It can be defined as a small, relatively inexpensive computer designed for an individual user. In price, personal computers range anywhere from a few hundred pounds to over five thousand pounds. All are based on the microprocessor technology that enables manufacturers to put an entire CPU on one chip. Businesses use personal computers for word processing, accounting, desktop publishing, and for running spreadsheet and database management applications. At home, the most popular use for personal computers is for playing games and recently for surfing the Internet.

Personal computers first appeared in the late 1970s. One of the first and most popular personal computers was the Apple II, introduced in 1977 by Apple Computer. During the late 1970s and early 1980s, new models and competing operating systems seemed to appear daily. Then, in 1981, IBM entered the fray with its first personal computer, known as the IBM PC. The IBM PC quickly became the personal computer of choice, and most other personal computer manufacturers fell by the wayside. P.C. is short for personal computer or IBM PC.

One of the few companies to survive IBM's onslaught was Apple Computer, which remains a major player in the personal computer marketplace. Other companies adjusted to IBM's dominance by building IBM clones, computers that were internally almost the same as the IBM PC, but that cost less. Because IBM clones used the same microprocessors as IBM PCs, they were capable of running the same software. Over the years, IBM has lost much of its influence in directing the evolution of PCs.

Therefore after the release of the first PC by IBM the term PC increasingly came to mean IBM or IBM-compatible personal computers, to the exclusion of other types of personal computers, such as Macintoshes. In recent years, the term PC has become more and more difficult to pin down. In general, though, it applies to any personal computer based on an Intel microprocessor, or on an Intel-compatible microprocessor.

Tower Model

The term refers to a computer in which the power supply, motherboard, and mass storage devices are stacked on top of each other in a cabinet. This is in contrast to desktop models, in which these components are housed in a more compact box. The main advantage of tower models is that there are fewer space constraints, which makes installation of additional storage devices easier.

Desktop Model

A computer designed to fit comfortably on top of a desk, typically with the monitor sitting on top of the computer. Desktop model computers are broad and low, whereas tower model computers are narrow and tall. Because of their shape, desktop model computers are generally limited to three internal mass storage devices. Desktop models designed to be very small are sometimes referred to as slimline models.

Notebook Computer

An extremely lightweight personal computer. Notebook computers typically weigh less than 6 pounds and are small enough to fit easily in a briefcase. Aside from size, the principal difference between a notebook computer and a personal computer is the display screen. Notebook computers use a variety of techniques, known as flat-panel technologies, to produce a lightweight and non-bulky display screen. The quality of notebook display screens varies considerably. In terms of computing power, modern notebook computers are nearly equivalent to personal computers. They have the same CPUs, memory capacity, and disk drives. However, all this power in a small package is expensive. Notebook computers cost about twice as much as equivalent regular-sized computers.

Laptop Computer

A small, portable computer—small enough that it can sit on your lap. Nowadays, laptop computers are more frequently called notebook computers.

Sub Notebook Computer

A portable computer that is slightly lighter and smaller than a full-sized notebook computer. Typically, subnotebook computers have a smaller keyboard and screen, but are otherwise equivalent to notebook computers.

Hand-held Computer

A portable computer that is small enough to be held in one's hand. Although extremely convenient to carry, handheld computers have not replaced notebook computers because of their small keyboards and screens. The most popular hand-held computers are those that are specifically designed to provide PIM (personal information manager) functions, such as a calendar and address book. Some manufacturers are trying to solve the small keyboard problem by replacing the keyboard with an electronic pen. However, these pen-based devices rely on handwriting recognition technologies, which are still in their infancy. Hand-held computers are also called PDAs, palmtops and pocket computers.

Palmtop

A small computer that literally fits in your palm.

Compared to full-size computers, palmtops are severely limited, but they are practical for certain functions such as phone books and calendars. Palmtops that use a pen rather than a keyboard for input are often called hand-held computers or PDAs. Because of their small size, most palmtop computers do not include disk drives. However, many contain PCMCIA slots in which you can insert disk drives, modems, memory, and other devices. Palmtops are also called PDAs, hand-held computers and pocket computers.

PDA

Short for personal digital assistant, a handheld device that combines computing, telephone/fax, and networking features. A typical PDA can function as a cellular phone, fax sender, and personal organizer. Unlike portable computers, most PDAs are pen-based, using a stylus rather than a keyboard for input. This means that they also incorporate handwriting recognition features. Some PDAs can also react to voice input by using voice recognition technologies. The field of PDA was pioneered by Apple Computer, which introduced the Newton MessagePad in 1993. Shortly thereafter, several other manufacturers offered similar products. To date, PDAs have had only modest success in the marketplace, due to their high price tags and limited applications. However, many experts believe that PDAs will eventually become common gadgets. PDAs are also called palmtops, hand-held computers and pocket computers.

CLASSIFICATION OF COMPUTERS

Computers are classified according to their data processing speed, amount of data that they can hold and price. Generally, a computer with high processing speed and large internal storage is called a big computer. Due to rapidly improving technology, we are always confused among the categories of computers.

Depending upon their speed and memory size, computers are classified into following four main groups.

- Supercomputer.

- Mainframe computer.
- Mini computer.
- Microcomputer.

SUPERCOMPUTER

Supercomputer is the most powerful and fastest, and also very expensive. It was developed in 1980s. It is used to process large amount of data and to solve the complicated scientific problems. It can perform more than one trillions calculations per second. It has large number of processors connected parallel. So parallel processing is done in this computer. In a single supercomputer thousands of users can be connected at the same time and the supercomputer handles the work of each user separately.

Supercomputer are mainly used for:

- Weather forecasting.
- Nuclear energy research.
- Aircraft design.
- Automotive design.
- Online banking.
- To control industrial units.

The supercomputers are used in large organizations, research laboratories, aerospace centers, large industrial units etc. Nuclear scientists use supercomputers to create and analyse models of nuclear fission and fusions, predicting the actions and reactions of millions of atoms as they interact. The examples of supercomputers are CRAY-1, CRAY-2, Control Data CYBER 205 and ETA A-10 etc.

MAINFRAME COMPUTERS

Mainframe computers are also large-scale computers but supercomputers are larger than mainframe. These are also very expensive. The mainframe computer specially requires a very large clean room with air-conditioner. This makes it very expensive to buy and operate. It can support a large number of various equipments It also has multiple processors. Large mainframe systems can handle the input and output requirements of several thousand of users. For example, IBM, S/390 mainframe can support 50,000 users simultaneously. The users often access then mainframe with terminals or personal computers. Tere are basically two types of terminals used with mainframe systems. These are:

Dumb Terminal

Dumb terminal does not have its own CPU and storage devices. This type of terminal uses the CPU and storage devices of mainframe system. Typically, a dumb terminal consists of monitor and a keyboard (or mouse).

Intelligent Terminal

Intelligent terminal has its own processor and can perform some processing operations. Usually, this type of terminal does not have its own storage. Typically, personal computrers are used as intelligent terminals. A personal computer as an intelligent terminal gives facility to access data and other services from mainframe system. It also enables to store and process data locally.

The mainframe computers are specially used as servers on the World Wide Web. The mainframe computers are used in large organizations such as Banks, Airlines and Universities etc. where many people (users) need frequent access to the same data, which is usually organized into one or more huge databases. IBM is the major manufacturer of mainframe computers. The examples of mainframes are IBM S/390, Control Data CYBER 176 and Amdahl 580 etc.

MINICOMPUTERS

These are smaller in size, have lower processing speed and also have lower cost than mainframe. These computers are known as minicomputers because of their small size as compared to other computers at that time. The capabilities of a minicomputer are between mainframe and personal computer. These computers are also known as midrange computers.

The minicomputers are used in business, education and many other government departments. Although some minicomputers are designed for a single user but most are designed to handle multiple terminals. Minicomputers are commonly used as servers in network environment and hundreds of personal computers can be connected to the network with a minicomputer acting as server like mainframes, minicomputers are used as web servers. Single user minicomputers are used for sophisticated design tasks.

The first minicomputer was introduced in the mid-1960s by Digital Equipment Corporation (DEC). After this IBM Corporation (AS/400 computers) Data General Corporation and Prime Computer also designed the mini computers.

MICROCOMPUTER

The microcomputers are also known as personal computers or simply PCs. Microprocessor is used in this type of computer. These are very small in size and cost. The IBM's first microcomputer was designed in 1981 and was named as IBM-PC. After this many computer hardware companies copied the design of IBM-PC. The term "PC-compatible" refers any personal computer based on the original IBM personal computer design.

The most popular types of personal computers are the PC and the Apple. PC and PC-compatible computers have processors with different architectures than processors in Apple computers. These two types of computers also use different operating systems. PC and PC-compatible computers use the Windows operating system while Apple computers use the Macintosh operating system (MacOS). The majority of microcomputers sold today are part of IBM-compatible. However the Apple computer is neither an IBM nor a compatible. It is another family of computers made by Apple computer. Personal computers are available in two models.

These are:

- Desktop PCs
- Tower PCs

A desktop personal computer is most popular model of personal computer. The system unit of the desktop personal computer can lie flat on the desk or table. In desktop personal computer, the monitor is usually placed on the system unit.

Microcomputer are further divided into following categories:

- Laptop computer
- Workstation
- Network computer
- Handheld computer

Laptop computer

Laptop computer is also known as notebook computer. It is small size (85-by-11 inch notebook computer and can fit inside a briefcase. The laptop computer is operated on a special battery and it does not have to be plugged in like desktop computer. The laptop computer is portable and fully functional microcomputer. It is mostly used during journey. It can be used on your lap in an airplane. It is because it is referred to as laptop computer.

The memory and storage capacity of laptop computer is almost equivalent to the PC or desktop computer. It also has the hard dist, floppy disk drive, Zip disk drive, CD-ROM drive, CD-writer etc. it has built-in keyboard and built-in trackball as pointing device. Laptop computer is also available with the same processing speed as the most powerful personal computer. It means that laptop computer has same features as personal computer. Laptop computers are more expensive than desktop computers. Normally these computers are frequently used in business travellers.

Workstations

Workstations are special single user computers having the same features as personal computer but have the processing speed equivalent to minicomputer or mainframe computer. A workstation computer can be fitted on a desktop. Scientists, engineers, architects and graphic designers mostly use these computers.

Workstation computers are expensive and powerful computers. These have advanced processors, more RAM and storage capacity than personal computers. These are usually used as single-user applications but these are used as servers on computer network and web servers as well.

Network Computers

Network computers are also version of personal computers having less processing power, memory and storage. These are specially designed as terminals for network environment. Some types of network computers have no storage.

The network computers are designed for network, Internet or Intranet for data entry or to access data on the network.

The network computers depend upon the network's server for data storage and to use software. These computers also use the network's server to perform some processing tasks. Network computers are cheaper to purchase and to maintain than personal computers.

Handheld Computer

In the mid 1990s, many new types of small personal computing devices have been introduced and these are referred to as handheld computers. These computers are also referred to as Palmtop Computers. The handheld computers sometimes called Mini-Notebook Computers. The type of computer is named as handheld computer because it can fit in one hand while you can operate it with the other hand. Because of its reduced size, the screen of handheld computer is quite small.

Similarly it also has small keyboard. The handheld computers are preferred by business traveller. Some handheld computers have a specialized keyboard. These computers are used by mobile employees, such as meter readers and parcel delivery people, whose jobs require them to move from place to place.

The examples of handheld computers are:

- Personal Digital Assistance
- Cellular telephones
- H/PC Pro devices

FUNCTIONAL UNITS OF A COMPUTER SYSTEM

Digital computer systems consist of three distinct units. *These units are as follows*:

- Input unit
- Central Processing unit
- Output unit

These units are interconnected by electrical cables to permit communication between them. This allowsthe computer to function as a system.

INPUT UNIT

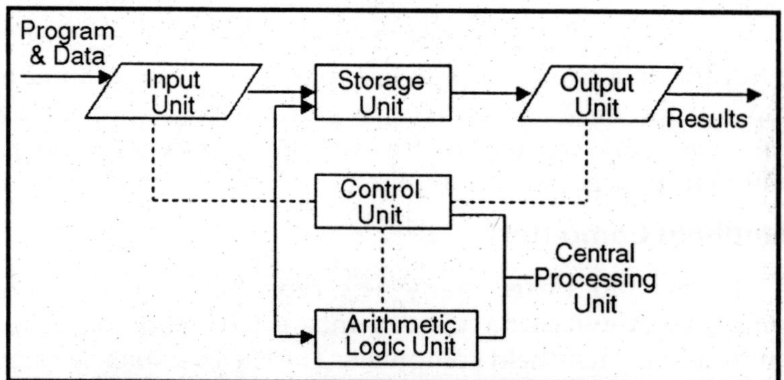

A computer must receive both data and programme statements to function properly and be able to solve problems. The method of feeding data and programs to a computer is accomplished by an input device. Computer input devices read data from a source, such as magnetic disks, and translate that data into electronic impulses for transfer into the CPU. Some typical input devices are a keyboard, a mouse, or a scanner.

CENTRAL PROCESSING UNIT

The brain of a computer system is the central processing unit (CPU). The CPU processes data transferred to it from one of the various input devices. It then transfers either an intermediate or final result of the CPU to one or more output devices. A central control section and work areas are required to perform calculations or manipulate data. The CPU is the computing centre of the system. It consists of a control section, an arithmetic-logic section as shown in fig, and an internal storage section (main memory). Each section within the CPU serves a specific function and has a particular relationship with the other sections within the

CPU.Control Section

The control section directs the flow of traffic (operations) and data. It also maintains order within the computer. The flow of control is indicated by dotted arrows. The control section selects one programme statement at a time from the programme storage area, interprets the statement, and sends the appropriate electronic impulses to the arithmetic-logic and storage sections so they can carryout the instructions. The control section does not perform actual processing operations on the data. The control section instructs the input device on when to start and stop transferring data to the input storage area. It also tells the output device when to start and stop receiving data from the output storage area.

Arithmetic-logic Section

The arithmetic-logic section performs arithmetic operations, such as addition, subtraction, multiplication, and division. Through internal logic capability, it tests various conditions encountered during processing and takes action based on the result.As indicated by the solid arrows, data flows between the arithmetic-logic section and the internal storage section during processing. Specifically, data is transferred as needed from the storage section to the arithmetic-logic section, processed, and returned to internal storage. At no time does processing take placein the storage section.

Internal Storage Section

The internal storage section is sometimes called primary storage, main storage, or main memory, because this section functions similar to our own human memory. The storage section serves four purposes; three relate to retention (holding) of data during processing. First, as indicated by the solid arrow as shown in fig, data is transferred from an input device to the INPUTSTORAGE AREA where it remains until the computers ready to process it. Second, a WORKINGSTORAGE AREA ("scratch pad" memory) within the storage section holds both the data being processed and the intermediate results of the arithmetic-logic operations. Third, the storage section retains the processing results in the OUTPUT STORAGE AREA. From there the processing results can be transferred to an output device. The fourth storage section, the PROGRAMME STORAGE AREA, contains the programme statements transferred from an input device to process the data. Please note that the four areas (input, working storage, output, and programme storage) are NOT famed in size or location but are determined by individual programme requirements.

OUTPUT UNIT

As programme statements and data are received by the CPU from an input device, the results of the processed data are sent from the CPU to an OUTPUT DEVICE. These results are transferred from the output storage area onto an output medium, such as a floppy disk, hard drive, video display, printer, and so on.

BUSES AND ARCHITECTURE

BUS

A set of parallel conductors, which allow devices attached to it to communicate with the CPU.

The bus consists of three main parts:

- Control lines
- Address lines
- Data lines

Control Lines

These allow the CPU to control which operations the devices attached should perform, *I.E.* read or write.

Address Lines

Allows the CPU to reference certain (Memory) locations within the device.

Data Lines

The meaningful data which is to be sent or retrieved from a device is placed on to these lines. The Bus is set to run at a specified speed which is measured in MHz

REGISTERS

Registers are fast memory, almost always connected to circuitry that allows various arithmetic, logical, control, and other manipulations, as well as possibly setting internal flags.

Most early computers had only one data register that could be used for arithmetic and logic instructions. Often there would be additional special purpose registers set aside either for temporary fast internal storage or assigned to logic circuits to implement certain instructions. Some early computers had one or two address registers that pointed to a memory location for memory accesses (a pair of address registers typically would act as source and destination pointers for memory operations).

Computers soon had multiple data registers, address registers, and sometimes other special purpose registers. Some computers have general purpose registers that can be used for both data and address operations. Every digital computer using a von Neumann architecture has a register (called the programme counter) that points to the next executable instruction. Many computers have additional control registers for implementing various control capabilities. Often some or all of the internal flags are combined into a flag or status register.

ACCUMULATORS

Accumulators are registers that can be used for arithmetic, logical, shift, rotate, or other similar operations. The first computers typically only had one accumulator. Many times there were related special purpose registers that contained the source data for an accumulator. Accumulators were replaced with data registers and general purpose registers.

Accumulators reappeared in the first microprocessors.

- *Intel 8086/80286*: one word (16 bit) accumulator; named AX (high order byte of the AX register is named AH and low order byte of the AX register is named AL)
- *Intel 80386*: one doubleword (32 bit) accumulator; named EAX (low order word uses the same names as the accumulator on the Intel 8086 and 80286 [AX] and low order and high order bytes of the low order words of four of the registers use the same names as the accumulator on the Intel 8086 and 80286 [AH and AL])
- *Mix*: one accumulator; named A-register; five bytes plus sign

DATA REGISTERS

Data registers are used for temporary scratch storage of data, as well as for data manipulations (arithmetic, logic, etc.). In some processors, all data registers act in the same manner, while in other processors different operations are performed are specific registers.

- *Mix*: one extension register; named X-register; five bytes plus sign; can be concatenated on the right hand side of the A-register (accumulator)
- *Motorola 680x0, 68300*: 8 longword (32 bit) data registers; named D0, D1, D2, D3, D4, D5, D6, and D7

ADDRESS REGISTERS

Address registers store the addresses of specific memory locations. Often many integer and logic operations can be performed on address registers directly (to allow for computation of addresses). Sometimes the contents of address register(s) are combined with other special purpose registers to compute the actual physical address. This allows for the hardware implementation of dynamic memory pages, virtual memory, and protected memory. The number of bits of an address register (possibly combined with information from other registers) limits the maximum amount of addressable memory. A 16-bit address register can address 64K of physical memory. A 24-bit address register can address address 16 MB of physical memory. A 32-bit address register can address 4 GB of physical memory. A 64-bit address register can address 1.8446744×10^{19} of physical memory. Addresses are always unsigned binary numbers.

- *Mix*: one jump registers; named J-register; two bytes and sign is always positive
- *Motorola 680x0, 68300*: 8 longword (32 bit) address registers; named A0, A1, A2, A3, A4, A5, A6, and A7 (also called the stack pointer)

GENERAL PURPOSE REGISTERS

General purpose registers can be used as either data or address registers.

- *DEC VAX*: 16 word (32 bit) general purpose registers; named R0 through R15
- *IBM 360/370*: 16 full word (32 bit) general purpose registers; named 0, 1, 2, 3, 4, 5, 6, 7, 8, 9, A (or 10), B (or 11), C (or 12), D (or 13), E (or 14), and F (or 15)
- *Intel 8086/80286*: 8 word (16 bit) general purpose registers; named AX, BX, CX, DX, BP, SP, SI, and DI (high order bytes of the AX, BX, CX, and DX registers have the names AH, BH, CH, and DH and low order bytes of the AX, BX, CX, and DX registers have the names AL, BL, CL, and DL)
- *Intel 80386*: 8 doubleword (32 bit) general purpose registers; named EAX, EBX, ECX, EDX, EBP, ESP, ESI, and EDI (low order words use the same names as the general purpose registers on the Intel 8086 and 80286 and low order and high order bytes of the low order words of four of the registers use the same names as the general purpose registers on the Intel 8086 and 80286)
- *Motorola 88100*: 32 word (32 bit) general purpose registers; named r0 through r31

CONSTANT REGISTERS

Constant registers are special read-only registers that

store a constant. Attempts to write to a constant register are illegal or ignored.

In some RISC processors, constant registers are used to store commonly used values (such as zero, one, or negative one) — for example, a constant register containing zero can be used in register to register data moves, providing the equivalent of a clear instruction without adding one to the instruction set.

Constant registers are also often used in floating point units to provide such value as pi or e with additional hidden bits for greater accuracy in computations.

- Motorola 88100: r0 (general purpose register 0) contains the constant 32 bit integer zero

FLOATING POINT REGISTERS

Floating point registers are special registers set aside for floating point math.

INDEX REGISTERS

Index registers are used to provide more flexibility in addressing modes, allowing the programmer to create a memory address by combining the contents of an address register with the contents of an index register (with displacements, increments, decrements, and other options). In some processors, there are specific index registers (or just one index register) that can only be used only for that purpose. In some processors, any data register, address register, or general register (or some combination of the three) can be used as an index register.

- *IBM 360/370*: any of the 16 general purpose registers may be used as an index register
- *Intel 80x86*: 7 of the 8 general purpose registers may be used as an index register (the ESP is the exception)
- *Mix*: five index registers; named I-registers I1, I2, I3, I4, and I5; five bytes plus sign
- *Motorola 680x0, 68300*: any of the 8 data registers or the 8 address registers may be used as an index register

BASE REGISTERS

Base registers or segment registers are used to segment memory. Effective addresses are computed by adding the contents of the base or segment register to the rest of the effective address computation. In some processors, any register can serve as a base register.

In some processors, there are specific base or segment registers (one or more) that can only be used for that purpose. In some processors with multiple base or segment registers, each base or segment register is used for different kinds of memory accesses (such as a segment register for data accesses and a different segment register for programme accesses).

- *IBM 360/370*: Any of the 16 general purpose registers may be used as a base register
- *Intel 80x86*: 6 dedicated segment registers: CS (code segment), SS (stack segment), DS (data segment), ES (extra segment, a second data segment register), FS (third data segment register), and GS (fourth data segment register)
- *Motorola 680x0, 68300*: any of the 8 address registers may be used as a base register

CONTROL REGISTERS

Control registers control some aspect of processor operation. The most universal control register is the programme counter.

PROGRAMME COUNTER

Almost every digital computer ever made uses a programme counter. The programme counter points to the memory location that stores the next executable instruction. Branching is implemented by making changes to the programme counter.

Some processor designs allow software to directly change the programme counter, but usually software only indirectly changes the programme counter (for example, a JUMP instruction will insert the operand into the programme counter).

An assembler has a location counter, which is an internal pointer to the address (first byte) of the next location in storage (for instructions, data areas, constants, etc.) while the source code is being converted into object code.

The VAX uses the 16th of 16 general purpose registers as the programme counter (PC). Almost the entire instruction set can directly manipulate the programme counter, allowing a very rich set of possible kinds of branching.

The programme counter in System/360 and 370 machines is contained in bits 40-63 of the programme status word (PSW), which is directly accessible by some instructions.

- *IBM 360/370*: Programme counter is bits 40-63 of the programme status word (PSW)
- *Intel 8086/80286*: 16-bit instruction pointer (IP)
- *Intel 80386*: 32-bit instruction pointer (EIP)
- *Motorola 680x0, 68300*: 32-bit programme counter (PC)

PROCESSOR FLAGS

Processor flags store information about specific processor functions. The processor flags are usually kept in a flag register or a general status register. This can include result flags that record the results of certain kinds of testing, information about data that is moved, certain kinds of information about the results of compations or transformations, and information about some processor states. Closely related and often stored in the same processor word or status register (although often in a privileged portion) are control flags that control processor actions or processor states or the actions of certain instructions.

- *IBM 360/370*: programme status word (PSW)
- *Intel 8086/80286*: 16-bit flag register (FLAGS); system flags, control flag, and status flags)
- *Intel 80386*: 32-bit flag register (EFLAGS); system flags, control flag, and status flags)
- *Mix*: an overflow toggle and a comparison indicator
- *Motorola 680x0, 68300*: 16-bit status register (SR); high byte is system byte and requires privileged access, low byte is user byte or condition code register (CCR)

STACK POINTER

Stack pointers are used to implement a processor stack in memory. In many processors, address registers can be used as generic data stack pointers and queue pointers. A specific stack pointer or address register may be hardwired for certain instructions. The most common use is to store return addresses, processor state information, and temporary variables for subroutines.

- *IBM 360/370*: any of the 16 general purpose registers may be used as a stack pointer
- *Intel 8086/80286*: dedicated stack pointer (SP) combined with stack segment pointer (SS) to create address of stack
- *Intel 80386*: dedicated stack pointer (ESP) combined with stack segment pointer (SS) and the stack-frame base pointer (EBP) to create address of stack
- *Motorola 680x0, 68300*: dedicated user stack pointer (USP, A7) and system stack pointer (SSP, A7) for implicit stack pointer operations, as well as allowing any of the 8 address registers to be as explicit stack pointers

SUBROUTINE RETURN POINTER

Some RISC processors include a special subroutine return pointer rather than using a stack in memory. The return address for subroutine calls is stored in this register rather than in memory. More than one level of subroutine calls requires storing and saving the contents of this register to and from memory.

- *Motorola 88100*: r1 is a 32 bit register containing the return pointer generated by bsr and jsr instructions; the register can be read or overwritten by software and can even be used as a temporary general purpose data register

STOCK ORGANIZATION

A useful feature that is included in the CPU of most computers is a stack or last-in first out (LIFO) list. A stack is a storage device that stores information in such a manner that the item stored last is the first item retrieved. The operation a stack can be companied to a stack of trays.

The stack in Digital Computer is essentially a memory unit with an address register that can count only (after an initial value is loaded into it.) The register that holds the address for the stack is called a Stack Pointer (SP) because its values always points at the top item in the stack.

The two operations – PUSH (insert)
– Pop (delete)

REGISTER STACK

A stack can be placed in a portion of a large memory as it can be organized as a collection of a finite number of memory words as register. In a 64- word stack, the stack pointer contains 6 bits because $2^6 = 64$. The one bit register FULL is set to 1 when the stack is full, and the one-bit register EMTY is set to 1 when the stack is empty. DR is the data register that holes the binary data to be written into on read out of the stack. Initially, SP is decide to O, EMTY is set to 1, FULL = 0, so that SP points to the word at address O and the stack is masked empty and not full.

PUSH	SP → SP + 1	increment stack pointer
	M [SP] → DR	unit item on top of the Stack
	It (SP = 0)	then (FULL → 1) check it stack is full
	EMTY → 0	mask the stack not empty.
POP	DR → [SP]	read item trans the top of stack
	SP → SP –1	decrement SP
	It (SP = 0)	then (EMTY → 1) check it stack is empty
	FULL → 0	mark the stack not full.

INSTRUCTION FORMATS

The most common fields found in instruction format are:

- An operation code field that specified the operation to be performed
- An address field that designates a memory address or a processor registers.

- A mode field that specifies the way the operand or the effective address is determined.

Computers may have instructions of several different lengths containing varying number of addresses. The number of address field in the instruction format of a computer depends on the internal organization of its registers. Most computers fall into one of three types of CPU organization.

- Single Accumulator organization
  ADD X AC → AC + M [×]
- General Register Organization ADD
  R1, R2, R3 R → R2 + R3
- Stack Organization PUSH X

Three address Instruction

Computer with three addresses instruction format can use each address field to specify either processor register are memory operand.

ADD R_1, A, B	$A_1 \rightarrow M [A] + M [B]$
ADD R_2, C, D	$R_2 \rightarrow M [C] + M [B]$ X = (A + B) * (C + A)
MUL X, R_1, R_2	M [X] R_1 * R_2

The advantage of the three address formats is that it results in short programme when evaluating arithmetic expression. The disadvantage is that the binary-coded instructions require too many bits to specify three addresses.

Two Address Instruction

Most common in commercial computers. Each address field can specify either a processes register on a memory word.

MOV	R_1, A	$R_1 \rightarrow M [A]$	
ADD	R_1, B	$R_1 \rightarrow R_1 + M [B]$	
MOV	R_2, C	$R_2 \rightarrow M [C]$	X = (A + B) * (C + D)
ADD	R_2, D	$R_2 \rightarrow R_2 + M [D]$	
MUL	R_1, R_2	$R_1 \rightarrow R_1 * R_2$	
MOV	X_1 R_1	$M [X] \rightarrow R_1$	

One Address instruction

It used an implied accumulator (AC) register for all data

manipulation. For multiplication/division, there is a need for a second register.

LOAD	A	AC → M [A]	
ADD	B	AC → AC + M [B]	
STORE	T	M [T] → AC	X = (A +B) × (C + A)

All operations are done between the AC register and a memory operand. It's the address of a temporary memory location required for storing the intermediate result.

LOAD	C	AC → M (C)
ADD	D	AC → AC + M (D)
ML	T	AC → AC + M (T)
STORE	X	M [×]→ AC

Zero – Address Instruction

A stack organized computer does not use an address field for the instruction ADD and MUL. The PUSH and POP instruction, however, need an address field to specify the operand that communicates with the stack (TOS → top of the stack).

PUSH	A	TOS → A
PUSH	B	TOS → B
ADD		TOS → (A + B)
PUSH	C	TOS → C
PUSH	D	TOS → D
ADD		TOS → (C + D)
MUL		TOS → (C + D) * (A + B)
POP	X	M [X] TOS

ADDRESSING MODES

The operation field of an instruction specifies the operation to be performed. This operation must be executed on some data stored in computer register as memory words. The way the operands are chosen during programme execution is dependent on the addressing mode of the instruction.

The addressing mode specifies a rule for interpreting or modifying the address field of the instruction between the operand is activity referenced. Computer use addressing mode technique for the purpose of accommodating one or both of the following provisions.

- To give programming versatility to the uses by providing such facilities as pointer to memory, counters for top control, indexing of data, and programme relocation.
- To reduce the number of bits in the addressing fields of the instruction.

OPERATION CYCLE OF COMPUTER

- Fetch the instruction from memory
- Decode the instruction
- Execute the instruction

Programme Counter (PC) keeps track of the instruction in the programme stored in memory.

PC holds the address of the instruction to be executed next and in incremented each time an instruction is fetched from memory.

- Implied mode
- Auto increment/Auto decrement mode
- Immediate mode
- Direct Address mode
- Register mode
- Indirect Address mode
- Register mode
- Relative Address ınode
- Register – indirect
- Indexed Addressing mode mode
- Base Register Addressing mode

Opcode	Mode	Address

INSTRUCTION FORMAT WITH MODE FIELD

Relative Address

The content of PC is added to the address part of the instruction in order to obtain the effective address,

Ex:- PC = 825 + 1 + 24

Indexed Addressing Mode

The content of index register is added to the address part of the instruction in order to obtain the effective address.

Base Register Addressing Mode

The content of a base register is added to the address bank of the instruction to obtain the effective address.

Indirect Address

Effective Address = Address part of instruction + content of CPU register

DATA TRANSFER AND MANIPULATION

Computer provides an extensive set of instructions to give the user the flexibility to carryout various computational task. Most computer instruction can be classified into three categories.

- Data transfer instruction
- Data manipulation instruction
- Programme control instruction

Data transfer instruction cause transferred data from one location to another without changing the binary instruction content. Data manipulation instructions are those that perform arithmetic logic, and shift operations. Programme control instructions provide decision-making capabilities and change the path taken by the programme when executed in the computer.

Data Transfer Instruction

Data transfer instruction move data from one place in the computer to another without changing the data content. The most common transfers are between memory and processes registers, between processes register and input or output, and between processes register themselves.

Table. Typical Data Transfer Instruction

Name	Mnemonic	Name	Mnemonic
Load	LD	Store	ST
Move	MOV	Exchange	XCH
Input	IN	Output	OUT
Push	PUSH	Pop	POP

Data Manipulation Instruction

It performs operations on data and provides the computational capabilities for the computer. The data manipulation instructions in a typical computer are usually divided into three basic types.

- Arithmetic Instruction
- Logical bit manipulation Instruction
- Shift Instruction.

Arithmetic Instruction

Name	Mnemonic
Increment	INC
Decrement	DEC
Add	Add
Subtract	Sub
Multiply	MUL
Divide	DIV
Add with Carry	ADDC
Subtract with Basses	SUBB
Negate (2's Complement)	NEG

Logical and Bit Manipulation Instruction

Name	Mnemonic
Clear	CLR
Complement	COM
AND	AND
OR	OR
Exclusive-Or	XOR
Clear Carry	CLRC
Set Carry	SETC
Complement Carry	COMC
Enable Interrupt	ET
Disable Interrupt	OI

Shift Instruction

Instructions to shift the content of an operand are quite

useful and one often provided in several variations. Shifts are operation in which the bits of a word are moved to the left or right. The bit-shifted in at the and of the word determines the type of shift used. Shift instruction may specify either logical shift, arithmetic shifts, or rotate type shifts.

Name	Mnemonic
Logical Shift right	SHR
Logical Shift left	SHL
Arithmetic shift right	SHRA
Arithmetic shift left	SHLA
Rotate right	ROR
Rotate left	ROL
Rotate mgmt through carry	RORC
Rotate left through carry	ROLC

RISC and CISC ARCHITECTURE

Characteristics of CISC architecture are:

- A large no. of instruction-typically from 100 to 250 instruction.
- Some instruction that perform specialized tasks and one used infrequently.
- A large variety of addressing modes – typically from 5 to 20 different modes.
- Variable length instruction format
- Instruction that manipulate operates in memory.

3

Concept and Structure

OVERVIEW

Operating Systems are resource managers. The main resource is computer hardware in the form of processors, storage, input/output devices, communication devices, and data. Some of the operating system functions are: implementing the user interface, sharing hardware among users, allowing users to share data among themselves, preventing users from interfering with one another, scheduling resources among users, facilitating input/output, recovering from errors, accounting for resource usage, facilitating parallel operations, organizing data for secure and rapid access, and handling network communications.

OBJECTIVES

Modern Operating systems generally have following three major goals. Operating systems generally accomplish these goals by running processes in low privilege and providing service calls that invoke the operating system kernel in high-privilege state.

There are several reasons for abstraction.

- *First,* the code needed to control peripheral devices is not standardized. Operating systems provide subroutines called device drivers that perform operations on behalf of programs for example, input/output operations.
- *Second,* the operating system introduces new functions as it abstracts the hardware. For instance,

operating system introduces the file abstraction so that programs do not have to deal with disks.

- *Third,* the operating system transforms the computer hardware into multiple virtual computers, each belonging to a different programme. Each programme that is running is called a process. Each process views the hardware through the lens of abstraction.
- *Fourth,* the operating system can enforce security through abstraction.
  - To allocate resources to processes (Manage resources) An operating system controls how processes (the active agents) may access resources (passive entities).
  - Provide a pleasant and effective user interface. The user interacts with the operating systems through the user interface and usually interested in the "look and feel" of the operating system. The most important components of the user interface are the command interpreter, the file system, on-line help, and application integration. The recent trend has been towards increasingly integrated graphical user interfaces that encompass the activities of multiple processes on networks of computers.

HISTORY

Historically operating systems have been tightly related to the computer architecture, it is good idea to study the history of operating systems from the architecture of the computers on which they run. Operating systems have evolved through a number of distinct phases or generations which corresponds roughly to the decades.

THE 1940'S-FIRST GENERATIONS

The earliest electronic digital computers had no operating systems. Machines of the time were so primitive that programs were often entered one bit at time on rows of mechanical switches (plug boards). Programming languages were unknown (not even assembly languages). Operating systems were unheard of.

THE 1950'S-SECOND GENERATION

By the early 1950's, the routine had improved somewhat with the introduction of punch cards. The General Motors Research Laboratories implemented the first operating systems in early 1950's for their IBM 701. The system of the 50's generally ran one job at a time. These were called single-stream batch processing systems because programs and data were submitted in groups or batches.

THE 1960'S-THIRD GENERATION

The systems of the 1960's were also batch processing systems, but they were able to take better advantage of the computer's resources by running several jobs at once. So operating systems designers developed the concept of multiprogramming in which several jobs are in main memory at once; a processor is switched from job to job as needed to keep several jobs advancing while keeping the peripheral devices in use.

For example, on the system with no multiprogramming, when the current job paused to wait for other I/O operation to complete, the CPU simply sat idle until the I/O finished. The solution for this problem that evolved was to partition memory into several pieces, with a different job in each partition. While one job was waiting for I/O to complete, another job could be using the CPU.

Another major feature in third-generation operating system was the technique called spooling. In spooling, a high-speed device like a disk interposed between a running programme and a low-speed device involved with the programme in input/output. Instead of writing directly to a printer, for example, outputs are written to the disk. Programs can run to completion faster, and other programs can be initiated sooner when the printer becomes available, the outputs may be printed.

Another feature present in this generation was time-sharing technique, in which each user has an on-line terminal. Because the user is present and interacting with the computer, the computer system must respond quickly to user requests, otherwise user productivity could suffer. Timesharing systems were developed to multiprogram large number of simultaneous interactive users.

FOURTH GENERATION

With the development of LSI (Large Scale Integration) circuits, chips, operating system entered in the system entered in the personal computer and the workstation age. Microprocessor technology evolved to the point that it become possible to build desktop computers as powerful as the mainframes of the 1970s. Two operating systems have dominated the personal computer scene: MS-DOS, written by Microsoft, Inc. for the IBM PC and other machines using the Intel 8088 CPU and its successors, and UNIX, which is dominant on the large personal computers using the Motorola 6899 CPU family.

STRUCTURE

SYSTEM COMPONENTS

Even though, not all systems have the same structure many modern operating systems share the same goal of supporting the following types of system components.

Process Management

The operating system manages many kinds of activities ranging from user programs to system programs like printer spooler, name servers, file server etc. Each of these activities is encapsulated in a process. A process includes the complete execution context (code, data, PC, registers, OS resources in use etc.). It is important to note that a process is not a programme. A process is only ONE instant of a programme in execution. There are many processes can be running the same programme.

The five major activities of an operating system in regard to process management are:

- Creation and deletion of user and system processes.
- Suspension and resumption of processes.
- A mechanism for process synchronization.
- A mechanism for process communication.
- A mechanism for deadlock handling.

Main-Memory Management

Primary-Memory or Main-Memory is a large array of words or bytes. Each word or byte has its own address. Main-memory provides storage that can be access directly by the CPU. That is to say for a programme to be executed, it must in the main memory.

The major activities of an operating in regard to memory-management are:

- Keep track of which part of memory are currently being used and by whom.
- Decide which process are loaded into memory when memory space becomes available.
- Allocate and deallocate memory space as needed.

File Management

A file is a collected of related information defined by its creator. Computer can store files on the disk (secondary storage), which provide long term storage. Some examples of storage media are magnetic tape, magnetic disk and optical disk. Each of these media has its own properties like speed, capacity, data transfer rate and access methods.

A file systems normally organized into directories to ease their use. These directories may contain files and other directions.

The five main major activities of an operating system in regard to file management are:

- The creation and deletion of files.
- The creation and deletion of directions.
- The support of primitives for manipulating files and directions.

- The mapping of files onto secondary storage.
- The back up of files on stable storage media.

I/O System Management

I/O subsystem hides the peculiarities of specific hardware devices from the user. Only the device driver knows the peculiarities of the specific device to whom it is assigned.

SECONDARY-STORAGE MANAGEMENT

Generally speaking, systems have several levels of storage, including primary storage, secondary storage and cache storage. Instructions and data must be placed in primary storage or cache to be referenced by a running programme.

Because main memory is too small to accommodate all data and programs, and its data are lost when power is lost, the computer system must provide secondary storage to back up main memory.

Secondary storage consists of tapes, disks, and other media designed to hold information that will eventually be accessed in primary storage (primary, secondary, cache) is ordinarily divided into bytes or words consisting of a fixed number of bytes. Each location in storage has an address; the set of all addresses available to a programme is called an address space.

The three major activities of an operating system in regard to secondary storage management are:

- Managing the free space available on the secondary-storage device.
- Allocation of storage space when new files have to be written.
- Scheduling the requests for memory access.

Networking

A distributed systems is a collection of processors that do not share memory, peripheral devices, or a clock. The processors communicate with one another through communication lines called network. The communication-network design must consider routing and connection strategies, and the problems of contention and security.

Protection System

If a computer systems has multiple users and allows the concurrent execution of multiple processes, then the various processes must be protected from one another's activities. Protection refers to mechanism for controlling the access of programs, processes, or users to the resources defined by a computer systems.

Command Interpreter System

A command interpreter is an interface of the operating system with the user. The user gives commands with are executed by operating system (usually by turning them into system calls). The main function of a command interpreter is to get and execute the next user specified command. Command-Interpreter is usually not part of the kernel, since multiple command interpreters (shell, in UNIX terminology) may be support by an operating system, and they do not really need to run in kernel mode.

OPERATING SYSTEMS SERVICES

Following are the five services provided by an operating systems to the convenience of the users.

Programme Execution

The purpose of a computer systems is to allow the user to execute programs. So the operating systems provides an environment where the user can conveniently run programs. The user does not have to worry about the memory allocation or multitasking or anything. These things are taken care of by the operating systems.

Running a programme involves the allocating and deallocating memory, CPU scheduling in case of multiprocess. These functions cannot be given to the user-level programs. So user-level programs cannot help the user to run programs independently without the help from operating systems.

I/O Operations

Each programme requires an input and produces output. This involves the use of I/O. The operating systems hides the user the details of underlying hardware for the I/O. All the user sees is that the I/O has been performed without any details. So the operating systems by providing I/O makes it convenient for the users to run programs.

For efficiently and protection users cannot control I/O so this service cannot be provided by user-level programs.

File System Manipulation

The output of a programme may need to be written into new files or input taken from some files. The operating systems provides this service. The user does not have to worry about secondary storage management. User gives a command for reading or writing to a file and sees his her task accomplished. Thus operating systems makes it easier for user programs to accomplished their task.

This service involves secondary storage management. The speed of I/O that depends on secondary storage management is critical to the speed of many programs and hence I think it is best relegated to the operating systems to manage it than giving individual users the control of it. It is not difficult for the user-level programs to provide these services but for above mentioned reasons it is best if this service s left with operating system.

Communications

There are instances where processes need to communicate with each other to exchange information. It may be between processes running on the same computer or running on the different computers. By providing this service the operating system relieves the user of the worry of passing messages between processes.

In case where the messages need to be passed to processes on the other computers through a network it can be done by the user programs. The user programme may be customised to the specifics of the hardware through which the message transits and provides the service interface to the operating system.

Error Detection

An error is one part of the system may cause malfunctioning of the complete system. To avoid such a situation the operating system constantly monitors the system for detecting the errors. This relieves the user of the worry of errors propagating to various part of the system and causing malfunctioning.

SYSTEM CALLS AND SYSTEM PROGRAMS

System calls provide an interface between the process an the operating system. System calls allow user-level processes to request some services from the operating system which process itself is not allowed to do. In handling the trap, the operating system will enter in the kernel mode, where it has access to privileged instructions, and can perform the desired service on the behalf of user-level process.

It is because of the critical nature of operations that the operating system itself does them every time they are needed. For example, for I/O a process involves a system call telling the operating system to read or write particular area and this request is satisfied by the operating system.

System programs provide basic functioning to users so that they do not need to write their own environment for programme development (editors, compilers) and programme execution (shells). In some sense, they are bundles of useful system calls.

LAYERED APPROACH DESIGN

In this case the system is easier to debug and modify, because changes affect only limited portions of the code, and programmer does not have to know the details of the other layers.

Information is also kept only where it is needed and is accessible only in certain ways, so bugs affecting that data are limited to a specific module or layer.

MECHANISMS AND POLICIES

The policies what is to be done while the mechanism specifies how it is to be done. For instance, the timer construct for ensuring CPU protection is mechanism. On the other hand, the decision of how long the timer is set for a particular user is a policy decision. The separation of mechanism and policy is important to provide flexibility to a system. If the interface between mechanism and policy is well defined, the change of policy may affect only a few parameters. On the other hand, if interface between these two is vague or not well defined, it might involve much deeper change to the system.

PROCESS

DEFINITION

The term "process" was first used by the designers of the MULTICS in 1960's. Since then, the term process, used somewhat interchangeably with 'task' or 'job'.

The process has been given many definitions for instance:

- A programme in Execution.
- An asynchronous activity.
- The 'animated sprit' of a procedure in execution.
- The entity to which processors are assigned.
- The 'dispatchable' unit.

and many more definitions have given. As we can see from above that there is no universally agreed upon definition, but the definition *"Programme in Execution"* seem to be most frequently used. And this is a concept are will use in the present study of operating systems.

Now that we agreed upon the definition of process, the question is what is the relation between process and programme. It is same beast with different name or when this beast is sleeping (not executing) it is called programme and when it is executing becomes process.

Process is not the same as programme. A process is more than a programme code. A process is an 'active' entity as oppose to programme which consider to be a 'passive' entity. As we all know that a programme is an algorithm expressed in some suitable notation, (*e.g.*, programming language). Being a passive, a programme is only a part of process.

Process, on the other hand, includes:

- Current value of Programme Counter (PC)
- Contents of the processors registers
- Value of the variables
- The process stack (SP) which typically contains temporary data such as subroutine parameter, return address, and temporary variables.
- A data section that contains global variables.

A process is the unit of work in a system. In Process model, all software on the computer is organized into a number of sequential processes. A process includes PC, registers, and variables. Conceptually, each process has its own virtual CPU. In reality, the CPU switches back and forth among processes.

PROCESS STATE

The process state consist of everything necessary to resume the process execution if it is somehow put aside temporarily.

The process state consists of at least following:

- Code for the programme.
- Program's static data.
- Program's dynamic data.
- Program's procedure call stack.
- Contents of general purpose registers.
- Contents of programme counter (PC)
- Contents of programme status word (PSW).
- Operating Systems resource in use.

PROCESS OPERATIONS

Process Creation

In general-purpose systems, some way is needed to create processes as needed during operation. There are four principal events led to processes creation.

- System initialization.

- Execution of a process Creation System calls by a running process.
- A user request to create a new process.
- Initialization of a batch job.

Foreground processes interact with users. Background processes that stay in background sleeping but suddenly springing to life to handle activity such as e-mail, webpage, printing, and so on. Background processes are called daemons. This call creates an exact clone of the calling process. A process may create a new process by some create process such as 'fork'. It choose to does so, creating process is called parent process and the created one is called the child processes. Only one parent is needed to create a child process. Note that unlike plants and animals that use sexual representation, a process has only one parent.

Process Termination

A process terminates when it finishes executing its last statement. Its resources are returned to the system, it is purged from any system lists or tables, and its process control block (PCB) is erased *i.e.*, the PCB's memory space is returned to a free memory pool.

The new process terminates the existing process, usually due to following reasons:

- *Normal exist*: Most processes terminates because they have done their job. This call is exist in UNIX.
- *Error exist*: When process discovers a fatal error. For example, a user tries to compile a programme that does not exist.
- *Fatal error*: An error caused by process due to a bug in programme for example, executing an illegal instruction, referring non-existing memory or dividing by zero.
- *Killed by another process*: A process executes a system call telling the Operating Systems to terminate some other process. In UNIX, this call is kill. In some systems when a process kills all processes it created are killed as well (UNIX does not work this way).

Process States

A process goes through a series of discrete process states.

- *New state*: The process being created.
- *Terminated state*: The process has finished execution.
- *Blocked (waiting) state*: When a process blocks, it does so because logically it cannot continue, typically because it is waiting for input that is not yet available. Formally, a process is said to be blocked if it is waiting for some event to happen (such as an I/O completion) before it can proceed. In this state a process is unable to run until some external event happens.
- *Running state*: A process is said t be running if it currently has the CPU, that is, actually using the CPU at that particular instant.
- *Ready state*: A process is said to be ready if it use a CPU if one were available. It is runable but temporarily stopped to let another process run.

Process State Transitions

Following are six(6) possible transitions among above mentioned five (5) states:

- Transition 1 occurs when process discovers that it cannot continue. If running process initiates an I/O operation before its allotted time expires, the running process voluntarily relinquishes the CPU.
  This state transition is:
  - Block (process-name): Running '! Block.
- Transition 2 occurs when the scheduler decides that the running process has run long enough and it is time to let another process have CPU time.
  This state transition is:
  - *Time-Run-Out (process-name)*: Running '! Ready.
- Transition 3 occurs when all other processes have had their share and it is time for the first process to run again
  This state transition is:
  - *Dispatch (process-name)*: Ready '! Running.

- Transition 4 occurs when the external event for which a process was waiting (such as arrival of input) happens.
  This state transition is:
  – *Wakeup (process-name)*: Blocked '! Ready.
- Transition 5 occurs when the process is created.
  This state transition is:
  – *Admitted (process-name)*: New '! Ready.
- Transition 6 occurs when the process has finished execution.
  This state transition is:
  – *Exit (process-name)*: Running '! Terminated.

PROCESS CONTROL BLOCK

A process in an operating system is represented by a data structure known as a process control block (PCB) or process descriptor.

The PCB contains important information about the specific process including:

- The current state of the process *i.e.*, whether it is ready, running, waiting, or whatever.
- Unique identification of the process in order to track "which is which" information.
- A pointer to parent process.
- Similarly, a pointer to child process (if it exists).
- The priority of process (a part of CPU scheduling information).
- Pointers to locate memory of processes.
- A register save area.
- The processor it is running on.

The PCB is a certain store that allows the operating systems to locate key information about a process. Thus, the PCB is the data structure that defines a process to the operating systems.

THREADS

THREADS

Despite of the fact that a thread must execute in process,

the process and its associated threads are different concept. Processes are used to group resources together and threads are the entities scheduled for execution on the CPU.

A thread is a single sequence stream within in a process. Because threads have some of the properties of processes, they are sometimes called *lightweight processes.*

In a process, threads allow multiple executions of streams. In many respect, threads are popular way to improve application through parallelism. The CPU switches rapidly back and forth among the threads giving illusion that the threads are running in parallel.

Like a traditional process *i.e.,* process with one thread, a thread can be in any of several states (Running, Blocked, Ready or Terminated). Each thread has its own stack. Since thread will generally call different procedures and thus a different execution history.

This is why thread needs its own stack. An operating system that has thread facility, the basic unit of CPU utilization is a thread. A thread has or consists of a programme counter (PC), a register set, and a stack space. Threads are not independent of one other like processes as a result threads shares with other threads their code section, data section, OS resources also known as task, such as open files and signals.

PROCESSES VS THREADS

As we mentioned earlier that in many respect threads operate in the same way as that of processes. Some of the similarities and differences are:

Similarities

- Like processes threads share CPU and only one thread active (running) at a time.
- Like processes, threads within a processes, threads within a processes execute sequentially.
- Like processes, thread can create children.
- And like process, if one thread is blocked, another thread can run.

Differences

- Unlike processes, threads are not independent of one another.
- Unlike processes, all threads can access every address in the task.
- Unlike processes, thread are design to assist one other. Note that processes might or might not assist one another because processes may originate from different users.

Why Threads

Following are some reasons why we use threads in designing operating systems.

- A process with multiple threads make a great server for example printer server.
- Because threads can share common data, they do not need to use interprocess communication.
- Because of the very nature, threads can take advantage of multiprocessors.

Threads are cheap in the sense that:

- They only need a stack and storage for registers therefore, threads are cheap to create.
- Threads use very little resources of an operating system in which they are working. That is, threads do not need new address space, global data, programme code or operating system resources.
- Context switching are fast when working with threads. The reason is that we only have to save and/ or restore PC, SP and registers.

But this cheapness does not come free-the biggest drawback is that there is no protection between threads.

User-Level Threads

User-level threads implement in user-level libraries, rather than via systems calls, so thread switching does not need to call operating system and to cause interrupt to the kernel. In fact, the kernel knows nothing about user-level threads and manages them as if they were single-threaded processes.

Kernel-Level Threads

In this method, the kernel knows about and manages the threads. No runtime system is needed in this case. Instead of thread table in each process, the kernel has a thread table that keeps track of all threads in the system. In addition, the kernel also maintains the traditional process table to keep track of processes. Operating Systems kernel provides system call to create and manage threads.

Application that Benefits from Threads

A proxy server satisfying the requests for a number of computers on a LAN would be benefited by a multi-threaded process. In general, any programme that has to do more than one task at a time could benefit from multitasking. For example, a programme that reads input, process it, and outputs could have three threads, one for each task.

Context Switch

To give each process on a multiprogrammed machine a fair share of the CPU, a hardware clock generates interrupts periodically. This allows the operating system to schedule all processes in main memory (using scheduling algorithm) to run on the CPU at equal intervals. Each time a clock interrupt occurs, the interrupt handler checks how much time the current running process has used. If it has used up its entire time slice, then the CPU scheduling algorithm (in kernel) picks a different process to run. Each switch of the CPU from one process to another is called a context switch.

Major Steps of Context Switching

- The values of the CPU registers are saved in the process table of the process that was running just before the clock interrupt occurred.
- The registers are loaded from the process picked by the CPU scheduler to run next.

Action of Kernel to Context Switch Among Threads

The threads share a lot of resources with other peer

threads belonging to the same process. So a context switch among threads for the same process is easy. It involves switch of register set, the programme counter and the stack. It is relatively easy for the kernel to accomplished this task.

SOLARIS

INTRODUCTION

The solaris-2 Operating Systems supports:

- threads at the user-level.
- threads at the kernel-level.
- symmetric multiprocessing and
- real-time scheduling.

AT USER-LEVEL

- The user-level threads are supported by a library for the creation and scheduling and kernel knows nothing of these threads.
- These user-level threads are supported by lightweight processes (LWPs). Each LWP is connected to exactly one kernel-level thread is independent of the kernel.
- Many user-level threads may perform one task. These threads may be scheduled and switched among LWPs without intervention of the kernel.
- User-level threads are extremely efficient because no context switch is needs to block one thread another to start running.

RESOURCE NEEDS OF USER-LEVEL THREADS

- A user-thread needs a stack and programme counter. Absolutely no kernel resource are required.
- Since the kernel is not involved in scheduling these user-level threads, switching among user-level threads are fast and efficient.

AT INTERMEDIATE-LEVEL

The lightweight processes (LWPs) are located between the user-level threads and kernel-level threads. These LWPs serve as a "Virtual CPUs" where user-threads can run. Each task contains at least one LWp. The user-level threads are multiplexed on the LWPs of the process.

RESOURCE NEEDS OF LWP

An LWP contains a process control block (PCB) with register data, accounting information and memory information. Therefore, switching between LWPs requires quite a bit of work and LWPs are relatively slow as compared to user-level threads.

AT KERNEL-LEVEL

The standard kernel-level threads execute all operations within the kernel. There is a kernel-level thread for each LWP and there are some threads that run only on the kernels behalf and have associated LWP. For example, a thread to service disk requests. By request, a kernel-level thread can be pinned to a processor (CPU). The kernel-level threads are scheduled by the kernel's scheduler and user-level threads blocks. In modern solaris-2 a task no longer must block just because a kernel-level threads blocks, the processor (CPU) is free to run another thread.

RESOURCE NEEDS OF KERNEL-LEVEL THREAD

A kernel thread has only small data structure and stack. Switching between kernel threads does not require changing memory access information and therefore, kernel-level threads are relating fast and efficient.

CPU/PROCESS SCHEDULING

The assignment of physical processors to processes allows processors to accomplish work. The problem of determining when processors should be assigned and to which processes is called processor scheduling or CPU scheduling.

When more than one process is runable, the operating system must decide which one first. The part of the operating system concerned with this decision is called the scheduler. and algorithm it uses is called the scheduling algorithm.

GOALS OF SCHEDULING (OBJECTIVES)

In this section we try to answer following question: What the scheduler try to achieve? Many objectives must be considered in the design of a scheduling discipline. In particular, a scheduler should consider fairness, efficiency, response time, turnaround time, throughput, etc., Some of these goals depends on the system one is using for example batch system, interactive system or real-time system, etc. but there are also some goals that are desirable in all systems.

GENERAL GOALS

Fairness

Fairness is important under all circumstances. A scheduler makes sure that each process gets its fair share of the CPU and no process can suffer indefinite postponement. Note that giving equivalent or equal time is not fair. Think of *safety control* and *payroll* at a nuclear plant.

Policy Enforcement

The scheduler has to make sure that system's policy is enforced. For example, if the local policy is safety then the *safety control processes* must be able to run whenever they want to, even if it means delay in *payroll processes*.

Efficiency

Scheduler should keep the system (or in particular CPU) busy cent per cent of the time when possible. If the CPU and all the Input/Output devices can be kept running all the time, more work gets done per second than if some components are idle.

Response Time

A scheduler should minimize the response time for interactive user.

Turnaround

A scheduler should minimize the time batch users must wait for an output.

Throughput

A scheduler should maximize the number of jobs processed per unit time. A little thought will show that some of these goals are contradictory.

It can be shown that any scheduling algorithm that favours some class of jobs hurts another class of jobs. The amount of CPU time available is finite, after all.

PREEMPTIVE VS NONPREEMPTIVE SCHEDULING

The Scheduling algorithms can be divided into two categories with respect to how they deal with clock interrupts.

Nonpreemptive Scheduling

A scheduling discipline is nonpreemptive if, once a process has been given the CPU, the CPU cannot be taken away from that process.

Following are some characteristics of nonpreemptive scheduling:

- In nonpreemptive system, short jobs are made to wait by longer jobs but the overall treatment of all processes is fair.
- In nonpreemptive system, response times are more predictable because incoming high priority jobs can not displace waiting jobs.
- In nonpreemptive scheduling, a schedular executes jobs in the following two situations.
  - When a process switches from running state to the waiting state.
  - When a process terminates.

Preemptive Scheduling

A scheduling discipline is preemptive if, once a process has been given the CPU can taken away. The strategy of allowing processes that are logically runable to be temporarily suspended is called Preemptive Scheduling and it is contrast to the "run to completion" method.

SCHEDULING ALGORITHMS

FIFCFS SCHEDULING

Other names of this algorithm are:

- First-In-First-Out (FIFO)
- Run-to-Completion
- Run-Until-Done

Perhaps, First-Come-First-Served algorithm is the simplest scheduling algorithm is the simplest scheduling algorithm. Processes are dispatched according to their arrival time on the ready queue. Being a nonpreemptive discipline, once a process has a CPU, it runs to completion. The FCFS scheduling is fair in the formal sense or human sense of fairness but it is unfair in the sense that long jobs make short jobs wait and unimportant jobs make important jobs wait.

ROUND ROBIN SCHEDULING

One of the oldest, simplest, fairest and most widely used algorithm is round robin (RR). In the round robin scheduling, processes are dispatched in a FIFO manner but are given a limited amount of CPU time called a time-slice or a quantum. If a process does not complete before its CPU-time expires, the CPU is preempted and given to the next process waiting in a queue. The preempted process is then placed at the back of the ready list.

Round Robin Scheduling is preemptive (at the end of time-slice) therefore it is effective in time-sharing environments in which the system needs to guarantee reasonable response times for interactive users.

SHORTEST-JOB-FIRST (SJF) SCHEDULING

Other name of this algorithm is Shortest-Process-Next (SPN). Shortest-Job-First (SJF) is a non-preemptive discipline in which waiting job (or process) with the smallest estimated run-time-to-completion is run next. In other words, when CPU is available, it is assigned to the process that has smallest next CPU burst. The SJF scheduling is especially appropriate for batch jobs for which the run times are known in advance.

Since the SJF scheduling algorithm gives the minimum average time for a given set of processes, it is probably optimal. The SJF algorithm favours short jobs (or processors) at the expense of longer ones. The obvious problem with SJF scheme is that it requires precise knowledge of how long a job or process will run, and this information is not usually available.

PRIORITY SCHEDULING

The basic idea is straightforward: each process is assigned a priority, and priority is allowed to run. Equal-Priority processes are scheduled in FCFS order. The shortest-Job-First (SJF) algorithm is a special case of general priority scheduling algorithm. An SJF algorithm is simply a priority algorithm where the priority is the inverse of the (predicted) next CPU burst. That is, the longer the CPU burst, the lower the priority and vice versa. Priority can be defined either internally or externally. Internally defined priorities use some measurable quantities or qualities to compute priority of a process.

Examples of Internal priorities are:

- Time limits.
- Memory requirements.
- File requirements,

  for example, number of open files.
- CPU Vs I/O requirements.

Externally defined priorities are set by criteria that are external to operating system such as:

- The importance of process.
- Type or amount of funds being paid for computer use.
- The department sponsoring the work.
- Politics.

Priority scheduling can be either preemptive or non preemptive:

- A preemptive priority algorithm will preemptive the CPU if the priority of the newly arrival process is higher than the priority of the currently running process.
- A non-preemptive priority algorithm will simply put the new process at the head of the ready queue.

MULTILEVEL QUEUE SCHEDULING

A multilevel queue scheduling algorithm partitions the ready queue in several separate queues, for instance. In a multilevel queue scheduling processes are permanently assigned to one queues.

The processes are permanently assigned to one another, based on some property of the process, such as:

- Memory size
- Process priority
- Process type

Algorithm choose the process from the occupied queue that has the highest priority, and run that process either:

- Preemptive or
- Non-preemptively

MULTILEVEL FEEDBACK QUEUE SCHEDULING

Multilevel feedback queue-scheduling algorithm allows a process to move between queues. It uses many ready queues and associate a different priority with each queue. The Algorithm chooses to process with highest priority from the occupied queue and run that process either preemptively or unpreemptively. If the process uses too much CPU time it will moved to a lower-priority queue. Similarly, a process that wait too long in the lower-priority queue may be moved to a higher-priority queue may be moved to a highest-priority queue.

Example:

- A process entering the ready queue is placed in queue 0.
- If it does not finish within 8 milliseconds time, it is moved to the tail of queue 1.
- If it does not complete, it is preempted and placed into queue 2.
- Processes in queue 2 run on a FCFS basis, only when queue 2 run on a FCFS basis, only when queue 0 and queue 1 are empty.'

FUNCTIONS OF OPERATING SYSTEM

The operating system (sometimes referred to by its

abbreviation *OS*), is responsible for creating the link between the material resources, the user and the applications (word processor, video game, etc.). When a programme wants to access a material resource, it does not need to send specific information to the peripheral device but it simply sends the information to the operating system, which conveys it to the relevant peripheral via its driver. If there are no drivers, each programme has to recognise and take into account the communication with each type of peripheral! The operating system thus allows the "dissociation" of programmes and hardware, mainly to simplify resource management and offer the user a simplified Man-machine interface (MMI) to overcome the complexity of the actual machine.

An operating system is a software component that acts as the core of a computer system. It performs various functions and is essentially the interface that connects your computer and its supported components. In this article, we will discuss the basic functions of the operating system, along with security concerns for the most popular types. Drivers play a major role in the operating system. A driver is a programme designed to comprehend the functions of a particular device installed on the system.

The operating system performs other functions with system utilities that monitor performance, debug errors and maintain the system. It also includes a set of libraries often used by applications to perform tasks to enable direct interaction with system components. These common functions run seamlessly and are transparent to most users. Types of operating systems: There are several types of operating systems, with Windows, Linux and Macintosh suites being the most widely used.

The operating system has various roles:

- *Management of the processor*: The operating system is responsible for managing allocation of the processor between the different programmes using a scheduling algorithm. The type of scheduler is totally dependent on the operating system, according to the desired objective.

- *Management of the random access memory*: The operating system is responsible for managing the memory space allocated to each application and, where relevant, to each user. If there is insufficient physical memory, the operating system can create a memory zone on the hard drive, known as "virtual memory". The virtual memory lets you run applications requiring more memory than there is available RAM on the system. However, this memory is a great deal slower.
- *Management of input/output*: the operating system allows unification and control of access of programmes to material resources via drivers (also known as peripheral administrators or input/output administrators).
- *Management of execution of applications*: The operating system is responsible for smooth execution of applications by allocating the resources required for them to operate. This means an application that is not responding correctly can be "killed".
- *Management of authorisations*: The operating system is responsible for security relating to execution of programmes by guaranteeing that the resources are used only by programmes and users with the relevent authorisations.
- *File management*: The operating system manages reading and writing in the file system and the user and application file access authorisations.
- *Information management*: The operating system provides a certain number of indicators that can be used to diagnose the correct operation of the machine.

CHARATERISTICS OF OPERATING SYSTEM

The definition of an operating system is "the software that controls the hardware". However, today, due to microcode we need a better definition. We see an operating system as the programs that make the hardware useable. In brief, an operating system is the set of programs that controls a computer. Some examples of operating systems are UNIX, Mach, MS-DOS, MS-Windows, Windows/NT, Chicago, OS/2, MacOS, VMS, MVS, and VM.

Controlling the computer involves software at several levels. We will differentiate kernel services, library services, and application-level services, all of which are part of the operating system. Processes run Applications, which are linked together with libraries that perform standard services. The kernel supports the processes by providing a path to the peripheral devices.

The kernel responds to service calls from the processes and interrupts from the devices. The core of the operating system is the kernel, a control programme that functions in privileged state (an execution context that allows all hardware instructions to be executed), reacting to interrupts from external devices and to service requests and traps from processes. Generally, the kernel is a permanent resident of the computer. It creates and terminates processes and responds to their request for service.

OBJECTIVES

Modern Operating systems generally have following three major goals. Operating systems generally accomplish these goals by running processes in low privilege and providing service calls that invoke the operating system kernel in high-privilege state.

Hiding of Hardware

An abstraction is software that hides lower level details and provides a set of higher-level functions. An operating system transforms the physical world of devices, instructions, memory, and time into virtual world that is the result of abstractions built by the operating system. There are several reasons for abstraction.

- *First,* the code needed to control peripheral devices is not standardized. Operating systems provide subroutines called device drivers that perform operations on behalf of programs for example, input/output operations.

- *Second,* the operating system introduces new functions as it abstracts the hardware. For instance, operating system introduces the file abstraction so that programs do not have to deal with disks.
- *Third,* the operating system transforms the computer hardware into multiple virtual computers, each belonging to a different programme. Each programme that is running is called a process. Each process views the hardware through the lens of abstraction.
- *Fourth,* the operating system can enforce security through abstraction.

Manage Resources

An operating system controls how processes (the active agents) may access resources (passive entities).

Effective user interface

The user interacts with the operating systems through the user interface and usually interested in the "look and feel" of the operating system. The most important components of the user interface are the command interpreter, the file system, on-line help, and application integration. The recent trend has been towards increasingly integrated graphical user interfaces that encompass the activities of multiple processes on networks of computers.

TYPES OF OPERATING SYSTEMS

As computers have progressed and developed so have the types of operating systems. Below is a basic list of the different types of operating systems and a few examples of operating systems that fall into each of the categories. Many computer operating systems will fall into more than one of the below categories.

GUI

Graphical User Interface, a GUI Operating System contains

graphics and icons and is commonly navigated by using a computer mouse. See our GUI dictionary definition for a complete definition. Below are some examples of GUI Operating Systems.

System 7.x

Mac OS 9 is the latest public release of the Apple operating system, which includes new and unique features not found in any other operating system. Below are some of the new features found with this new operating system.

- *Sherlock* 2: Which offers the capability of quickly searching and purchasing online.
- *3D acceleration*: Support for technologies such as OpenGL, allowing improved video and a wider gaming experience.
- *Share files*: Share files and folders over the Internet with other Mac users.
- *Colorsync* 3.0: Manages colour even more efficiently.
- *Synchronize*: Synchronizes with Palm computing products using HotSync software.
- *TCP/IP*: Provides access to TCP/IP networks.
- *Lock system*: Ensures that System Folders and Applications do not accidentally get reconfigured by having the capability of locking the system.

Windows 98

Microsoft Windows 98 is the upgrade to Microsoft Windows 95. While this was not as big as release as Windows 95, Windows 98 has significant updates, fixes and support for new peripherals. Below is a list of some of its new features.

- *Protection*: Windows 98 includes additional protection for important files on your computer such as backing up your registry automatically.
- *Improved support:* Improved support for new devices such as AGP, DirectX, DVD, USB, MMX,
- *FAT32*: Windows 98 has the capability of converting your drive to FAT32 without losing any information.
- *Interface*: Users of Windows 95 and NT will enjoy the same easy interface.

- *PnP*: Improved PnP support, to detect devices even better than Windows 95.
- *Internet Explorer 4.0*: Included Internet Explorer 4.0
- *Customizable Taskbar*: Windows adds many nice new features to the taskbar that 95 and NT do not have.
- *Includes Plus!*: Includes features only found in Microsoft Plus! free.
- *Active Desktop*: Includes Active Desktop that allows for users to customise their desktop with the look of the Internet.

Includes the same additional features as Windows 98; however, includes additional fixes and all of Year 2000 patches have been included in Windows 98 Second Edition. Below is a listing of the various new features Windows 98 SE includes.

Windows CE

Microsoft Windows CE 1.0 was originally released in 1996 to compete in the Palm Device Assistant Category. Windows CE, as shown below, has many of the same features as Windows 95. In addition to the look of Windows 95, Windows CE also includes similar applications such as Pocket Excel, Pocket Word, and Pocket Power.

MULTI-USER

A multi-user operating system allows for multiple users to use the same computer at the same time and/or different times. See our multi-user dictionary definition for a complete definition for a complete definition. Below are some examples of multi-user operating systems.

Linux

Unix, which is not an acronym, was developed by some of the members of the Multics team at the bell labs starting in the late 1960's by many of the same people who helped create the Cprogramming language. The Unix today, however, is not just the work of a couple of programmers. Many other organizations, institutes and various other individuals contributed significant additions to the system we now know today.

Unix

Unix, which is not an acronym, was developed by some of the members of the Multics team at the bell labs starting in the late 1960's by many of the same people who helped create the Cprogramming language. The Unix today, however, is not just the work of a couple of programmers. Many other organizations, institutes and various other individuals contributed significant additions to the system we now know today.

Windows 2000

Windows 2000 is based of the Windows NT Kernel and is sometimes referred to as Windows NT 5.0. Windows 2000 contains over 29 Million lines of code, mainly written in C++. 8 Million of those lines alone are written for drivers. Currently, Windows 2000 is by far one of the largest commercial projects ever built.

Some of the significant features of Windows 2000 Professional are:

- Support for FAT16, FAT32 and NTFS.
- Increased uptime of the system and significantly fewer OS reboot scenarios.
- Windows Installer tracks applications and recognizes and replaces missing components.
- Protects memory of individual apps and processes to avoid a single app bringing the system down.
- Encrypted File Systems protects sensitive data.
- Secure Virtual Private Networking (VPN) supports tunneling in to private LAN over public Internet.

MULTIPROCESSING

An operating system capable of supporting and utilizing more than one computer processor. Below are some examples of multiprocessing operating systems.

Unix

Unix, which is not an acronym, was developed by some of the members of the Multics team at the bell labs starting in the late 1960's by many of the same people who helped create the Cprogramming language. The Unix today, however, is not just the work of a couple of programmers. Many other organizations, institutes and various other individuals contributed significant additions to the system we now know today.

Windows 2000

Windows 2000 is based of the Windows NT Kernel and is sometimes referred to as Windows NT 5.0. Windows 2000 contains over 29 Million lines of code, mainly written in C++. 8 Million of those lines alone are written for drivers. Currently, Windows 2000 is by far one of the largest commercial projects ever built.

Some of the significant features of Windows 2000 Professional are:

- Support for FAT16, FAT32 and NTFS.
- Increased uptime of the system and significantly fewer OS reboot scenarios.
- Windows Installer tracks applications and recognizes and replaces missing components.
- Protects memory of individual apps and processes to avoid a single app bringing the system down.
- Encrypted File Systems protects sensitive data.
- Secure Virtual Private Networking (VPN) supports tunneling in to private LAN over public Internet.
- Personalized menus adapt to the way you work.

MULTITASKING

An operating system that is capable of allowing multiple software processes to run at the same time. Below are some examples of multitasking operating systems.

Unix

Unix, which is not an acronym, was developed by some of the members of the Multics team at the bell labs starting in the late 1960's by many of the same people who helped create the Cprogramming language. The Unix today, however, is not just the work of a couple of programmers. Many other organizations, institutes and various other individuals contributed significant additions to the system we now know today.

Windows 2000

Windows 2000 is based of the Windows NT Kernel and is sometimes referred to as Windows NT 5.0. Windows 2000 contains over 29 Million lines of code, mainly written in C++. 8 Million of those lines alone are written for drivers. Currently, Windows 2000 is by far one of the largest commercial projects ever built.

Some of the significant features of Windows 2000 Professional are:

- Support for FAT16, FAT32 and NTFS.
- Increased uptime of the system and significantly fewer OS reboot scenarios.
- Windows Installer tracks applications and recognizes and replaces missing components.
- Protects memory of individual apps and processes to avoid a single app bringing the system down.
- Encrypted File Systems protects sensitive data.
- Secure Virtual Private Networking (VPN) supports tunneling in to private LAN over public Internet.

MULTITHREADING

Operating systems that allow different parts of a software programme to run concurrently.

Operating systems that would fall into this category are:

- Linux
- Unix
- Windows 2000

INTERPROCESS COMMUNICATION

Since processes frequently needs to communicate with other processes therefore, there is a need for a well-structured communication, without using interrupts, among processes.

RACE CONDITIONS

In operating systems, processes that are working together

share some common storage (main memory, file etc.) that each process can read and write. When two or more processes are reading or writing some shared data and the final result depends on who runs precisely when, are called race conditions. Concurrently executing threads that share data need to synchronize their operations and processing in order to avoid race condition on shared data. Only one 'customer' thread at a time should be allowed to examine and update the shared variable.

CRITICAL SECTION

Avoiding race conditions

The key to preventing trouble involving shared storage is find some way to prohibit more than one process from reading and writing the shared data simultaneously. That part of the programme where the shared memory is accessed is called the *Critical Section*. To avoid race conditions and flawed results, one must identify codes in *Critical Sections* in each thread. The characteristic properties of the code that form a *Critical Section* are

- Codes that reference one or more variables in a "read-update-write" fashion while any of those variables is possibly being altered by another thread.
- Codes that alter one or more variables that are possibly being referenced in "read-updata-write" fashion by another thread.
- Codes use a data structure while any part of it is possibly being altered by another thread.
- Codes alter any part of a data structure while it is possibly in use by another thread.

MUTUAL EXCLUSION

A way of making sure that if one process is using a shared modifiable data, the other processes will be excluded from doing the same thing.

Formally, while one process executes the shared variable, all other processes desiring to do so at the same time moment should be kept waiting; when that process has finished executing the shared variable, one of the processes waiting; while that process has finished executing the shared variable, one of the processes waiting to do so should be allowed to proceed.

In this fashion, each process executing the shared data (variables) excludes all others from doing so simultaneously. This is called Mutual Exclusion.

Mutual Exclusion Conditions

If we could arrange matters such that no two processes were ever in their critical sections simultaneously, we could avoid race conditions. We need four conditions to hold to have a good solution for the critical section problem (mutual exclusion).

- No two processes may at the same moment inside their critical sections.
- No assumptions are made about relative speeds of processes or number of CPUs.
- No process should outside its critical section should block other processes.
- No process should wait arbitrary long to enter its critical section.

SEMAPHORES

Definition

A semaphore is a protected variable whose value can be accessed and altered only by the operations P and V and initialization operation called 'Semaphoiinitislize'. Binary Semaphores can assume only the value 0 or the value 1 counting semaphores also called general semaphores can assume only nonnegative values.

The P (or wait or sleep or down) operation on semaphores S, written as P(S) or wait (S), operates as follows:

P(S): IF S > 0
THEN S:= S-1
ELSE (wait on S)

The V (or signal or wakeup or up) operation on semaphore S, written as V(S) or signal (S), operates as follows:

V(S): IF (one or more process are waiting on S)
THEN (let one of these processes proceed)
ELSE S:= S +1

Operations P and V are done as single, indivisible, atomic action. It is guaranteed that once a semaphore operations has stared, no other process can access the semaphore until operation has completed. Mutual exclusion on the semaphore, S, is enforced within P(S) and V(S).

If several processes attempt a P(S) simultaneously, only process will be allowed to proceed. The other processes will be kept waiting, but the implementation of P and V guarantees that processes will not suffer indefinite postponement.

DEADLOCK

A set of process is in a deadlock state if each process in the set is waiting for an event that can be caused by only another process in the set.

In other words, each member of the set of deadlock processes is waiting for a resource that can be released only by a deadlock process. None of the processes can run, none of them can release any resources, and none of them can be awakened.

It is important to note that the number of processes and the number and kind of resources possessed and requested are unimportant.

The resources may be either physical or logical. Examples of physical resources are Printers, Tape Drivers, Memory Space, and *CPU* Cycles. Examples of logical resources are Files, Semaphores, and Monitors.

PREEMPTABLE AND NONPREEMPTABLE RESOURCES

Resources come in two flavours: preemptable and nonpreemptable. A preemptable resource is one that can be taken away from the process with no ill effects. Memory is an example of a preemptable resource. On the other hand, a nonpreemptable resource is one that cannot be taken away from process (without causing ill effect). For example, *CD* resources are not preemptable at an arbitrary moment. Reallocating resources can resolve deadlocks that involve preemptable resources.

Deadlocks that involve nonpreemptable resources are difficult to deal with.

NECESSARY AND SUFFICIENT DEADLOCK CONDITIONS

Coffman identified four (4) conditions that must hold simultaneously for there to be a deadlock.

1. *Mutual Exclusion Condition*: The resources involved are non-shareable.
   - *Explanation*: At least one resource (thread) must be held in a non-shareable mode, that is, only one process at a time claims exclusive control of the resource. If another process requests that resource, the requesting process must be delayed until the resource has been released.
2. *Hold and Wait Condition*: Requesting process hold already, resources while waiting for requested resources.
   - *Explanation*: There must exist a process that is holding a resource already allocated to it while waiting for additional resource that are currently being held by other processes.
3. *No-Preemptive Condition*: Resources already allocated to a process cannot be preempted.
   - *Explanation*: Resources cannot be removed from the processes are used to completion or released voluntarily by the process holding it.
4. *Circular Wait Condition*: The processes in the system form a circular list or chain where each process in the list is waiting for a resource held by the next process in the list. As an example, consider the traffic deadlock.

DEALING WITH DEADLOCK PROBLEM

In general, there are four strategies of dealing with deadlock problem:

1. *The Ostrich Approach*: Just ignore the deadlock problem altogether.
2. *Deadlock Detection and Recovery*: Detect deadlock and, when it occurs, take steps to recover.
3. *Deadlock Avoidance*: Avoid deadlock by careful resource scheduling.
4. *Deadlock Prevention*: Prevent deadlock by resource scheduling so as to negate at least one of the four conditions.

DEADLOCK DETECTION

Deadlock detection is the process of actually determining that a deadlock exists and identifying the processes and resources involved in the deadlock. The basic idea is to check allocation against resource availability for all possible allocation sequences to determine if the system is in deadlocked state a. Of course, the deadlock detection algorithm is only half of this strategy.

Once a deadlock is detected, there needs to be a way to recover several alternatives exists:

- Temporarily prevent resources from deadlocked processes.
- Back off a process to some check point allowing preemption of a needed resource and restarting the process at the checkpoint later.
- Successively kill processes until the system is deadlock free.

These methods are expensive in the sense that each iteration calls the detection algorithm until the system proves to be deadlock free. The complexity of algorithm is$O(N^2)$ where N is the number of proceeds. Another potential problem is starvation; same process killed repeatedly.

MEMORY MANAGEMENT

CONCEPT

The memory management subsystem is one of the most

important parts of the operating system. Since the early days of computing, there has been a need for more memory than exists physically in a system. Strategies have been developed to overcome this limitation and the most successful of these is virtual memory. Virtual memory makes the system appear to have more memory than it actually has by sharing it between competing processes as they need it.

LARGE ADDRESS SPACES

The operating system makes the system appear as if it has a larger amount of memory than it actually has. The virtual memory can be many times larger than the physical memory in the system,

PROTECTION

Each process in the system has its own virtual address space. These virtual address spaces are completely separate from each other and so a process running one application cannot affect another. Also, the hardware virtual memory mechanisms allow areas of memory to be protected against writing. This protects code and data from being overwritten by rogue applications.

MEMORY MAPPING

Memory mapping is used to map image and data files into a processes address space. In memory mapping, the contents of a file are linked directly into the virtual address space of a process.

FAIR PHYSICAL MEMORY ALLOCATION

The memory management subsystem allows each running process in the system a fair share of the physical memory of the system,

SHARED VIRTUAL MEMORY

Although virtual memory allows processes to have separate (virtual) address spaces, there are times when you need processes to share memory. For example there could be several processes in the system running the bash command shell. Rather than have several copies of bash, one in each processes virtual address space, it is better to have only one copy in physical memory and all of the processes running bash share it. Dynamic libraries are another common example of executing code shared between several processes.

ABSTRACT MODEL OF VIRTUAL MEMORY

Before considering the methods that Linux uses to support virtual memory it is useful to consider an abstract model that is not cluttered by too much detail. As the processor executes a programme it reads an instruction from memory and decodes it. In decoding the instruction it may need to fetch or store the contents of a location in memory. The processor then executes the instruction and moves onto the next instruction in the programme. In this way the processor is always accessing memory either to fetch instructions or to fetch and store data.

DEMAND PAGING

As there is much less physical memory than virtual memory the operating system must be careful that it does not use the physical memory inefficiently. One way to save physical memory is to only load virtual pages that are currently being used by the executing programme. For example, a database programme may be run to query a database. In this case not all of the database needs to be loaded into memory, just those data records that are being examined. If the database query is a search query then it does not make sense to load the code from the database programme that deals with adding new records. This technique of only loading virtual pages into memory as they are accessed is known as demand paging.

SWAPPING

If a process needs to bring a virtual page into physical memory and there are no free physical pages available, the operating system must make room for this page by discarding another page from physical memory. If the page to be discarded from physical memory came from an image or data file and has not been written to then the page does not need to be saved. Instead it can be discarded and if the process needs that page again it can be brought back into memory from the image or data file.

However, if the page has been modified, the operating system must preserve the contents of that page so that it can be accessed at a later time. This type of page is known as a *dirty* page and when it is removed from memory it is saved in a special sort of file called the swap file. Accesses to the swap file are very long relative to the speed of the processor and physical memory and the operating system must juggle the need to write pages to disk with the need to retain them in memory to be used again.

SHARED VIRTUAL MEMORY

Virtual memory makes it easy for several processes to share memory. All memory access are made via page tables and each process has its own separate page table. For two processes sharing a physical page of memory, its physical page frame number must appear in a page table entry in both of their page tables shows two processes that each share physical page frame number 4. For process *X* this is virtual page frame number 4 whereas for process *Y* this is virtual page frame number 6. This illustrates an interesting point about sharing pages: the shared physical page does not have to exist at the same place in virtual memory for any or all of the processes sharing it.

PHYSICAL AND VIRTUAL ADDRESSING MODES

It does not make much sense for the operating system itself to run in virtual memory. This would be a nightmare situation where the operating system must maintain page tables for itself. Most multi-purpose processors support the notion of a physical address mode as well as a virtual address mode. Physical addressing mode requires no page tables and the processor does not attempt to perform any address translations in this mode. The Linux kernel is linked to run in physical address space.

ACCESS CONTROL

The page table entries also contain access control information. As the processor is already using the page table entry to map a processes virtual address to a physical one, it can easily use the access control information to check that the process is not accessing memory in a way that it should not. There are many reasons why you would want to restrict access to areas of memory. Some memory, such as that containing executable code, is naturally read only memory; the operating system should not allow a process to write data over its executable code. By contrast, pages containing data can be written to but attempts to execute that memory as instructions should fail. Most processors have at least two modes of execution: *kernel* and *user*.

CACHES

If you were to implement a system using the above theoretical model then it would work, but not particularly efficiently. Both operating system and processor designers try hard to extract more performance from the system. Apart from making the processors, memory and so on faster the best approach is to maintain caches of useful information and data that make some operations faster. Linux uses a number of memory management related caches:

Buffer Cache

The buffer cache contains data buffers that are used by the block device drivers. These buffers are of fixed sizes (for example 512 bytes) and contain blocks of information that have either been read from a block device or are being written to it. A block device is one that can only be accessed by reading and writing fixed sized blocks of data. All hard disks are block devices.

The buffer cache is indexed via the device identifier and the desired block number and is used to quickly find a block of data. Block devices are only ever accessed via the buffer cache. If data can be found in the buffer cache then it does not need to be read from the physical block device, for example a hard disk, and access to it is much faster.

PAGE ALLOCATION AND DEALLOCATION

There are many demands on the physical pages in the system. For example, when an image is loaded into memory the operating system needs to allocate pages. These will be freed when the image has finished executing and is unloaded. Another use for physical pages is to hold kernel specific data structures such as the page tables themselves. The mechanisms and data structures used for page allocation and deallocation are perhaps the most critical in maintaining the efficiency of the virtual memory subsystem.

Each element of free_area contains information about blocks of pages. The first element in the array describes single pages, the next blocks of 2 pages, the next blocks of 4 pages and so on upwards in powers of two. The list element is used as a queue head and has pointers to the page data structures in the mem_maparray. Free blocks of pages are queued here. map is a pointer to a bitmap which keeps track of allocated groups of pages of this size.

MEMORY MAPPING

When an image is executed, the contents of the executable image must be brought into the processes virtual address space. The same is also true of any shared libraries that the executable image has been linked to use. The executable file is not actually brought into physical memory, instead it is merely linked into the processes virtual memory. Then, as the parts of the programme are referenced by the running application, the image is brought into memory from the executable image.

DEMAND PAGING

Once an executable image has been memory mapped into a processes virtual memory it can start to execute. As only the very start of the image is physically pulled into memory it will soon access an area of virtual memory that is not yet in physical memory. When a process accesses a virtual address that does not have a valid page table entry, the processor will report a page fault to Linux.

Linux must find the vm_area_struct that represents the area of memory that the page fault occurred in. As searching through the vm_area_struct data structures is critical to the efficient handling of page faults, these are linked together in an AVL (Adelson-Velskii and Landis) tree structure. If there is no vm_area_structdata structure for this faulting virtual address, this process has accessed an illegal virtual address. Linux will signal the process, sending a SIGSEGV signal, and if the process does not have a handler for that signal it will be terminated.

SWAPPING OUT AND DISCARDING PAGES

When physical memory becomes scarce the Linux memory management subsystem must attempt to free physical pages. This task falls to the kernel swap daemon (*kswapd*). The kernel swap daemon is a special type of process, a kernel thread. Kernel threads are processes have no virtual memory, instead they run in kernel mode in the physical address space. The kernel swap daemon is slightly misnamed in that it does more than merely swap pages out to the system's swap files. Its role is make sure that there are enough free pages in the system to keep the memory management system operating efficiently. The Kernel swap daemon (*kswapd*) is started by the kernel init process at startup time and sits waiting for the kernel swap timer to periodically expire.

4

Generalisation of Computer Software

COMPUTER SOFTWARE

Computer software is a general term that describes computer programs. Related terms such as software programs, applications, scripts, and instruction sets all fall under the category of computer software. Therefore, installing new programs or applications on your computer is synonymous with installing new software on your computer.

Software can be difficult to describe because it is "virtual," or not physical like computer hardware. Instead, software consists of lines of code written by computer programmers that have been compiled into a computer programme. Software programs are stored as binary data that is copied to a computer's hard drive, when it is installed. Since software is virtual and does not take up any physical space, it is much easier (and often cheaper) to upgrade than computer hardware.

While at its most basic level, software consists of binary data, CD-ROMs, DVDs, and other types of media that are used to distribute software can also be called software. Therefore, when you buy a software programme, it often comes on a disc, which is a physical means of storing the software.

CATEGORIES OF SOFTWARE

Software is a generic term for organized collections of

computer data and instructions, often broken into two major categories: system software that provides the basic non-task-specific functions of the computer, and application software which is used by users to accomplish specific tasks.

System Software

System software is a set of programs that control the operations of a computer and devices attached with the computer. It creates links between user and computer as well as controls the execution of application programs. System software are essential for a computer to do work, Without this software no link can be created between user and computer.

The examples of system software are:

- Operating systems.
- Utility programs.
- Device Drivers.
- Language Processors.

Application Software

A set of programs used to solve particular problems of user through computer is called Application software. It is also known as application package. The ready packages are also available in market on CDs for various purposes. These are used by user who does not know the computer programming. The users solve their problems by using ready packages more easily and quickly.

Some of application packages are:

- Word processing software.
- Spreadsheet software.
- Database Management System software.
- Graphics software.
- Communication software.

Word Processing Software

This software is used to create and to edit documents such as letters, reports, essays etc. The word processing software provides several features for document editing and formatting. In. editing process, text is entered into the document, deleted, copied or moved to another location etc. In formatting process, different formats can be applied on the text to make the document more attractive before to print on the printer. The most popular word processing software programs are: Microsoft Word, Word Perfect etc.

Spreadsheet Software

Spreadsheet software is used to store and process data in an electronic sheet having columns and rows. The data is entered into the cells of the sheet. The intersection of a row and a column is known as cell. Each cell is a unique address. The numbers and formulas are entered into the cells and the computer can automatically perform the calculation on numerical data in cells. The spreadsheet software is commonly used for business application such as for performing financial calculations and recording transactions. The most popular example of spreadsheet software is Microsoft Excel etc.

Database Management Software

Database management software is used to create and manage databases. A database is a collection of related information or records on any subject such as records of the books in a library, information about the students of a college etc. Database Management Software stores and manages records in databases. These records can be accessed very quickly when required. The Microsoft Access, Oracle etc. are most popular examples of Database Management Software.

Presentation Graphics Software

The presentation graphic software is used to create slides for making presentations. The presentation graphic software also has pre-drawn clip art images, which can be inserted into slides and can be modified. The PowerPoint is an example of presentation graphic software.

Communication Software

The Communication software is used to exchange

information electronically. It is most commonly used software to send and receive information on the Internet. It also allows for sending and receiving faxes directly. The computer files can also be transferred from one PC to another through this software. The Internet Explorer is an example of this software.

Application software may consist of a single programme, such as an image viewer; a small collection of programs (often called a software package) that work closely together to accomplish a task, such as a spreadsheet or text processing system; a larger collection (often called a software suite) of related but independent programs and packages that have a common user interface or shared data format, such as Microsoft Office, which consists of closely integrated word processor, spreadsheet, database, etc.; or a software system, such as a database management system, which is a collection of fundamental programs that may provide some service to a variety of other independent applications.

Software is created with programming languages and related utilities, which may come in several of the above forms: single programs like script interpreters, packages containing a compiler, linker, and other tools; and large suites (often called Integrated Development Environments) that include editors, debuggers, and other tools for multiple languages.

The following diagram shows the flow between system software and application software residing in memory in a multiuser computer. The operating system (OS), TP monitor, database manager and interpreter are considered system software. The applications and interactive DBMS query and edit would be considered application software.

SOFTWARE GENERATIONS

First Generation

During the 1950's the first computers were programmed by changing the wires and set tens of dials and switches. One for every bit sometimes these settings could be stored on paper tapes that looked like a ticker tape from the telegraph-a punch tape-or punched card. With these tapes and or cards the machine was told what, how and when to do something.

To have a flawless programme a programmer needed to have a very detailed knowledge of the computer where he or she worked on. A small mistake caused the computer to crash.

Second Generation

Because the first generation "languages" were regarded as very user unfriendly people set out to look for something else, faster and easier to understand. The result was the birth of the second generation languages (2GL) at the mid of the 1950's. These generation made use of symbols and are called assemblers. An assembler is a programme that translates symbolic instructions to processor instructions. But deep in the 1950's there was still not a single processor but a whole assembly rack with umpteen tubes and or relays. A programmer did no longer have to work with one's and zero's when using an assembly language. He or she can use symbols instead. These symbols are called mnemonics because of the mnemonic character these symbols had (STO = store). Each mnemonic stands for one single machine instruction.

Third Generation

At the end of the 1950's the 'natural language' interpreters and compilers were made. But it took some time before the new languages were accepted by enterprises.

About the oldest 3GL is FORTRAN (Formula Translation) which was developed around 1953 by IBM. This is a language primarily intended for technical and scientific purposes. Standardization of FORTRAN started 10 years later, and a recommendation was finally published by the International Standardization Organization (ISO) in 1968.

Fortran 77 is now standardized

COBOL (= Common Business Oriented Language) was developed around 1959 and is like its name says primarily used, up till now, in the business world.

With a 3GL there was no longer a need to work in symbolics. Instead a programmer could use a programming language what resembled more to natural language. Be it a stripped version with some two or three hundred 'reserved' words. This is the period (1970's) were the now well known so called 'high level' languages like BASIC,PASCAL, ALGOL, FORTRAN, PL/I, and C have been born.

Fourth Generation

A 4GL is an aid witch the end user or programmer can use to build an application without using a third generation programming language. Therefore knowledge of a programming language is strictly spoken not needed. The primary feature is that you do not indicate HOW a computer must perform a task but WHAT it must do. In other words the assignments can be given on a higher functional level.

A few instructions in a 4GL will do the same as hundreds of instructions in a lower generation language like COBOLor BASIC. Applications of 4GL's are concentrating on the daily performed tasks such like screen forms, requests for data, change data, and making hard copies. In most of these cases one deals with Data Base Management Systems (DBMS).

The main advantage of this kind of languages is that a trained user can create an application in a much shorter time for development and debugging than would be possible with older generation programming language. Also a customer can be involved earlier in the project and can actively take part in the development of a system, by means of simulation runs, long before the application is actually finished.

Today the disadvantage of a 4GL lays more in the technological capacities of hardware. Since programs written in a 4GL are quite a bit larger they are needing more disk space and demanding a larger part of the computer's memory capacity than 3GL's. But hardware of technologically high standard is made more available every day, not necessarily cheaper, so in the long run restrictions will disappear.

Considering the arguments one can say that the costs saved in development could now be invested in hardware of higher performance and stimulate the development of the 4GL's.

Fifth Generation

This term is often misused by software companies that build programming environments. Till today one can only see vague contours. When one sees a nice graphical interface it is tempting to call that a fifth generation. But alas changing the makeup does not make a butterfly into an eagle.

Many attempts are made but are stranding on the limitations of hardware, and strangely enough on the views and insight of the use of natural language. But it is a direction that will be taken by these languages: no longer prohibiting for the use of natural language and intuitive approach towards the programme (language) to be developed

The basis of this is laid in the 1990's by using sound, moving images and agents-a kind of advanced macro's of the 1980's. And it is only natural that neural networks will play an important role. Software for the end user will be (may be) based on principles of knowbot-agents.

COMPUTER LANGUAGES

INTRODUCTION

The term computer language includes a wide variety of languages used to communicate with computers. It is broader than the more commonly-used term programming language. Programming languages are a subset of computer languages. For example, HTML is a markup language and a computer language, but it is not traditionally considered a programming language. Machine code is a computer language. It can technically be used for programming, and has been (*e.g.* the original bootstrapped for Altair BASIC), though most would not consider it a programming language. Computer languages can be divided into two groups: high-level languages and low-level languages. High-level languages are designed to be easier to use, more abstract, and more portable than low-level languages. Syntactically correct programs in some languages are then compiled to low-level language and executed by the computer. Computer languages could also be grouped based on other criteria. Another distinction could be made between human-readable and non-human-readable languages. Human-readable languages are designed to be used directly by humans to communicate with the computer.

TYPES OF COMPUTER LANGUAGES

Language can be categories broadly into three categories.

Machine Language

The most elementary and first type of computer, which was invented, was machine language. Machine language was machine dependent. A programme written in machine language cannot be run on another type of computer without significant alterations. Machine language is some times also referred as the binary language i-e, the language of 0 and 1 where 0 stands for the absence of electric pulse and i stands for the presence of electric pulse.

Assembly Language

As computer became more popular, it became quite apparent that machine language programming was simply too slow slow tedious for most programmers. Assembly languages are also called as low level language instead of using the string of members programmers began using English like abbreviation to represent the elementary operation.

High Level Language

The assembly languages started using English like words,m but still it was difficult to learn these languages. High level languages are the computer language in which it is much easier to write a programme than the low level language. A programme written in high level language is just like gibing instruction to person in daily life.

5

Types of Operating System

BACKGROUND

An operating system is a programme designed to run other programs on a computer. A computer's operating system is its most important programme. It is considered the backbone of a computer, managing both software and hardware resources. Operating systems are responsible for everything from the control and allocation of memory to recognizing input from external devices and transmitting output to computer displays. They also manage files on computer hard drives and control peripherals, like printers and scanners. The operating system of a large computer system has even more work to do.

There are multiuser, multiprocessing, multitasking, multithreading, and real-time operating systems. A multiuser operating system enables multiple users to run programs simultaneously. This type of operating system may be used for just a few people or hundreds of them. In fact, there are some operating systems that are used to allow thousands of people to run programs at the same time.

A multiprocessing operating system allows a programme to run on more than one central processing unit (CPU) at a time. This can come in very handy in some work environments, at schools, and even for some home-computing situations. Multitasking operating systems work a little differently; they make it possible to run more than one programme at a time. Multithreading operating systems are even more different, allowing varied parts of one programme to be used simultaneously. Real-time operating systems are designed to allow computers to process and respond to input instantly. Usually, general-purpose operating systems, such as disk operating system (DOS), are not considered real time, as they may require seconds or minutes to respond to input. Real-time operating systems are typically used when computers must react to the consistent input of information without delay. For example, real-time operating systems may be used in navigation.

Operating Systems are resource managers. The main resource is computer hardware in the form of processors, storage, input/output devices, communication devices, and data.

Some of the operating system functions are: implementing the user interface, sharing hardware among users, allowing users to share data among themselves, preventing users from interfering with one another, scheduling resources among users, facilitating input/output, recovering from errors, accounting for resource usage, facilitating parallel operations, organizing data for secure and rapid access, and handling network communications.

OBJECTIVES OF OPERATING SYSTEMS

Modern Operating systems generally have following three major goals. Operating systems generally accomplish these goals by running processes in low privilege and providing service calls that invoke the operating system kernel in high-privilege state.

Hide Details of Hardware by Creating Abstraction

An abstraction is software that hides lower level details and provides a set of higher-level functions. An operating system transforms the physical world of devices, instructions, memory, and time into virtual world that is the result of abstractions built by the operating system. There are several reasons for abstraction.

- *First,* the code needed to control peripheral devices is not standardized. Operating systems provide subroutines called device drivers that perform operations on behalf of programs for example, input/ output operations.

- *Second,* the operating system introduces new functions as it abstracts the hardware. For instance, operating system introduces the file abstraction so that programs do not have to deal with disks.
- *Third,* the operating system transforms the computer hardware into multiple virtual computers, each belonging to a different programme. Each programme that is running is called a process. Each process views the hardware through the lens of abstraction.
- *Fourth,* the operating system can enforce security through abstraction.

Allocate Resources to Processes (Manage

An operating system controls how processes (the active agents) may access resources (passive entities).

Provide a Pleasant and Effective User Interface

The user interacts with the operating systems through the user interface and usually interested in the "look and feel" of the operating system. The most important components of the user interface are the command interpreter, the file system, on-line help, and application integration. The recent trend has been towards increasingly integrated graphical user interfaces that encompass the activities of multiple processes on networks of computers.

One can view Operating Systems from two points of views: Resource manager and Extended machines. Form Resource manager point of view Operating Systems manage the different parts of the system efficiently and from extended machines point of view Operating Systems provide a virtual machine to users that is more convenient to use. The structurally Operating Systems can be design as a monolithic system, a hierarchy of layers, a virtual machine system, an exokernel, or using the client-server model. The basic concepts of Operating Systems are processes, memory management, I/O management, the file systems, and security.

HISTORY

Historically operating systems have been tightly related to the computer architecture, it is good idea to study the history of operating systems from the architecture of the computers on which they run.

Operating systems have evolved through a number of distinct phases or generations which corresponds roughly to the decades.

The 1940's-First Generations

The earliest electronic digital computers had no operating systems. Machines of the time were so primitive that programs were often entered one bit at time on rows of mechanical switches (plug boards). Programming languages were unknown (not even assembly languages). Operating systems were unheard of.

The 1950's-Second Generation

By the early 1950's, the routine had improved somewhat with the introduction of punch cards. The General Motors Research Laboratories implemented the first operating systems in early 1950's for their IBM 701. The system of the 50's generally ran one job at a time. These were called single-stream batch processing systems because programs and data were submitted in groups or batches.

The 1960's-Third Generation

The systems of the 1960's were also batch processing systems, but they were able to take better advantage of the computer's resources by running several jobs at once. So operating systems designers developed the concept of multiprogramming in which several jobs are in main memory at once; a processor is switched from job to job as needed to keep several jobs advancing while keeping the peripheral devices in use.

For example, on the system with no multiprogramming, when the current job paused to wait for other I/O operation to complete, the CPU simply sat idle until the I/O finished. The solution for this problem that evolved was to partition memory into several pieces, with a different job in each partition. While one job was waiting for I/O to complete, another job could be using the CPU.

Another major feature in third-generation operating system was the technique called spooling (simultaneous peripheral operations on line). In spooling, a high-speed device like a disk interposed between a running programme and a low-speed device involved with the programme in input/output. Instead of writing directly to a printer, for example, outputs are written to the disk.

Fourth Generation

With the development of LSI (Large Scale Integration) circuits, chips, operating system entered in the system entered in the personal computer and the workstation age. Microprocessor technology evolved to the point that it become possible to build desktop computers as powerful as the mainframes of the 1970s. Two operating systems have dominated the personal computer scene: MS-DOS, written by Microsoft, Inc. for the IBM PC and other machines using the Intel 8088 CPU and its successors, and UNIX, which is dominant on the large personal computers using the Motorola 6899 CPU family.

STRUCTURE OF OPERATING SYSTEMS

As modern operating systems are large and complex careful engineering is required. There are four different structures that have shown in this document in order to get some idea of the spectrum of possibilities. These are by no mean s exhaustive, but they give an idea of some designs that have been tried in practice.

Monolithic Systems

This approach well known as "The Big Mess". The

structure is that there is no structure. The operating system is written as a collection of procedures, each of which can call any of the other ones whenever it needs to. When this technique is used, each procedure in the system has a well-defined interface in terms of parameters and results, and each one is free to call any other one, if the latter provides some useful computation that the former needs.

For constructing the actual object programme of the operating system when this approach is used, one compiles all the individual procedures, or files containing the procedures, and then binds them all together into a single object file with the linker. In terms of information hiding, there is essentially none- every procedure is visible to every other one *i.e.* opposed to a structure containing modules or packages, in which much of the information is local to module, and only officially designated entry points can be called from outside the module.

Layered System

A generalization of the approach for organizing the operating system as a hierarchy of layers, each one constructed upon the one below it. The system had 6 layers. Layer 0 dealt with allocation of the processor, switching between processes when interrupts occurred or timers expired. Above layer 0, the system consisted of sequential processes, each of which could be programmed without having to worry about the fact that multiple processes were running on a single processor. In other words, layer 0 provided the basic multiprogramming of the CPU.

Layer 1: Did the memory management. It allocated space for processes in main memory and on a 512k word drum used for holding parts of processes (pages)for which there was no room in main memory. Above layer 1, processes did not have to worry about whether they were in memory or on the drum; the layer 1 software took care of making sure pages were brought into memory whenever they were needed.

Layer 2: Handled communication between each process and the operator console. Above this layer each process effectively had its own operator console. Layer 3 took care of managing the I/O devices and buffering the information streams to and from them. Above layer 3 each process could deal with abstract I/O devices with nice properties, instead of real devices with many peculiarities. Layer 4 was where the user programs were found. They did not have to worry about process, memory, console, or I/O management. The system operator process was located I layer 5.

Virtual Machines

The heart of the system, known as the virtual machine monitor, runs on the bare hardware and does the multiprogramming, providing not one, but several virtual machines to the next layer up. However, unlike all other operating systems, these virtual machines are not extended machines, with files and other nice features. Instead, they are exact copies of the bare hardware, including kernel/user mod, I/O, interrupts, and everything else the real machine has.

For reason of Each virtual machine is identical to the true hardware, each one can run any operating system that will run directly on the hard ware. Different virtual machines can, and usually do, run different operating systems. Some run one of the descendants of OF/360 for batch processing, while other ones run a single-user, interactive system called CMS (conversational Monitor System) fro timesharing users.

Client-server Model

A trend in modern operating systems is to take this idea of moving code up into higher layers even further, and remove as much as possible from the operating system, leaving a minimal kernel. The usual approach is to implement most of the operating system functions in user processes. To request a service, such as reading a block of a file, a user process (presently known as the client process) sends the request to a server process, which then does the work and sends back the answer.

In client-Server Model, all the kernel does is handle the communication between clients and servers. By splitting the operating system up into parts, each of which only handles one fact of the system, such as file service, process service,

Terminal service, or memory service, each part becomes small and manageable; furthermore, because all the servers run as user-mode processes, and not in kernel mode, they do not have direct access to the hardware. As a consequence, if a bug in the file server is triggered, the file service may crash, but this will not usually bring the whole machine down.

TYPES OF OPERATING SYSTEM

Microsoft Windows isn't the only operating system for personal computers, or even the best... it's just the best-distributed. Its inconsistent behaviour and an interface that changes with every version are the main reasons people find computers difficult to use. Microsoft adds new bells and whistles in each release, and claims that this time they've solved the countless problems in the previous versions... but the hype is never really fulfilled. Windows 7 offers little new: it's basically Vista without quite so many mistakes built into it. The upgrade prices serve primarily to keep the cash flowing to Microsoft, to subsidize their efforts to take over other markets. A slew of intrusive "features" in the recent versions benefit Microsoft at the expensive of both your privacy and your freedom. Switching to Windows Vista or Windows 7 requires buying new hardware and learning a new system, so instead consider switching to something *better*. More than 1 in 10 people on the web already have.

- ≅ ç If you can't say "no" to Windows (which is understandable in many cases), you can still say "no more". The simplest alternative to Windows Vista/7 is a previously-installed version of Windows. Windows Vista/7 isn't a simple upgrade; it's a drastically different operating system, which may not even run your existing software, or work properly on hardware just a few years old, so installing the "upgrade" is a risk.

The Mac OS user interface inspired the creation of Windows, and is still the target Microsoft is trying to equal. As a popular consumer product, there's plenty of software available for it, and it's moving beyond its traditional niches of graphic design, education, and home use, into general business use (after all, Apple Corp. runs on it). OS X (ten), uses Unix technology, which makes it more stable and secure than Windows. But the real star is OS X's visual interface, which shows the difference between Microsoft's guesswork in this area and Apple's innovative *design work*: it's both beautiful and easy to use.

- ç⃠ Linux ("LIH-nux") is a free Unix-like operating system, originally developed by programmers who who simply love the challenge of solving problems and producing quality software... even if that means giving the resulting product away. Not coincidentally, there's also a wealth of free software for it. Unlike proprietary operating systems, which are usually controlled in every detail by a single company, Linux has a standard consistent core (called the "kernel") around which many varieties (known as "distributions") have been produced by various companies and organisations. Some are aimed at geeks, some focus on the needs of business users, and some are designed with typical home users in mind. Businesses might prefer RedHat/Fedora, Novell/SUSE, or CentOS. Geeks should check out Debian, Slackware, and Gentoo. Linux is a first-rate choice for servers; this site is a Linux system
- ç⃠ Google's Chrome OS is still vapourware so far, and it's arguably just another flavour of Linux, but it promises to be a viable alternative to Windows on

small portable "netbooks" which will come with it preinstalled. The user interface is going to be based on Google's web browser of the same name, and take advantage of technology to make online apps like Google Docs work even if you're not online.

- ≅ ç BeOS was designed with multimedia in mind, including the kinds of features that Microsoft is just recently tacking onto Windows. Although Microsoft successfully drove Be Corp. out of business through illegal interference with their marketing efforts, reports of BeOS's death are exaggerated: The source code for BeOS has been licensed to a European software firm whose Zeta is effectively the much-longed-for BeOS R6. The free BeOS R5 Personal Edition is still available to download, and has been packaged with all the latest drivers and free add-ons as BeOS Max Edition. And the Haiku project is creating an open duplicate of BeOS R5, which will then be enhanced
- ç⃠ FreeBSD is commonly called "the free Unix". It's descended from the classic 1970's Berkeley Software Distribution of Unix (from before the OS became "UNIX"®), making it one of the most mature and stable operating systems around. It's "free" as in "free beer" (you can download it for nothing) and as in "free speech" (you can do pretty much whatever you like with it... like when Microsoft took code from it to add better networking to Windows NT).
- ç⃠ OpenBSD is "the other free Unix". It's similar to FreeBSD both in the Berkeley code it's based on, and the licensing terms. One key advantage it has over its BSD siblings (and nearly any other OS) is that it's incredibly secure from attack, as implied by its blowfish mascot, and made explicit by their boast of only one remotely-exploitable hole-ever-in their default installation. (Compare that to Windows' hundreds.) "Open" is a reference to their code auditing process, not a welcome-mat forcrackers. It's

not as speedy as FreeBSD, but it's safer. It's also available for some hardware plaforms FreeBSD doesn't support, including Mac 68K, PPC.

- ç ⃠ NetBSD is "the *other* other free Unix". It's the work of another group of volunteer developers using the net to collaborate (hence the name of their product). Their mission is to get the OS to run-and run *well*-on hardware platforms no other Unix supports. In addition to most of the usual suspects above, it's been ported to run on the NeXT box, MIPSmachines, the good Atari computers, the BeBox, WinCE-compatible handhelds, ARM processors, and even game machines like the Playstation 2 or the orphaned Sega Dreamcast.
- ç ⃠ Darwin is a cousin of Free/Open/NetBSD, and the free foundation on which the commercial Mac OS X is built. Although its development was originally managed rather tightly by Apple (understandable, because their business depends on it) they've loosened the leash, making participation in the development more open. Darwin is making progress towards becoming an open-source OS in its own right.
- ç Syllable is a free alternative OS for standard PCs. It uses some of the better ideas from Unix, BeOS, AmigaOS, and others, and is compatible enough with portable software written for Unix that many have already been ported over to it. It's not a full-featured OS yet, but it's functional enough to be used with built-in web and e-mail clients, and media players.
- Amiga owners used to taunt PC and Mac users with their smoothly-multitasking graphical operating system, back when the Macs couldn't multitask, and PCs weren't even graphical. Even though the "classic" Amiga machines are no longer being produced, there's been a lot of activity in Amigaspace in the meantime: The OS has been updated to support current technology with Amiga OS 4, emulation

layers called AmigaOS XL and AMIthlon were created to run Amiga OS on modern PC hardware, Amiga Forever is an emulator for Windows and other operating systems, and a new hardware platform and OS called AmigaOne have been introduced to try to carry on the Amiga legacy.

- MorphOS began as a project to port the Amiga OS to the then-new PowerPC architecture, but has since morphed into an OS in its own right. It runs on certain PowerPC/G3/G4-based systems, and has better-than-standard-emulation support for Amiga OS 3.1 applications as well as native apps built for MorphOS.
- RISC OS is the operating system of the former Acorn line of computers (best known in the UK), which has been revived and updated for faster performance and to meet current OS standards (*e.g.* long filenames, large hard drives). It doesn't run on standard PCs, but on systems specifically designed for it (such as the RiscPC and A7000), using the high-speed StrongARM processors. The OS itself is stored in electronic ROM rather than having to be loaded into RAM from a hard drive
- ç⃠ GNU's Not Unix. In fact, that phrase is what G.N.U. is a (recursive) abbrevation for. It is a Unix-like operating system being developed as a long-term project by the Free Software Foundation to offer a fully-free alternative to the commercial and BSD versions of Unix. Although you'll find many key components of GNU used in Linux and BSD packages under the GNU General Public license (GPL), a fully GNU system will use the Hurd, GNU's own free-software kernel. The Hurd has some design advantages over the Linux kernel, but is still far from finished, and requires serious expertise with OS development to install.
- ç⃠ Minix is an open-source Unix-like operating system originally developed for educational purposes. Because of its relative simplicity and ample

documentation, its creator says that a few months studying the source code should teach you most of how such things work. (It inspired Linus Torvalds to create Linux.) Versions 1 and 2 serve primarily as teaching examples, but version 3 has also become useful in its own right, intended for highly reliable uses on low-end 386-level hardware.

- ⦸ There are also a bunch of commercial UNIX systems, which are typically customised to run on expensive, high-end, proprietary hardware sold by the same vendor. Most of them have names other than "Unix" due to old trademark issues. They're better as alternatives to the server versions of Windows, not the desktop versions of Windows such as 98/XP/Vista.
- ≅ IBM's OS/2warp was once supposed to replace MS Windows, back when Emperor IBM and Darth Microsoft were planning to rule the galaxy together. Then Darth decided he didn't need the Emperor, struck confidential deals with other hardware vendors and software developers, and made Windows (just barely) powerful enough to fill OS/2's intended role. Windows didn't really beat OS/2 technically, but it won the Marketing Wars, which is what mattered. Unfortunately, IBM has given up on OS/2's future. A third-party package called eComStation is a licensed effort to update and maintain OS/2.
- ç Believe it or not, DOS (with or without Windows 3.1) is still a viable option for many uses. There was an incredible amount of software developed for it, and it still works. Plus, DOS runs like a champ, on old hardware that no one else wants. You can even fit it on a diskette, to boot it on nearly any PC anywhere.

COMPUTER VIRUS

INTRODUCTION

A computer virus is a programme which reproduces

itself. It may attach to other programs, it may create copies of itself (as in companion viruses).

It may damage or corrupt data, change data, or degrade the performance of your system by utilizing resources such as memory or disk space.

A computer virus may be categorized with one or more of the following four designations:

- Boot sector computer virus
- Master Boot Record (MBR) computer virus
- File infector computer virus
- Macro computer virus

A computer virus which displays characteristics of more than one of these categories is known as a multi-partite computer virus.

- *Boot sector viruses*: A boot sector virus does not need to be able to successfully boot the victims computer to infect it. Because of this, even non-bootable media can spread a boot sector virus. Once the infected computer does successfully boot, the boot sector virus stays in memory and infects floppies and other media when they are written to by the infected computer. Boot sector viruses have become less common as floppy disks have become rarer.
- *Master Boot Record (MBR) viruses*: Master Boot Record (MBR) viruses are very similar to boot sector viruses, except that they infect the MBR (Master Boot Record) instead of the boot sector.
- *File infector viruses*: File infector viruses infect files which contain executables code, such as.EXE and.COM files.
- *Some file infectors are memory resident*: This means that the virus will stay in memory and continue to infect other programs. Other file infector viruses only infect other files when they are executed.
- *Macro viruses*: Macro viruses infect certain types of data files. Most macro viruses infect Microsoft Office files, such as Word Documents, Excel Spreadsheets, PowerPoint Presentations, and Access Databases.

HISTORY OF VIRUS

The first computer virus to openly make it to the public was a programme called "Elk Cloner". It was created by Rich Skrenta, a computer programmer who was in high school when this virus was created in 1982. Elk Cloner attached itself to the Apple DOS 3.3 operating system and was later spreaded by a floppy disk.

When the virus was created, it was intentionally made as a joke by the high school student, who inputted the virus into a game in which the virus was set off after the 50th time of using the game. When the virus was set off, a blank screen appeared and displayed a poem about the virus. The computer then became infected.

The first PC virus was a boot sector virus named (c) Brain. Two brothers, Basit and Amjad Farooq Alva, whose only intentions were to protect their work from piracy and to target copyright infringers, programmed it. However, according to analysts, the Ashar virus, which was a variant of Brain, possibly was created before the (c) Brain.

Before network computer expansion, most viruses were spreaded through removable media, such as floppy disks. These viruses infected programs stored in the disks, while others were inputted into the disk boot sectors, and activated when the user booted the computer from the disk. The traditional and typical virus characteristics common to us now emerged in the 1980s, where there was an increase of BBS (Bulletin Board System, where a computer system runs software that allows users to dial into the system over a phone line), modem use, and software sharing. BBS contributed greatly to the rapid spread of Trojan horses, and viruses were originally written to target popular software traders. Traders who were in a hurry to retrieve the latest software were usually the easiest prey to infect viruses with.

TYPES OF VIRUS

Computer viruses are generally defined as a programme inputted into a computer that allows replication of the programme installed. As it replicates, the programme intentionally infects the computer, typically without even the user knowing about the damage being done. A virus, unlike worms or Trojan horses, needs an aid to transfer them to computers. Viruses usually take a large amount of computer memory, resulting into system crashes. Viruses are categorized to several parts based on its features.

Macro Viruses

A macro virus, often scripted into common application programs such as Word or Excel, is spread by infecting documents. Macro viruses are known to be platform-independent since the virus itself are written in language of the application and not the operating system. When the application is running, this allows the macro virus to spread amongst the operating systems. There are thousands of macro viruses that exists, and each are considered major threats. Examples of these viruses are: Melissa.A and Bablas.

Network Viruses

Network viruses rapidly spreads through a Local Network Area (LAN), and sometimes throughout the internet. Generally, network viruses multiply through shared resources, *i.e.*, shared drives and folders. When the virus infects a computer, it searches through the network to attack its new potential prey. When the virus finishes infecting that computer, it moves on to the next and the cycle repeats itself. The most dangerous network viruses are Nimda and SQLSlammer.

Logic Bombs

The logic bomb virus is a piece of code that are inputted into a software system. When a certain and specific condition is met, such as clicking on an Internet browser or opening a particular file, the logic bomb virus is set off. Many programmers set the malicious virus off during days such as April Fools Day or Friday the 13th. When the virus is activated, then various activities will take place. For example, files are permanently deleted.

Companion Viruses

Companion viruses takes advantage of MS-DOS. This virus creates a new file with typically the.COM extensions, but sometimes the.EXD extension as well. When a user manually types in a programme they desire without adding.EXE or any other specific extention, DOS will make the assumption that the user want the file with the extension that comes first in alphabetical order, and thus running the virus. The companion virus is rare among Windows XP computers as this particular operating system does not use the MS-DOS.

Boot Sector Viruses

Boot sector viruses generally hide in the boot sector, either in the bootable disk or the hard drive. Unlike most viruses, this virus does not harm the files in the hard disk, but harm the hard disk itself. Boot sector viruses are uncommon at this day and age because these viruses are spread rapidly by floppy disks and not on CD-ROMs.

Multipartite Viruses

Multipartite viruses are spreaded through infected media and usually hides in the memory. Gradually, the virus moves to the boot sector of the hard drive and infects executable files on the hard drive and later across the computer system.

WORKING OF VIRUS

There are millions of viruses present these days, and new viruses originating every day. It is awfully tricky to provide you with a standard explanation of how viruses function, because they all have differences in the manner they infect or the method they spread. Hence, in this article, I have explained it bearing in mind few broad groups that are usually used to illustrate different types of viruses.

File Viruses or Parasitic Viruses

File viruses are pieces of code that attach themselves to executable files, driver files or compressed files, and they are triggered when the host programme is executed. Once the file virus or parasitic virus is activated, it may spread by attaching to new programs in the system, and also perform out the wicked actions it was programmed for. A large number of file/parasitic viruses spread by loading themselves in the system memory, and they start searching for additional programs located on the drive.

If it locates one, it transforms the program's code so that it encloses the virus code. Then it activates the virus's code next time it runs. It keeps doing this yet again until it crawls all over the system, and probably to additional systems that share the infected programme.

Besides spreading themselves, these viruses also hold various types of destructive elements that can be activated instantly or by a specific 'trigger'. The triggers could possibly be specific dates, or the number of times the virus has been replicated, or anything equally small.

Examples of file/parasitic viruses are Randex, Meve and MrKlunky.

Boot Sector Viruses

A boot sector virus infects the boot sector of a hard drive, which is a very critical component for the booting process. The boot sector is where all the information concerning the drive is stored, along with a programme that makes it possible for the operating system to boot up. By introducing the virus code into the boot sector, the virus ensures that it loads into the system memory at each boot cycle.

A boot virus does not infect files; instead, it infects the drive on which they are saved. Possibly this is the reason for their collapse. In earlier days, when the programs were carried around in floppy disks, the virus used to spread like a wild fire. However, with the upcoming of CD drives and CD ROMs, it became impossible for the boot sector virus to infect pre-written information on a CD, which in due course stopped such viruses from spreading and infecting.

Examples of boot sector viruses are Polyboot.B and AntiEXE.

Multipartite Viruses

Multipartite viruses are a mixture of boot sector viruses and file viruses. These viruses enter the system through infected media and dwell in the system memory. They then travel onto the boot sector of the hard drive. From there, the multipartite virus infects the executable files on the hard drive and spreads throughout the system. There aren't many multipartite viruses present these days, but in their era, they were responsible for a number of vital troubles due to their ability to combine different infection practices. A significant example of a multipartite virus is Ywinz.

Macro Viruses

Macro viruses infect files that are formed using certain applications or programs that include macros. Such applications comprises of Microsoft Office documents such as Word documents, Excel spreadsheets, PowerPoint presentations, Access databases and other related application files such as Corel Draw, AmiPro, etc.

As macro viruses are programmed in the language of the application and not in that of the operating system, they are recognized to be platform-independent, *i.e.* they can spread across operating systems such as Windows, Macintosh or any other systems, as long as they are running the necessary application. With the ever rising abilities of macro languages in applications, and the risk of hazardous infection spreading over the networks, this macro virus has become a critical threat. Examples of macro viruses are Relax, Melissa.A and Bablas.

Network Viruses

A network virus is very much skilled in rapidly spreading across a Local Area Network (LAN) or even over the internet. Generally, it circulates through shared resources, such as shared drives and folders. When it infects a fresh system, it hunts for possible victims by scanning the network for other defenceless systems. When a defenceless system is found, the network virus infects the additional systems and thus spreads over the network. Examples of some most dangerous viruses are Nimda and SQLStammer.

E-Mail Viruses

An e-mail virus can probably be a type of a macro virus that spreads itself to all the contacts located in the host's e-mail address book. If any of the e-mail recipients open the attachment of the infected mail, it spreads to the new host's address book contacts, and then proceeds to send itself to all those contacts as well. Nowadays, e-mail viruses can infect hosts even if the infected e-mail is previewed in a mail client. One of the most widespread and destructive e-mail viruses is the ILOVEYOU virus.

6

Windows Operating System

OVERVIEW

Microsoft has taken two separate approaches with the Windows operating system: one is suited for home users while the other is intended for the IT professional. The dual approach has resulted in home editions having more functionality in the way of multimedia support. However, Microsoft home-based operating systems tend to have less functionality in regard to security and networking. The professional versions for the server environment are limited in multimedia features but offer enhanced networking capability and security.

HISTORY

The first version of Windows was released in November of 1985. This programme wasn't very popular as it lacked functionality compared to the Apple operating system. Version 1.0 was not a complete system. Instead, it simply extended on MS-DOS.

Version 2.0 was released two years later and achieved slightly more popularity than its predecessor. Version 2.03 was released in January of 2008. This version offered a totally different look that resulted in Apple filing a lawsuit against Microsoft with accusations of infringement.

Windows version 3 0 was released in 1990, the first edition to reach commercial success by selling two million copies within its first six months. This version included numerous improvements to the user interface along with new multitasking capabilities. Version 3.1 offered a facelift and was made available in March, 1992.

The Windows NT operating system was released in July of 1993. This version was based on a new kernel and it was considered to be the first designed for a professional platform. NT was later upgraded to function as a home user operating system with the release of Windows XP.

The Microsoft operating system received a tremendous upgrade with Windows Vista on January 30, 2007. This version includes several new features with an emphasis on security. Vista offers an improved shell design and user interface along with numerous technical modifications. Despite its functionality, Windows Vista has received criticism.

1983: Microsoft Windows was announced November 10, 1983 and sells for $100.00.

1985: Microsoft Windows 1.0 is introduced in November, 1985 and is initially sold for $100.00.

1987: Microsoft Windows 2.0 was released December 9, 1987 and is initially sold for $100.00.

1987: Microsoft Windows/386 or Windows 386 is introduced December 9, 1987 and is initially sold for $100.00.

1988: Microsoft Windows/286 or Windows 286 is introduced June, 1988 and is initially sold for $100.00.

1990: Microsoft Windows 3.0 was released May, 22 1990. Microsoft Windows 3.0 full version was priced at $149.95 and the upgrade version was priced at $79.95.

1991: Following its decision not to develop operating systems cooperatively with IBM,Microsoft changes the name of OS/2 to Windows NT.

1991: Microsoft Windows 3.0 or Windows 3.0a with multimedia was released October, 1991.

1992: Microsoft Windows 3.1 was released April, 1992 and sells more than 1 Million copies within the first two months of its release.

1992: Microsoft Windows for Workgroups 3.1 was released October, 1992.

1993: Microsoft Windows NT 3.1 was released July 27, 1993.

1993: The number of licensed users of Microsoft Windows now totals more than 25 Million.

1994: Microsoft Windows for Workgroups 3.11 was released February, 1994.

1994: Microsoft Windows NT 3.5 was released September 21, 1994.

1995: Microsoft Windows NT 3.51 was released May 30, 1995.

1995: Microsoft Windows 95 was released August 24, 1995 and sells more than 1 Million copies within 4 days.

1996: Microsoft Windows NT 4.0 was released July 29, 1996.

1996: Microsoft Windows CE 1.0 was released November, 1996.

1997: Microsoft Windows CE 2.0 was released November, 1997.

1998: Microsoft Windows 98 was released June, 1998.

1998: Microsoft Windows CE 2.1 was released July, 1998.

1998: In October of 1998 Microsoft announced that future releases of Windows NT would no longer have the initials of NT and that the next edition would be Windows 2000.

1999: Microsoft Windows 98 SE (Second Edition) was released May 5, 1999.

1999: Microsoft Windows CE 3.0 was released 1999.

2000: On January 4th at CES Bill Gates announces the new version of Windows CE will be called Pocket PC.

2000: Microsoft Windows 2000 was released February 17, 2000.

2000: Microsoft Windows ME (Millennium) released June 19, 2000.

2001: Microsoft Windows XP is released October 25, 2001.

2001: Microsoft Windows XP 64-Bit Edition (Version 2002) for Itanium systems is released March 28, 2003.

2003: Microsoft Windows Server 2003 is released March 28, 2003.

2003: Microsoft Windows XP 64-Bit Edition (Version 2003) for Itanium 2 systems is released on March 28, 2003.

2003: Microsoft Windows XP Media Centre Edition 2003 is released on December 18, 2003.

2004: Microsoft Windows XP Media Centre Edition 2005 is released on October 12, 2004.

2005: Microsoft Windows XP Professional x64 Edition is released on April 24, 2005.

2005: Microsoft announces it's next operating system, codenamed "Longhorn" will be named Windows Vista on July 23, 2005.

2006: Microsoft releases Microsoft Windows Vista to corporations on November 30, 2006.

2007: Microsoft releases Microsoft Windows Vista and Office 2007 to the general public January 30, 2007.

2009: Microsoft releases Windows 7 October 22, 2009.

WORKING

When you turn on your computer, it's nice to think that you're in control. There's the trusty computer mouse, which you can move anywhere on the screen, summoning up your music library or Internet browser at the slightest whim. Although it's easy to feel like a director in front of your desktop or laptop, there's a lot going on inside, and the real man behind the curtain handling the necessary tasks is the operating system. Most desktop or laptop PCs come pre-loaded with Microsoft Windows. Macintosh computers come pre-loaded with Mac OS X. Many corporate servers use the Linux or UNIX operating systems. The operating system (OS) is the first thing loaded onto the computer—without the operating system, a computer is useless.

More recently, operating systems have started to pop up in smaller computers as well. If you like to tinker with electronic devices, you're probably pleased that operating systems can now be found on many of the devices we use every day, from cell phones to wireless access points. The computers used in these little devices have gotten so powerful that they can now actually run an operating system and applications. The computer in a typical modern cell phone is now more powerful than a desktop computer from 20 years ago, so this progression makes sense and is a natural development. The purpose of an operating system is to organize and control hardware and software so that the device it lives in behaves in a flexible but predictable way. In this article, we'll tell you what a piece of software must do to be called an operating system, show you how the operating system in your desktop computer works and give you some examples of how to take control of the other operating systems around you. Instead, the computer in a microwave oven simply runs a single hard-wired programme all the time.

For other devices, an operating system creates the ability to:

- Serve a variety of purposes
- Interact with users in more complicated ways
- Keep up with needs that change over time

All desktop computers have operating systems. The most common are the Windows family of operating systems developed by Microsoft, the Macintosh operating systems developed by Apple and the UNIX family of operating systems (which have been developed by a whole history of individuals, corporations and collaborators).

There are hundreds of other operating systems available for special-purpose applications, including specializations for mainframes, robotics, manufacturing, real-time control systems and so on.

OPERATING SYSTEM FUNCTIONS

At the simplest level, an operating system does two things:

- It manages the hardware and software resources of

the system. In a desktop computer, these resources include such things as the processor, memory, disk space and more (On a cell phone, they include the keypad, the screen, the address book, the phone dialer, the battery and the network connection).

- It provides a stable, consistent way for applications to deal with the hardware without having to know all the details of the hardware.

The first task, managing the hardware and software resources, is very important, as various programs and input methods compete for the attention of the central processing unit (CPU) and demand memory, storage and input/output (I/O) bandwidth for their own purposes. In this capacity, the operating system plays the role of the good parent, making sure that each application gets the necessary resources while playing nicely with all the other applications, as well as husbanding the limited capacity of the system to the greatest good of all the users and applications.

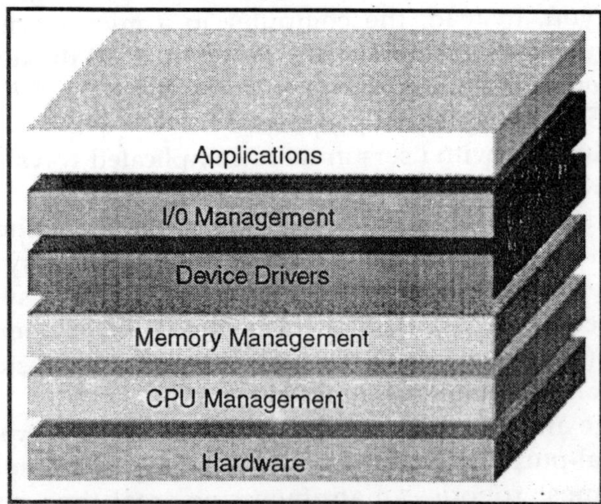

The second task, providing a consistent application interface, is especially important if there is to be more than one of a particular type of computer using the operating system, or if the hardware making up the computer is ever open to change. A consistent application programme interface

(API) allows a software developer to write an application on one computer and have a high level of confidence that it will run on another computer of the same type, even if the amount of memory or the quantity of storage is different on the two machines.

TYPES OF OPERATING SYSTEMS

Within the broad family of operating systems, there are generally four types, categorized based on the types of computers they control and the sort of applications they support. The categories are:

REAL-TIME OPERATING SYSTEM (RTOS)

Real-time operating systems are used to control machinery, scientific instruments and industrial systems. An RTOS typically has very little user-interface capability, and no end-user utilities, since the system will be a "sealed box" when delivered for use. A very important part of an RTOS is managing the resources of the computer so that a particular operation executes in precisely the same amount of time, every time it occurs. In a complex machine, having a part move more quickly just because system resources are available may be just as catastrophic as having it not move at all because the system is busy.

INGLE-USER, SINGLE TASK

As the name implies, this operating system is designed to manage the computer so that one user can effectively do one thing at a time. The Palm OS for Palm handheld computers is a good example of a modern single-user, single-task operating system.

SINGLE-USER, MULTI-TASKING

This is the type of operating system most people use on their desktop and laptop computers today. Microsoft's Windows and Apple's MacOS platforms are both examples of operating systems that will let a single user have several programs in operation at the same time. For example, it's entirely possible for a Windows user to be writing a note in a word processor while downloading a file from the Internet while printing the text of an e-mail message.

MULTI-USER

A multi-user operating system allows many different users to take advantage of the computer's resources simultaneously. The operating system must make sure that the requirements of the various users are balanced, and that each of the programs they are using has sufficient and separate resources so that a problem with one user doesn't affect the entire community of users. Unix, VMS and mainframe operating systems, such as *MVS*, are examples of multi-user operating systems.

It's important to differentiate between multi-user operating systems and single-user operating systems that support networking. Windows 2000 and Novell Netware can each support hundreds or thousands of networked users, but the operating systems themselves aren't true multi-user operating systems.

Thesystem administrator is the only "user" for Windows 2000 or Netware. The network support and all of the remote user logins the network enables are, in the overall plan of the operating system, a programme being run by the administrative user.

FEATURES OF WINDOWS OPERATING SYSTEM

WINDOWS CE

This operating system is designed for embedded devices such as Personal Digital Assistants (PDA's) and desktop boxes such as Web-TV.

General Features of Windows CE:

- Requirements specified by OEM
- Major use is in PDA's and embedded systems

WINDOWS 95

This operating system is designed for use as a

workstation client or desktop system, primarily for the home or mobile user. It is not intended to be used a server, but can be used in simple workgroups to share resources such as printers and files.

General Features of Windows 95

- Easier to use and learn than Windows 3.1
- More reliable than Windows 3.1
- Supports all major networking protocols including Novell IPX and TCP/IP
- Network clients are faster, more reliable, and use no conventional memory
- Simplified user interface
- Automated installation for all users and custom installations
- Remote administration features built in
- Supports multiple users on a single PC with customised settings for each individual
- Pre-emptive multitasking and multi-threading
- Plug and play support for hardware devices
- Dial-up networking (remote access services)
- Supports existing MS-DOS and Windows drivers and programs

WINDOWS 98

This operating system is designed for use as a workstation client or desktop system, primarily for the home or remote user.

It is not intended to be used a server, but can be used in simple workgroups to share resources such as printers and files. It is an upgraded enhanced version of Windows 95.

General Features of Windows 98:

- FAT32 enhanced file system
- Performance enhancements
- Fast startup and shutdown
- Intelligent update
- Wizards
- System file checker

- New hardware support, Universal Serial Bus
- Integrated browser/shell

WINDOWS NT V4 WORKSTATION

This operating system is designed for serious power users and desktop workstations, where users demand high reliability, pre-emptive multitasking of programs and support for OpenGL graphics applications. It can be used as a server in a workgroup, where the number of clients it supports is 10 or less.

General Features of Windows NT v4 Workstation

- Complete crash protection for 16- and 32-bit applications
- Built-in data protection
- Supports common networks and protocols
- Remote access service [client and/or server]
- Support for applications designed for MS-DOS®, Windows®, Windows 95, and other operating systems
- Preemptive multitasking
- OpenGL 3-D graphics
- Supports a wide range hardware devices
- Scalable [support for more than one processor]
- Multi-platform [support more than one processor type, eg, RISC]

WINDOWS NT 4 SERVER

This operating system is designed for robust scalable networks based on domains. It provides accounts for users and security logon using usernames and passwords. Where servers are required to handle more than 10 clients, NT Server is the best choice of operating system. It has been especially optimized to give good performance as an application server, and has additional tools to ease network administration problems.

WINDOWS 2000 PROFESSIONAL

This is the replacement for Windows NT 4 workstation,

designed for power users, remote users and high performance workstations. It has all the features of Windows NT 4 combined with the graphical desktop interface of Windows 98.

General Features of Windows 2000 Professional

- *File protection*: Core files are protected from being overwritten by software applications
- *Microsoft Installer*: This service helps users install, configure, upgrade and remove software
- *System preparation*: Entire computers can be cloned (copied) allowing multiple deployment of similar configurations to be done quickly and easily
- *Personalized menus*: The Start menu is adapted to the preferences of the user
- *Troubleshooters*: The troubleshooting wizards allow you to configure, optimize and troubleshoot Windows 2000
- *Encryption and security*: Files can be encrypted for greater protection. The standard security model for NT applies to all files, folders and system resources. Kerberos is also supported

WINDOWS 2000 SERVER

Organizations can use Windows 2000 server to build reliable scalable networks that support organizational requirements, such as file and application servers, Web and Intranet servers, e-mail and remote access servers and print servers.

WINDOWS 2000 ADVANCED SERVER

Windows 2000 Advanced Server includes all the features of Windows 2000 Server. It is designed for large-scale networks requiring high reliability and for the provision of e-commerce and line-of-business applications.

OPERATING SYSTEMS WIDELY USED ON PERSONAL COMPUTERS

The Operating System of a computer must be considered

when selecting Assistive Technology to be used to for accessing the computer, or accessing information displayed upon the computer monitor. It can be very frustrating to have purchased an application— and learn it is not compatible with the operating system of your computer.

The operating system of a computer performs basic tasks such as: recognizing information from the keyboard and mouse, sending information to the monitor, storing of information to the hard drive, and controlling device peripherals as printers and flatbed scanners.

Operating systems provide the basis for running common applications such as word processors and Internet browsers. Operating systems are also responsible for running Assistive Technology applications such as screen magnifiers, and applications that read text aloud.

ROLE

An "operating system" is a program that manages the resources of the computer. An operating system sets up a consistent way for programs to request resources, such as time on the processor, or space in memory, from the computer itself. Operating systems look after all the devices attached to the computer, such as printers, modems, disks, and terminals. Another part of an operating system's job is to maintain a file system; that is, to set up a consistent way for information to be stored and retrieved.

BACKGROUND

The first version of Windows was released in November of 1985. This program wasn't very popular as it lacked functionality compared to the Apple operating system. Version 1.0 was not a complete system. Instead, it simply extended on MS-DOS.

Version 2.0 was released two years later and achieved slightly more popularity than its predecessor. Version 2.03 was released in January of 2008. This version offered a totally different look that resulted in Apple filing a lawsuit against Microsoft with accusations of infringement.

Windows version 3.0 was released in 1990, the first edition to reach commercial success by selling two million copies within its first six months. This version included numerous improvements to the user interface along with new multitasking capabilities. Version 3.1 offered a facelift and was made available in March, 1992.

The Windows NT operating system was released in July of 1993. This version was based on a new kernel and it was considered to be the first designed for a professional platform. NT was later upgraded to function as a home user operating system with the release of Windows XP.

In August of 1995, Windows 95 was released. This operating system offered a consumer solution with significant changes to the user interface that also utilized preemptive multitasking.

Windows 95 was introduced to replace version 3.1 and Windows for Workgroups as well as MS-DOS. The first Microsoft operating system to use the plug and play system, Windows 95 revolutionized the desktop platform and achieved mass popularity.

Next up was Windows 98, released in June of 1998. This operating system was criticized for being slower and less reliable than version 95. Many of those issues were addressed a year later with the unveiling of Windows 98 Second Edition

Microsoft continued their line of professional operating systems with Windows 2000 in February of 2000. The consumer version was released as Windows ME in September of that year. ME integrated several new technologies, most notably the Universal Plug and Play.

Windows XP was released in October 2001. This version was based on the NT kernel and managed to retain the extreme functionality of its home-based predecessors. XP was widely embraced by the public and came in two different editions: Home and Professional. The Home Edition provided exceptionable multimedia support while the Professional edition offered excellent security and networking capabilities. XP has since been succeeded by Vista but support will continue through April of 2009.

WORKING

When you turn on your computer, it's nice to think that you're in control. There's the trusty computer mouse, which you can move anywhere on the screen, summoning up your music library or Internet browser at the slightest whim. Although it's easy to feel like a director in front of your desktop or laptop, there's a lot going on inside, and the real man behind the curtain handling the necessary tasks is the operating system.

Most desktop or laptop PCs come pre-loaded with Microsoft Windows. Macintosh computers come pre-loaded with Mac OS X. Many corporate servers use the Linux or UNIX operating systems. The operating system (OS) is the first thing loaded onto the computer—without the operating system, a computer is useless.

More recently, operating systems have started to pop up in smaller computers as well. If you like to tinker with electronic devices, you're probably pleased that operating systems can now be found on many of the devices we use every day, from cell phones to wireless access points. The computers used in these little devices have gotten so powerful that they can now actually run an operating system and applications. The computer in a typical modern cell phone is now more powerful than a desktop computer from 20 years ago, so this progression makes sense and is a natural development.

The purpose of an operating system is to organize and control hardware and software so that the device it lives in behaves in a flexible but predictable way. In this article, we'll tell you what a piece of software must do to be called an operating system, show you how the operating system in your desktop computer works and give you some examples of how to take control of the other operating systems around you.

Not all computers have operating systems. The computer that controls the microwave oven in your kitchen, for example, doesn't need an operating system. It has one set of tasks to perform, very straightforward input to expect (a numbered keypad and a few pre-set buttons) and simple, never-changing hardware to control. For a computer like this, an operating system would be unnecessary baggage, driving up the development and manufacturing costs significantly and adding complexity where none is required. Instead, the computer in a microwave oven simply runs a single hard-wired program all the time.

For other devices, an operating system creates the ability to:

- Serve a variety of purposes
- Interact with users in more complicated ways
- Keep up with needs that change over time

All desktop computers have operating systems. The most common are the Windows family of operating systems developed by Microsoft, the Macintosh operating systems developed by Apple and the UNIX family of operating systems (which have been developed by a whole history of individuals, corporations and collaborators). There are hundreds of other operating systems available for special-purpose applications, including specializations for mainframes, robotics, manufacturing, real-time control systems and so on.

In any device that has an operating system, there's usually a way to make changes to how the device works. This is far from a happy accident; one of the reasons operating systems are made out of portable code rather than permanent physical circuits is so that they can be changed or modified without having to scrap the whole device.

MICROSOFT WINDOWS AND OTHER USERS

A Windows user can still use the above MS-DOS steps if they wish to create a batch file. If, however, you're more comfortable using Microsoft Windows or your operating system, you can use any text editor, such as Notepad or WordPad, to create your batch files, as long as the file extension ends with. bat. In the below example we use the Windows notepad to create a batch file.

- Click Start
- Click Run
- *Type*: notepad and press enter.

- Once notepad is open, type the below lines in the file or copy and paste the below lines into notepad. @echo off echo Hello this is a test batch file pause dir c:\windows
- Click File and click Save; browse to where you want to save the file. For the file name, type "test.bat", and if your version of Windows has a "Save as type" option, choose "All files", otherwise it will save as a text file. Once all of this has been done click the Save button and exit notepad.
- Now, to run the batch file, simply double-click or run the file like any other program. Once the batch file has completed running it will close the window automatically.

WINDOWS SYSTEM PROTECTION

INTRODUCTION

From the beginning of electronic computing until 15 years ago, the 'game' of attack and defence was played on a system by system basis, with defenders relying on physical security and ad-hoc operating system protection methods and attackers guessing passwords or exploiting errors and omissions to bypass normal system controls.

Over the last 15 years, the computing environment has changed dramatically, with widespread physical distribution of computing power, almost complete loss of physical control over computing hardware, and a dramatic increase in the networking of computers, but defences have not changed substantially in terms of their reliance on physical security and ad-hoc defences.

As a result, we see new classes of attacks such as computer viruses, which exploit the lack of physical control and fundamental weakness of existing logical controls to spread transitively throughout the computing world. Even the best protection systems available today can quickly and easily be defeated by anyone with physical access and ample knowledge, or by the application of that expertise in a widespread computer virus attack. One of the major factors in the successful application of information protection techniques is the exploitation of computational advantage. Computational advantage shows up historically in cryptography, where Shannon's theory [Shan49] clearly demonstrates the effect of 'workload' on the complexity of cryptanalysis and introduces the concepts of diffusion and confusion as they relate to statistical attacks on cryptosystems.

Most modern cryptosystems exploit this as their primary defence The same basic principle applies in computer virus analysis in which evolutionary viruses drive the complexity of detection and eradication up dramatically and in password protection in which we try to drive the number of guesses required for a successful attack up by limiting the use of obvious passwords. As we will see, one of the major reasons attacks succeed is because of the static nature of defence, and the dynamic nature of attack.

THE ULTIMATE ATTACK

The ultimate attack against any system begins with physical access, and proceeds to disassembly and reverse engineering of whatever programmed defences are in place. Even with a cryptographic key provided by the user, an attacker can modify the mechanism to examine and exploit the key, given ample physical access. Eventually, the attacker can remove the defences by finding decision points and altering them to yield altered decisions.

Without physical protection, nobody has ever found a defence against this attack, and it is unlikely that anyone ever will. The reason is that any protection scheme other than a physical one depends on the operation of a finite state machine, and ultimately, any finite state machine can be examined and modified at will, given enough time and effort. The best we can ever do is delay attack by increasing the complexity of making desired alterations.

THE ULTIMATE DEFENCE

The ultimate defence is to drive the complexity of the

ultimate attack up so high that the cost of attack is too high to be worth performing. This is, in effect, security through obscurity, and it is our general conclusion that all technical information protection in computer systems relies at some level either on physical protection, security through obscurity, or combinations thereof.

The goal of security through obscurity is to make the difficulty of attack so great that in practice, it is not worth performing, even though it could eventually be successful. Successful attacks against obscurity defences depend on the ability to guess some key piece of information. The most obvious example is attacking and defending passwords, and since this problem demonstrates precisely the issues at hand, we will use it as an example. In password protection, there are generally three aspects to making attack difficult. One aspect is making the size of the password space large, so that the potential number of guesses required for an attack is enormous.

In the case of current operating systems, the size of the space is enormous, consisting of all programs that fit in the computer's memory, but the operating system may only have a very small number of versions, all of which are almost identical, yielding a highly coherent subspace consisting of only a few very closely tied points. Thus, only a few guesses are required to determine precisely which version of the operating system is in use, and even that may not be required for many attacks. Operating systems also provide no confusion in that the part of the program that performs any given operation is immediately apparent to the knowledgeable attacker. For this reason, low-level operating system attack is quite simple.

The problem for defenders is to find a way to increase the difficulty of operating system attack by reducing coherence. The ultimate goal is to obscure defences so as to make attackers require repeated use of the ultimate attack in order to impact substantial numbers of systems. One solution is to provide each computer with a sound and unique defence. This would tend to make it infeasible to design an automated attack that could systematically bypass all of the defences, but then we would have to design a new defence for each system, and the costs of defence would probably become intolerable. We could trade off costs for probability of attack by implementing some fixed number of different defences, thus requiring a fixed number of ultimate attacks for complete success. This is essentially the situation in the world today, where a wide variety of ad-hoc defences are on the market. Unfortunately, many of these defences fall to the same classes of attack, and the number is sufficiently small that defeating most of them requires relatively little effort or expense.

TECHNIQUES FOR PROGRAM IN WINDOWS

We will consider two programs equivalent if, given identical input sequences, they produce identical output sequences. The equivalence of two programs is undecidable as is the determination of whether one program can evolve from another. This result would seem to indicate that evolution has the potential for increasing complexity of analysis, and thus difficulty of attack. In a practical operating system design, we may also have very stringent requirements on the space and time used by the protection mechanism, and certain instruction sequences may be highly undesirable because they impact some other aspect of system operation or are incompatible across some similar machines. For this reason, we may not be able to reach the levels of complexity required to eliminate concerted human attack, but we may succeed in increasing the complexity of automated attacks to a level where the time required for attack is sufficient to have noticeable performance impacts, even to a level where no attacker is able to design a strong enough attack to defeat more than a small number of evolutions.

We know that evolution is as general as Turing machine computation, and that an exhaustive set of equivalent programs is easily described mathematically (*i.e.* the definition of equivalence), but this is not particularly helpful in terms of designing practical evolutionary schemes. We now describe a number of practical techniques we have explored for program evolution and some results regarding the space, time, and complexity issues introduced by these techniques.

STRUCTURE

SYSTEM COMPONENTS

Even though, not all systems have the same structure many modern operating systems share the same goal of supporting the following types of system components.

Process Management

The operating system manages many kinds of activities ranging from user programs to system programs like printer spooler, name servers, file server etc. Each of these activities is encapsulated in a process. A process includes the complete execution context (code, data, PC, registers, OS resources in use etc.).

It is important to note that a process is not a program. A process is only ONE instant of a program in execution. There are many processes can be running the same program. The five major activities of an operating system in regard to process management are:

- Creation and deletion of user and system processes.
- Suspension and resumption of processes.
- A mechanism for process synchronization.
- A mechanism for process communication.
- A mechanism for deadlock handling.

Main-Memory Management

Primary-Memory or Main-Memory is a large array of words or bytes. Each word or byte has its own address. Main-memory provides storage that can be access directly by the CPU. That is to say for a program to be executed, it must in the main memory.

The major activities of an operating in regard to memory-management are:

- Keep track of which part of memory are currently being used and by whom.

- Decide which processes are loaded into memory when memory space becomes available.
- Allocate and de allocate memory space as needed.

File Management

A file is a collected of related information defined by its creator. Computer can store files on the disk (secondary storage), which provide long term storage. Some examples of storage media are magnetic tape, magnetic disk and optical disk. Each of these media has its own properties like speed, capacity, data transfer rate and access methods.

A file systems normally organized into directories to ease their use. These directories may contain files and other directions.

The five main major activities of an operating system in regard to file management are:

- The creation and deletion of files.
- The creation and deletion of directions.
- The support of primitives for manipulating files and directions.
- The mapping of files onto secondary storage.
- The back up of files on stable storage media.

I/O System Management

I/O subsystem hides the peculiarities of specific hardware devices from the user. Only the device driver knows the peculiarities of the specific device to whom it is assigned.

Secondary-Storage Management

Generally speaking, systems have several levels of storage, including primary storage, secondary storage and cache storage. Instructions and data must be placed in primary storage or cache to be referenced by a running program. Because main memory is too small to accommodate all data and programs, and its data are lost when power is lost, the computer system must provide secondary storage to back up main memory. Secondary storage consists of tapes, disks, and other media designed to hold information that will eventually be accessed in primary storage (primary, secondary, cache) is ordinarily divided into bytes or words consisting of a fixed number of bytes. Each location in storage has an address; the set of all addresses available to a program is called an address space.

The three major activities of an operating system in regard to secondary storage management are:

- Managing the free space available on the secondary-storage device.
- Allocation of storage space when new files have to be written.
- Scheduling the requests for memory access.

Networking

A distributed systems is a collection of processors that do not share memory, peripheral devices, or a clock. The processors communicate with one another through communication lines called network. The communication-network design must consider routing and connection strategies, and the problems of contention and security.

Protection System

If a computer systems has multiple users and allows the concurrent execution of multiple processes, then the various processes must be protected from one another's activities. Protection refers to mechanism for controlling the access of programs, processes, or users to the resources defined by a computer systems.

Command Interpreter System

A command interpreter is an interface of the operating system with the user. The user gives commands with are executed by operating system (usually by turning them into system calls). The main function of a command interpreter is to get and execute the next user specified command. Command-Interpreter is usually not part of the kernel, since multiple command interpreters (shell, in UNIX terminology) may be support by an operating system, and they do not really need to run in kernel mode. There are two main advantages to separating the command interpreter from the kernel.

- If we want to change the way the command interpreter looks, *i.e.*, I want to change the interface of command interpreter, I am able to do that if the command interpreter is separate from the kernel. I cannot change the code of the kernel so I cannot modify the interface.
- If the command interpreter is a part of the kernel it is possible for a malicious process to gain access to certain part of the kernel that it showed not have to avoid this ugly scenario it is advantageous to have the command interpreter separate from kernel

OPERATING SYSTEMS SERVICES

Following are the five services provided by an operating systems to the convenience of the users.

Program Execution

The purpose of a computer systems is to allow the user to execute programs. So the operating systems provides an environment where the user can conveniently run programs. The user does not have to worry about the memory allocation or multitasking or anything. These things are taken care of by the operating systems.

Running a program involves the allocating and deallocating memory, CPU scheduling in case of multiprocess. These functions cannot be given to the user-level programs. So user-level programs cannot help the user to run programs independently without the help from operating systems.

I/O Operations

Each program requires an input and produces output. This involves the use of I/O. The operating systems hides the user the details of underlying hardware for the I/O. All the user sees is that the I/O has been performed without any details. So the operating systems by providing I/O makes it convenient for the users to run programs. For efficiently and protection users cannot control I/O so this service cannot be provided by user-level programs.

File System Manipulation

The output of a program may need to be written into new files or input taken from some files. The operating systems provides this service. The user does not have to worry about secondary storage management. User gives a command for reading or writing to a file and sees his her task accomplished.

Thus operating systems makes it easier for user programs to accomplished their task. This service involves secondary storage management. The speed of I/O that depends on secondary storage management is critical to the speed of many programs and hence it is best relegated to the operating systems to manage it than giving individual users the control of it. It is not difficult for the user-level programs to provide these services but for above mentioned reasons it is best if this service s left with operating system.

Communications

There are instances where processes need to communicate with each other to exchange information. It may be between processes running on the same computer or running on the different computers. By providing this service the operating system relieves the user of the worry of passing messages between processes. In case where the messages need to be passed to processes on the other computers through a network it can be done by the user programs. The user program may be customised to the specifics of the hardware through which the message transits and provides the service interface to the operating system.

Error Detection

An error is one part of the system may cause malfunctioning of the complete system. To avoid such a situation the operating system constantly monitors the system for detecting the errors. This relieves the user of the worry of errors propagating to various part of the system and causing malfunctioning.

This service cannot allowed to be handled by user programs because it involves monitoring and in cases altering area of memory or deallocation of memory for a faulty process. Or may be relinquishing the CPU of a process that goes into an infinite loop. These tasks are too critical to be handed over to the user programs. A user program if given these privileges can interfere with the correct (normal) operation of the operating systems.

SYSTEM CALLS AND SYSTEM PROGRAMS

System calls provide an interface between the process an the operating system. System calls allow user-level processes to request some services from the operating system which process itself is not allowed to do. In handling the trap, the operating system will enter in the kernel mode, where it has access to privileged instructions, and can perform the desired service on the behalf of user-level process. It is because of the critical nature of operations that the operating system itself does them every time they are needed. For example, for I/O a process involves a system call telling the operating system to read or write particular area and this request is satisfied by the operating system.

System programs provide basic functioning to users so that they do not need to write their own environment for program development (editors, compilers) and program execution (shells). In some sense, they are bundles of useful system calls.

LAYERED APPROACH DESIGN

In this case the system is easier to debug and modify, because changes affect only limited portions of the code, and programmer does not have to know the details of the other layers. Information is also kept only where it is needed and is accessible only in certain ways, so bugs affecting that data are limited to a specific module or layer.

MECHANISMS AND POLICIES

The policies what is to be done while the mechanism specifies how it is to be done. For instance, the timer construct for ensuring CPU protection is mechanism. On the other hand, the decision of how long the timer is set for a particular user is a policy decision.

The separation of mechanism and policy is important to provide flexibility to a system. If the interface between mechanism and policy is well defined, the change of policy may affect only a few parameters. On the other hand, if interface between these two is vague or not well defined, it might involve much deeper change to the system.

Once the policy has been decided it gives the programmer the choice of using his/her own implementation. Also, the underlying implementation may be changed for a more efficient one without much trouble if the mechanism and policy are well defined.

7

Network Operating System

INTRODUCTION

A network operating system (NOS) is a computer operating system system that is designed primarily to support workstation, personal computer, and, in some instances, older terminal that are connected on a local area network (LAN). Artisoft's LANtastic, Banyan VINES, Novell's NetWare, and Microsoft's LAN Manager are examples of network operating systems. In addition, some multi-purpose operating systems, such asWindows NT and Digital's OpenVMS come with capabilities that enable them to be described as a network operating system.

A network operating system provides printer sharing, common file system and database sharing, application sharing, and the ability to manage a network name directory, security, and other housekeeping aspects of a network.

A network operating system (NOS) is a software program that controls other software and hardware that runs on a network. It also allows multiple computers, also known as network computers, to communicate with one main computer and each other, so as to share resources, run applications, and send messages, among other things. A computer network can consist of a wireless network, local area network (LAN), a wide area network (WAN), or even two or three computer networks. The heart of any of these networks, however, is the network operating system.

There are different types of operating systems. Most individual computer users run client operating systems, like

Windows XP®, which run on a single computer. Personal computers that individuals use at home have a client operating system which manages the interactions and processes between the computer and its peripherals such as the keyboard, mouse, external monitor, and printer. In a sense, this is also a network, though it is different in scale than a network operating system which manages the interactions of many computers.

A network usually consists of many network computers that are connected to a central hub or router. The central hub, in turn, is connected to a larger, main computer. The network may also include other devices like printers, a tape-backup system, and a central storage facility. The main network computer runs all the connected computers and devices with the help of the operating system software.

A network administrator is the person who installs and manages the network and its operating system. He or she may configure the NOS to recognize a wireless network as well. If a WAN is involved, this would probably require more than one network administrator, as the network would likely be located offsite.

A network operating system has a menu-driven administration interface. From this interface, the network administrator may perform a variety of activities. He or she can use the interface to format hard drives, set up security restrictions, or establish log-in information for each user. The interface of a network operating system can also be used to attach shared printers to the network, or configure the system to automatically back data up on a daily basis.

An important component of a network is the file server. A file server is the device where data is stored for use by network computers. It can be a single computer or it can be a cluster of external hard drives hooked up in series to store data. A network operating system helps manage the flow of information between that file server and the network computers.

Examples of network operating systems include UNIX®, Windows 2000 Server ®, and Netware®. Each operating system runs differently, and as such has to be configured to perform the actions the network requires. A good knowledge of each operating system is necessary to work with them. Network administrators may need to be certified in order to manage particular network operating systems.

EXPLANATION

Network operating systems (NOS) typically are used to run computers that act as servers. They provide the capabilities required for network operation. Network operating systems are also designed for client computers and provide functions so the distinction between network operating systems and stand alone operating systems is not always obvious.

Network operating systems provide the following functions:

- File and print sharing.
- Account administration for users.
- Security.

INSTALLED COMPONENTS

- Client functionality
- Server functionality

FUNCTIONS PROVIDED

- Account Administration for users
- Security
- File and print sharing

NETWORK SERVICES

- File Sharing
- Print sharing
- User administration
- Backing up data

UNIX

DESCRIPTION

Is it possible for an Information Technology [IT] product

to be both mature and state-of-the-art at the same time? In the case of the UNIX® system, the answer is an unqualified "Yes." The UNIX system has continued to develop over the past twenty-five years. In millions of installations running on nearly every hardware platform made, the UNIX system has earned its reputation for stability and scalability. Over the years, UNIX system suppliers have steadily assimilated new technologies so that UNIX systems today provide more functionality as any other operating system. Perhaps the key to the continuing growth of the UNIX system is the free-market demands placed upon suppliers who produce and support software built to open standards. The "open systems" approach is in bold contrast to other operating environments that lock in their customers with resultant high switching costs. UNIX system suppliers, on the other hand, must constantly provide the highest quality systems in order to retain their customers. Those who become dissatisfied with one UNIX system implementation retain the ability to easily move to another UNIX system implementation.

The continuing success of the UNIX system should come as no surprise. No other operating environment enjoys the support of every major system supplier. Mention the UNIX system and IT professionals immediately think not only of the operating system itself, but also of the large family of application software that the UNIX system supports. In the IT marketplace, the UNIX system has been the catalyst for sweeping changes that have empowered consumers to seek the best-of-breed without the arbitrary constraints imposed by proprietary environments.

In a nutshell then, the UNIX system is the users' and suppliers' operating environment of choice. The UNIX system represents the best collective efforts of competing suppliers, the most refined standards in the public domain, and the rock-solid stability that comes from years of quality assurance testing, mission-critical use, and refinement.

This white paper examines the UNIX system with a special concern for both its extraordinary past and its equally extraordinary prospects for the future.

THE UNIX SYSTEM

The UNIX system has been around for a long time, and many people may remember it as it existed in the previous decades. Many IT professionals who encountered UNIX systems in the past found it uncompromising. While its power was impressive, its command-line interface required technical competence, its syntax was not intuitive, and its interface was unfriendly.

Moreover, in the UNIX system's early days, security was virtually nonexistent. Subsequently, the UNIX system became the first operating system to suffer attacks mounted over the nascent Internet. As the UNIX system matured, however, the organization of security shifted from centralized to distributed authentication and authorization systems.

Now, a single Graphical User Interface is shipped and supported by all major vendors has replaced command-line syntax, and security systems, up to and including B1, provide appropriate controls over access to the UNIX system.

THE VALUE OF STANDARDS

The UNIX system's increasing popularity spawned the development of a number of variations of the UNIX operating system in the 1980s, and the existence of these caused a mid-life crisis. Standardization had progressed slowly and methodically in domains such as telecommunications and third-generation languages; yet no one had addressed standards at the operating system level.

For suppliers, the thought of a uniform operating environment was disconcerting. Consumer lock-in was woven tightly into the fabric of the industry. Individual consumers, particularly those with UNIX system experience, envisioned standardized environments, but had no way to pull the market in their direction.

However, for one category of consumer -governments- the standardization of the UNIX system was both desirable and within reach. Governments have clout and are the largest consumers of information technology products and services in the world. Driven by the need to improve commonality, both US and European governments endorsed a shift to the UNIX system. The Institute of Electrical and Electronic Engineers POSIX family of standards, along with standards from ISO, ANSI and others, led the way. Consortia such as the X/Open Company (merged with the Open Software Foundation in 1995 to form The Open Group) hammered out draft standards to accelerate the process.

In 1994, the definitive specification of what constitutes a UNIX system was finalized through X/Open Company's consensus process. The Single UNIX Specification was born-not from a theoretical, ivory tower approach, but by analyzing the applications that were in use in businesses across the world.

With the active support of government and commercial buyers alike, vendors began to converge on products that implement the Single UNIX Specification, and now all major vendors have products labeled UNIX 95, which indicates that the vendor guarantees that the product conforms to the Single UNIX Specification.

Vendors continue to add value to the UNIX system, particularly in areas of new technology, however that value will always be built upon a single, consensus standard. Meanwhile, the functionality of the UNIX system was established and the mid-life crisis was resolved. Suppliers today provide UNIX systems that are built upon a single, consensus standard.

It is also important to remember that even when variance among UNIX systems was at its worst, IT professionals agreed that migration among UNIX system variants was far easier than migration among the proprietary alternatives.

Now with UNIX 95 branded products available from all major systems vendors, the buyer can for the first time buy systems from different manufacturers, safe in the knowledge that each one is guaranteed to implement the complete functionality of the Single UNIX Specification and will continue to do so.

UNIX system suppliers can assure customers that they own a standards-based system by registering them to use the

Open Brand. Below is a list of suppliers who give users this guarantee.

UNIX 95 REGISTERED PRODUCTS

- *DIGITAL*: Digital UNIX® Version 4.0 running Digital's AlphaStations and Digital's Alpha Servers
- *HITACHI*: Hitachi 3050RX, 3500/3X, 3500/4XX running HI-UX/WE2 Version 06-01 and later HITACHI: Hitachi 3500 running HI-UX/WE2 Version 07-01 and later
- *Hewlett-Packard*: HP-UX Release 10.20 and later on all HP9000 Series 700 and 800
- HP-UX Release 11.00 or later (in both 32 and 64-bit configurations) on HP9000 Series (all models)
- *IBM*: IBM POWER, POWER2, and Power PCTM Systems with IBM AIX® Version 4.2 or later IBM: OS/390 Version 1 Release 2 or later with OS/390 V1R2 or later Security Server and OS/390 V1R2 or later C/ C++ Compiler on IBM System/390 Processors that support OS/390 Version 1 Release 2 NCR: NCR UNIX System V Release 4 MP-RAS Release 3.02 or later on NCR World Mark Series and System 3000 Series NEC: UX/4800 R12.3 and later on UP4800 and EWS4800 Series SCO: SCO UnixWare Family R2.1.1 and later for single and multiprocessor IntelTM 386/ 486 or Pentium® PCs conforming to PC/AT architectures
- *SGI*: IRIX 6.5 running on Silicon Graphics systems using the MIPS R4000, R5000, R8000 and R10,000 family of processors
- *SNI*: Business Servers running BS2000/OSD V3.0 and higher.
- *SNI*: Reliant UNIX V5.43 running on RM Server Family, all Models RM200/300/400/600
- *Siemens Pyramid*: Reliant UNIX Version 5.43 running on Reliant RM1000® Cluster Server
- *SUN*: Solaris 2.6 on SPARC based systems
- *SUN*: Solaris 2.6 on x86pc based systems

UNIX AND WINDOWS NT

It is common these days to read analysts' accounts and IS professionals' experiences that compare and contrast the UNIX system with Microsoft Corporation's latest operating system, called Windows NT. Opinions vary, of course, but a number of common themes have emerged. The key differences between these operating environments are as follows: The UNIX system today is more robust, reliable and scalable. Analysts say this observation, which is widely reported from many different viewpoints, makes practical sense. Engineers at Microsoft are retracing the steps that the UNIX system has completed. How else could it be?

In sharp contrast to the open standards that define the UNIX system, Windows NT technology remains fiercely proprietary. Microsoft remains ambivalent to the world of standards. Choosing NT entangles customers with nonstandard utilities, directories, and software tools that do not conform to any de jure or consensus standards.

The UNIX system today is available on a wide spectrum of computer hardware. Particularly when high performance is at issue, hardware suppliers suggest the UNIX system, rather than Windows NT. The primary appeal of NT is for low-end, office-centered, departmental applications.

Unit shipment growth rates for Windows NT exceed the rates for the UNIX system, which is to be expected for a new product. However, revenue growth in UNIX systems sales is much higher than NT. It is reasonable to expect Windows NT to take a share in the operating systems market, along with other more specialized operating systems. There is no evidence today to indicate that NT will be dominant; in fact, most IT professionals predict that it will not.

Windows NT Server 4.0 is still not a full-function server operating system. While it does support multi-user computing via third-party add-on tools, it lacks certain fundamental features that the UNIX system is known for providing, such as directory services for managing user access and peripherals over a distributed enterprise network. The presence of the UNIX system in the marketplace has been good for Windows

NT. The UNIX system established the market for cross-platform client and server operating environments that NT seeks to address. In turn, NT will improve the market for UNIX systems in the future. That is, competition among UNIX system providers will be enhanced by competition with NT. The choice between open and proprietary products will be quite crisp.

TODAY'S UNIX SYSTEM

The key to the continuing growth of the UNIX system is the free-market demands placed upon suppliers who produce and support software built to public standards. The "open systems" approach is in bold contrast to other operating environments that lock in their customers with high switching costs.

UNIX system suppliers, on the other hand, must constantly provide the highest quality systems in order to retain their customers. Those who become dissatisfied with one UNIX system implementation retain the ability to easily move to another UNIX system implementation.

The continuing success of the UNIX system should come as no surprise. No other operating environment enjoys the support of every major system supplier. Mention the UNIX system and IT professionals immediately think not only of the operating system itself, but also of the large family of hardware and application software that the UNIX system supports. In the IT marketplace, the UNIX system has been the catalyst for sweeping changes that have empowered consumers to seek the best-of-breed without the arbitrary constraints imposed by proprietary environments.

The market's pull for the UNIX system was amplified by other events as well. The availability of relational database management systems, the shift to the client/server architecture, and the introduction of low-cost UNIX system servers together set the stage for business applications to flourish. For client/server systems, the networking strengths of the UNIX system shine. Standardized relational database engines delivered on low-cost high-performance UNIX system servers offered substantial cost savings over proprietary alternatives.

UNIX SYSTEM EXISTENCE

For the last two and a half decades, the UNIX system has upheld a tradition of providing its customers with early access to new technologies.

For example:

- UNIX systems provided early access to RISC technology. Applications in CAD/CAM, multimedia, and large-scale publishing that demanded high performance workstations have always used the UNIX system platform.
- The UNIX system provided early access to symmetric multiprocessing [SMP] computers. UNIX system-based SMP parallel processors radically improved the price/performance of midsize and high-range servers.
- The UNIX system first enabled distributed transaction processing in conjunction with TP monitors from independent software suppliers. The server side of client/server technology was launched on the UNIX system.
- The UNIX system launched the Internet and the World Wide Web.

UNIX system suppliers also have a proud tradition of integration with legacy systems as well as innovation to uphold. No other system can ensure that disparate systems-usually proprietary systems-can be integrated, allowing the buyer's investment in data and information to be realised with minimal disruption and reinvestment.

There is every reason to believe that the UNIX system will continue to be the platform of choice for innovative development. In the near term, for example, UNIX system vendors will define the scope of Java and provide the distributed computing environment into which the Network Computer terminal will fit and enable it to thrive and grow.

How will Java and the Network Computer terminal manifest themselves? The exact answer is unknown; however, in open computing, the process for finding that answer is well understood. The UNIX system community has set aside (via consensus standards) the wasteful task of developing arbitrary differences among computing environments. Rather than building proprietary traps, this community is actively seeking ways to add value to the UNIX system with improved scalability, reliability, price/performance, and customer service.

Java and the Network Computer terminal offer several potential advantages for consumers. One key advantage is a smaller, lighter, standards-based client. A second advantage is a specification that is not controlled by one company, but is developed to the benefit of all by an open, consensus process. Thirdly, greater code reuse and a component software market based on Object technology, such as CORBA and Java. All of these options and more are being deployed first by members of the UNIX system community.

INDUSTRIAL STRENGTH UNIX SYSTEM

Today's UNIX system is robust, scalable, and it continues to provide uniform access to a wide variety of computing hardware. For these reasons the UNIX system continues to be the operating system of choice for mission-critical systems. The UNIX system is the key enabler for enterprises that wish to keep switching costs as low as possible. That is, the UNIX system remains the only open alternative to locking in on a proprietary operating system.

Scalability is here today, enabling application to run on small-scale systems through to the largest servers necessary. The UNIX system is available on hardware ranging from low-cost PC-class servers on through parallel architectures that harness together 60 or more processors. This range is wider and the choices of hardware more cost effective than any other system. The UNIX system is the only option for Massively Parallel Processing (MPP).

A robust operating system is tough enough to perform successfully under a variety of different operating conditions. By virtue of its worldwide deployment by an international community of system vendors, the UNIX system has earned the reputation for robustness.

Uniform operating system services are at the heart of the standardized UNIX system. Many enterprise systems are assembled with hardware from several different sources. Atop these different hardware platforms, the UNIX operating system provides a uniform platform for database management systems and application software.

The market for the UNIX system continues to expand. IDC estimates the market at US$ 39 billion in 1996 and forecasts the market to be US$ 50 billion in the year 2000. In addition, the installed base of the UNIX system has an estimated value of US$ 122 billion. These market estimates lead to several conclusions about the UNIX system, as follows:

An annual market of US$ 39 billion is large enough to remain attractive to many suppliers and to provide sufficient revenue to fund continuing high levels of investment in support and product enhancement.

The UNIX system's growth rates, which appear modest in comparison to the unit shipment growth of newer products, are anchored by an enormous installed base. High unit shipment growth rates are typical of new entries in a marketplace.

In key benchmarks and mission-critical applications, the UNIX system consistently performs better. The UNIX system is the dominant software platform for Relational Database Management Systems. Investment in developing and enhancing UNIX system products is significantly larger than in any other operating environment.

SINGLE UNIX SPECIFICATION

Today, The Open Group's UNIX 95 brand may be applied to any operating system product that is guaranteed to meet the Single UNIX Specification. The Single UNIX Specification is designed to give software developers a single set of APIs to be supported by every UNIX system.

The most significant consequence of the Single UNIX Specification initiative is that it shifts the focus of attention away from incompatible UNIX system product implementations on to compliance with a single, agreed-upon set of APIs. If an operating system meets the specification, and commonly available applications can run on it, then it can reliable viewed as open.

So, the future looks as though it will be about a set of sturdy and dependable specifications standing as a firm foundation upon which many competing product implementations will be built.

By developing a single specification for the UNIX system, The Open Group and the computer industry have completed the foundation of open systems. The next version of the Single UNIX Specification, known as Version 2 was announced in March 1997. Products guaranteed to conform to this specification will carry the label UNIX 98.

SINGLE UNIX SPECIFICATION

The Single UNIX Specification, Version 2 contains the following enhancements:

- Year 2000 Alignment-changes to minimize the impact of the Millennium Rollover.
- Threads: POSIX 1003.1c-1995. The Threads extensions permit development of applications to make significant performance gains on multiprocessor hardware.
- Large File Summit extensions to permit UNIX systems to support files of arbitrary sizes, this is of particular relevance to database applications.
- Networking Services: The specifications are aligned with the POSIX 1003.1g standard.
- *MSE*: The Multibyte Support Extension is now aligned with ISO C amendment 1, 1995.
- Dynamic linking extensions to permit applications to share common code across many applications, and ease maintenance of bug fixes and performance enhancements for applications.
- N-bit cleanup (64 bit and beyond), to remove any architectural dependencies in the Single UNIX

Specification. This is of particular relevance with the ongoing move to 64 bit CPUs.

- The real-time extensions are an optional feature group, allowing procurement of X/Open real-time systems with predictable, bounded behaviour.
- Inclusion of the existing specifications for the graphical user interface, CDE as an option in the UNIX 98 brand.

BENEFITS FOR APPLICATION DEVELOPERS

- Improved portability.
- Faster development through the increased number of standard interfaces.
- More innovation is possible, due to the reduced time spent porting applications.

BENEFITS FOR USERS

The Single UNIX Specification will evolve and develop in response to market needs protecting users investment in existing systems and applications. The availability of the UNIX system from multiple suppliers gives users freedom of choice rather than being locked in to a single supplier. And the wide range of applications-built on the UNIX system's strengths of scalability, availability and reliability-ensure that mission critical business needs can be met.

SUMMARY

When the history of the information age is written, the extraordinary dynamics of the UNIX system marketplace will be seen as playing an important role. The UNIX system was developed at just the right time and place to be the critical enabler for a revolution in information technology. Client/server architectures, the Internet, object databases, heterogeneous transaction processing, and Web computing all emerged on the shoulders of the UNIX system.

Most importantly, the UNIX system continues to be a driving force for innovation because of its commitment to standards. When proprietary differences are set aside, and with the wide implementation of the Single UNIX Specification they are set aside, suppliers compete by adding value. This fundamental tenet is the reason that the UNIX system has thrived-and will continue to thrive in the years to come.

HISTORY OF UNIX

Unix was originally developed in the 1960s and 1970s by a group of AT&T employees at Bell Labs. Today, Unix systems are split into different branches which have developed over time by AT&T and by commercial vendors and non-profit organizations. Many variations (usually called "flavours") of Unix and Unix-like Operating Systems were released during the dot com boom of the 1990's. The dot com bust caused many of these to consolidate. As a result, of the dozens of commercial variations of Unix that were developed in the 1980s, only Solaris, HP-UX, and AIX are still doing relatively well in the market. Of these, Solaris currently holds the highest market share.

A system is termed UNIX only if it complies fully with (and is certified by) the Single Unix Specification (SUS) standards. Similar systems that do not comply fully or are not certified are termed "Unix-like" operating systems. Examples of popular Unix-like systems include Linux and Xenix.

INTRODUCTION TO LINUX

Linux is quite possibly the most important free software achievement since the original Space War, or, more recently, Emacs. It has developed into an operating system for business, education, and personal productivity. Linux is no longer only for UNIX wizards who sit for hours in front of a glowing console (although we assure you that many users fall into this category). This book will help you get the most from Linux.

Linux (pronounced with a short i, as in LIH-nucks) is a UNIX operating system clone which runs on a variety of platforms, especially personal computers with Intel 80386 or better processors. It supports a wide range of software, from TeX, to the X Window System, to the GNU C/C++ compiler, to TCP/IP. It's a versatile, bona fide implementation of UNIX, freely distributed under the terms of the GNU General Public License.

Linux can turn any 80386 or better personal computer into a workstation that puts the full power of UNIX at your fingertips. Businesses install Linux on entire networks of machines, and use the operating system to manage financial and hospital records, distributed computing environments, and telecommunications. Universities worldwide use Linux to teach courses on operating system programming and design. Computing enthusiasts everywhere use Linux at home for programming, productivity, and all-around hacking.

What makes Linux so different is that it is a free implementation of UNIX. It was and still is developed cooperatively by a group of volunteers, primarily on the Internet, who exchange code, report bugs, and fix problems in an open-ended environment. Anyone is welcome to join the Linux development effort. All it takes is interest in hacking a free UNIX clone, and some programming know-how.

HISTORY OF LINUX

UNIX is one of the most popular operating systems worldwide because of its large support base and distribution. It was originally developed at AT&T as a multitasking system for minicomputers and mainframes in the 1970's, but has since grown to become one of the most widely-used operating systems anywhere, despite its sometimes confusing interface and lack of central standardization.

Many hackers feel that UNIX is the Right Thing--the One True Operating System. Hence, the development of Linux by an expanding group of UNIX hackers who want to get their hands dirty with their own system.

Versions of UNIX exist for many systems, from personal computers to supercomputers like the Cray Y-MP. Most versions of UNIX for personal computers are expensive and cumbersome. At the time of this writing, a one-machine version of UNIX System V for the 386 runs about US$1500. Linux is a free version of UNIX developed primarily by Linus Torvalds at the University of Helsinki in Finland, with the help of many UNIX programmers and wizards across the Internet. Anyone with enough know-how and gumption can develop and change the system.

The Linux kernel uses no code from AT&T or any other proprietary source, and much of the software available for Linux was developed by the GNU project of the Free Software Foundation in Cambridge, Massachusetts, U.S.A. However, programmers from all over the world have contributed to the growing pool of Linux software.

Linux was originally developed as a hobby project by Linus Torvalds. It was inspired by Minix, a small UNIX system developed by Andy Tanenbaum. The first discussions about Linux were on the Usenet newsgroup, comp.os.minix. These discussions were concerned mostly with the development of a small, academic UNIX system for Minix users who wanted more.

The very early development of Linux mostly dealt with the task-switching features of the 80386 protected-mode interface, all written in assembly code. Linus writes,

``After that it was plain sailing: hairy coding still, but I had some devices, and debugging was easier. I started using C at this stage, and it certainly speeds up development. This is also when I started to get serious about my megalomaniac ideas to make `a better Minix than Minix.' I was hoping I'd be able to recompile gcc under Linux someday...

Two months for basic setup, but then only slightly longer until I had a disk driver (seriously buggy, but it happened to work on my machine) and a small file system. That was about when I made 0.01 available (around late August of 1991): it wasn't pretty, it had no floppy driver, and it couldn't do much of anything. I don't think anybody ever compiled that version. But by then I was hooked, and didn't want to stop until I could chuck out Minix.

No announcement was ever made for Linux version 0.01. The 0.01 sources weren't even executable. They contained only the bare rudiments of the kernel source and assumed that you had access to a Minix machine to compile and experiment with them.

On October 5, 1991, Linus announced the first ``official'' version of Linux, which was version 0.02. At that point, Linus was able to run bash (the GNU Bourne Again Shell) and gcc (the GNU C compiler), but not much else. Again, this was intended as a hacker's system. The primary focus was kernel development--user support, documentation, and distribution had not yet been addressed. Today, the Linux community still seems to treat these issues as secondary to ``real programming''--kernel development.

After version 0.03, Linus bumped up the version number to 0.10, as more people started to work on the system. After several further revisions, Linus increased the version number to 0.95 in March, 1992, to reflect his expectation that the system was ready for an ``official'' release soon. (Generally, software is not assigned the version number 1.0 until it is theoretically complete or bug-free.). Almost a year and a half later, in late December of 1993, the Linux kernel was still at version 0.99.pl14--asymptotically approaching 1.0. At the time of this writing, the current stable kernel version is 2.0 patchlevel 33, and version 2.1 is under development.

Most of the major, free UNIX software packages have been ported to Linux, and commercial software is also available. More hardware is supported than in the original kernel versions. Many people have executed benchmarks on 80486 Linux systems and found them comparable with mid-range workstations from Sun Microsystems and Digital Equipment Corporation. Who would have ever guessed that this ``little'' UNIX clone would have grown up to take on the entire world of personal computing?

SYSTEM FEATURES

Linux supports features found in other implementations of UNIX, and many which aren't found elsewhere. In this section, we'll take a nickel tour of the features of the Linux kernel.

Linux is a complete multitasking, multiuser operating system, as are all other versions of UNIX. This means that many users can log into and run programs on the same machine simultaneously.

The Linux system is mostly compatible with several UNIX standards (inasmuch as UNIX has standards) at the source level, including IEEE POSIX.1, UNIX System V, and Berkely System Distribution UNIX. Linux was developed with source code portability in mind, and it's easy to find commonly used features that are shared by more than one platform.

Much of the free UNIX software available on the Internet and elsewhere compiles under Linux ``right out of the box." In addition, all of the source code for the Linux system, including the kernel, device drivers, libraries, user programs, and development tools, is freely distributable.

Other specific internal features of Linux include POSIX job control (used by shells like csh and bash), pseudoterminals (pty devices), and support for dynamically loadable national or customised keyboard drivers. Linux supports virtual consoles that let you switch between login sessions on the same system console. Users of the screen program will find the Linux virtual console implementation familiar.

The kernel can emulate 387-FPU instructions, and systems without a math coprocessor can run programs that require floating-point math capability. Linux supports various file systems for storing data, like the ext2 file system, which was developed specifically for Linux. The Xenix and UNIX System V file systems are also supported, as well as the Microsoft MS-DOS and Windows 95 VFAT file systems on a hard drive or floppy. The ISO 9660 CD-ROM file system is also supported.

Linux provides a complete implementation of TCP/IP networking software. This includes device drivers for many popular Ethernet cards, SLIP (Serial Line Internet Protocol) and PPP (Point-to-Point Protocol), which provide access to a TCP/IP network via a serial connection, PLIP (Parallel Line Internet Protocol), and NFS (Network File System).

The Linux kernel is developed to use protected-mode features of Intel 80386 and better processors. In particular, Linux uses the protected-mode, descriptor based, memory-management paradigm, and other advanced features. Anyone familiar with 80386 protected-mode programming knows that this chip was designed for multitasking systems like UNIX. Linux exploits this functionality.

The kernel supports demand-paged, loaded executables. Only those segments of a program which are actually in use are read into memory from disk. Also, copy-on-write pages are shared among executables. If several instances of a program are running at once, they share physical memory, which reduces overall usage. When the system requires more physical memory, it swaps inactive pages to disk, letting you run larger applications and support more users. However, swapping data to disk is no substitute for physical RAM, which is much faster.

The Linux kernel also implements a unified memory pool for user programs and disk cache. All free memory is used by the cache, which is reduced when running large programs.

Executables use dynamically linked, shared libraries: code from a single library on disk. This is not unlike the SunOS shared library mechanism. Executable files occupy less disk space, especially those which use many library functions. There are also statically linked libraries for object debugging and maintaining ``complete'' binary files when shared libraries are not installed. The libraries are dynamically linked at run time, and the programmer can use his or her own routines in place of the standard library routines.

To facilitate debugging, the kernel generates core dumps for post-mortem analysis. A core dump and an executable linked with debugging support allows a developer to determine what caused a program to crash.

SOFTWARE FEATURES

Virtually every utility one would expect of a standard UNIX implementation has been ported to Linux, including basic commands like ls, awk, tr, sed, bc, and more. The familiar working environment of other UNIX systems is duplicated on Linux. All standard commands and utilities are included. (Novice UNIX or Linux users should introduction to basic UNIX commands.)

Many text editors are available, including vi, ex, pico, jove, and GNU emacs, and variants like Lucid emacs, which incorporates extensions of the X Window System, and joe. The text editor you're accustomed to using has more than likely been ported to Linux.

The choice of a text editor is an interesting one. Many UNIX users prefer ``simple'' editors like vi. (The original author wrote this book with vi.) But vi has many limitations due to its age, and modern editors like emacs have gained popularity. emacs supports a complete, Lisp based macro language and interpreter, powerful command syntax, and other extensions. There are emacs macro packages which let you read electronic mail and news, edit directory contents, and even engage in artificially intelligent psychotherapy sessions (indispensible for stressed-out Linux hackers).

Most of the basic Linux utilities are GNU software. GNU utilities support advanced features that are not found in the standard versions of BSD and UNIX System V programs. For example, the GNU vi clone, elvis, includes a structured macro language that differs from the original implementation. However, GNU utilities are intended to remain compatible with their BSD and System V counterparts. Many people consider the GNU versions to be superior to the originals.

A shell is a program which reads and executes commands from the user. In addition, many shells provide features like job control, managing several processes at once, input and output redirection, and a command language for writing shell scripts. A shell script is a program in the shell's command language and is analogous to a MS-DOS batch file.

Many types of shells are available for Linux. The most important difference between shells is the command language. For example, the C SHell (csh) uses a command language similar to the C programming language. The classic Bourne SHell sh uses another command language. The choice of a shell is often based on the command language it provides, and determines, to a large extent, the qualities of your working environment under Linux.

The GNU Bourne Again Shell (bash) is a variation of the Bourne Shell which includes many advanced features like job control, command history, command and filename completion, an emacs-like interface for editing command lines, and other powerful extensions to the standard Bourne Shell language. Another popular shell is tcsh, a version of the C Shell with advanced functionality similar to that found in bash. Other shells include zsh, a small Bourne-like shell; the Korn Shell (ksh); BSD's ash; and rc, the Plan 9 shell.

If you're the only person using the system and refer to use vi and bash exclusively as your editor and shell, there's no reason to install other editors or shells. This ``do it yourself'' attitude is prevalent among Linux hackers and users.

TextProcessing and Word Processing

Almost every computer user needs a method of preparing documents. In the world of personal computers, word processing is the norm: editing and manipulating text in a ``What-You-See-Is-What-You-Get'' (WYSIWYG) environment and producing printed copies of the text, complete with graphics, tables, and ornamentation.

Commercial word processors from Corel, Applix, and Star Division are available in the UNIX world, but text processing, which is quite different conceptually, is more common. In text processing systems, text is entered in a page-description language, which describes how the text should be formatted. Rather than enter text within a special word processing environment, you can modify text with any editor, like vi or emacs. Once you finish entering the source text (in the typesetting language), a separate program converts the source to a format suitable for printing. This is somewhat analogous to programming in a language like C, and ``compiling'' the document into printable form.

Many text processing systems are available for Linux. One is groff, the GNU version of the classic troff text formatter originally developed by Bell Labs and still used on many UNIX systems worldwide. Another modern text processing system is TeX, developed by Donald Knuth of computer science fame. Dialects of TeX, like LaTeX, are also available.

Text processors like TeX and groff differ mostly in the syntax of their formatting languages. The choice of one formatting system over another is based upon what utilities are available to satisfy your needs, as well as personal taste.

Many people consider groff's formatting language to be a bit obscure and use find TeX more readable. However, groff produces ASCII output which can be viewed on a terminal more easily, while TeX is intended primarily for output to a printing device. Various add-on programs are required to produce ASCII output from TeX formatted documents, or convert TeX input to groff format.

Another program is texinfo, an extension to TeX which is used for software documentation developed by the Free Software Foundation. texinfo can produce printed output, or an online-browsable hypertext ``Info" document from a single source file. Info files are the main format of documentation used in GNU software like emacs.

Text processors are used widely in the computing community for producing papers, theses, magazine articles, and books. (This book is produced using LaTeX.) The ability to process source language as a text file opens the door to many extensions of the text processor itself. Because a source document is not stored in an obscure format that only one word processor can read, programmers can write parsers and translators for the formatting language, and thus extend the system.

What does a formatting language look like? In general, a formatted source file consists mostly of the text itself, with control codes to produce effects like font and margin changes, and list formatting.

Programming Languages and Utilities

Linux provides a complete UNIX programming environment which includes all of the standard libraries, programming tools, compilers, and debuggers which you would expect of other UNIX systems.

Standards like POSIX.1 are supported, which allows software written for Linux to be easily ported to other systems. Professional UNIX programmers and system administrators use Linux to develop software at home, then transfer the software to UNIX systems at work.

This not only saves a great deal of time and money, but also lets you work in the comfort of your own home. (One of the authors uses his system to develop and test X Window System applications at home, which can be directly compiled on workstations elsewhere.) Computer Science students learn UNIX programming and explore other aspects of the system, like kernel architecture.

With Linux, you have access to the complete set of libraries and programming utilities and the complete kernel and library source code. Within the UNIX software world, systems and applications are often programmed in C or C++. The standard C and C++ compiler for Linux is GNU gcc, which is an advanced, modern compiler that supports C++, including AT&T 3.0 features, as well as Objective-C, another object-oriented dialect of C.

Besides C and C++, other compiled and interpreted programming languages have been ported to Linux, like Smalltalk, FORTRAN, Java, Pascal, LISP, Scheme, and Ada (if you're masochistic enough to program in Ada, we aren't going to stop you). In addition, various assemblers for writing protected-mode 80386 code are available, as are UNIX hacking favourites like Perl (the script language to end all script languages) and Tcl/Tk (a shell-like command processing system which has support for developing simple X Window System applications).

The advanced gdb debugger can step through a program one line of source code at a time, or examine a core dump to find the cause of a crash. The gprof profiling utility provides performance statistics for your program, telling you where your program spends most of its execution time. As mentioned above, the emacs text editor provides interactive editing and compilation environments for various programming languages. Other tools include GNU make and imake, which manage compilation of large applications, and RCS, a system for source code locking and revision control.

Finally, Linux supports dynamically linked, shared libraries (DLLs), which result in much smaller binaries. The common subroutine code is linked at run-time. These DLLs let you override function definitions with your own code. For example, if you wish to write your own version of the malloc() library routine, the linker will use your new routine instead of the one in the libraries.

X Window System

The X Window System, or simply X, is a standard graphical user interface (GUI) for UNIX machines and is a powerful environment which supports many applications. Using the X Window System, you can have multiple terminal windows on the screen at once, each having a different login session. A pointing device like a mouse is often used with X, although it isn't required.

Many X-specific applications have been written, including games, graphics and programming utilities, and documentation tools. Linux and X make your system a bona fide workstation. With TCP/IP networking, your Linux machine can display X applications running on other machines.

The X Window System was originally developed at the Massachusetts Institute of Technology and is freely distributable. Many commercial vendors have distributed proprietary enhancements to the original X Window System as well.

The version of X for Linux is XFree86, a port of X11R6 which is freely distributable. XFree86 supports a wide range of video hardware, including VGA, Super VGA, and accelerated video adaptors. XFree86 is a complete distribution of the X Windows System software, and contains the X server itself, many applications and utilities, programming libraries, and documents.

Standard X applications include xterm, a terminal emulator used for most text-based applications within a window, xdm, which handles logins, xclock, a simple clock display, xman, a X-based manual page reader, and xmore. The many X applications available for Linux are too numerous to mention here, but their number includes spreadsheets, word processors, graphics programs, and web browsers like the Netscape Navigator. Many other applications are available separately. Theoretically, any application written for X should compile cleanly under Linux.

The interface of the X Window System is controlled largely by the window manager. This user-friendly program is in charge of the placement of windows, the user interface for resizing and moving them, changing windows to icons, and the appearance of window frames, among other tasks. XFree86 includes twm, the classic MIT window manager, and advanced window managers like the Open Look Virtual Window Manager (olvwm) are available. Popular among Linux users is fvwm--a small window manager that requires less than half the memory of twm.

It provides a 3-dimensional appearance for windows and a virtual desktop. The user moves the mouse to the edge of the screen, and the desktop shifts as though the display were much larger than it really is. fvwm is greatly customizable and allows access to functions from the keyboard as well as mouse. Many Linux distributions use fvwm as the standard window manager. A version of fvwm called fvwm95-2 offers Microsoft Windows 95-like look and feel.

The XFree86 distribution includes programming libraries for wily programmers who wish to develop X applications. Widget sets like Athena, Open Look, and Xaw3D are supported. All of the standard fonts, bitmaps, manual pages, and documentation are included. PEX (a programming interface for 3-dimensional graphics) is also supported.

Many X application programmers use the proprietary Motif widget set for development. Several vendors sell single and multiple user licenses for binary versions of Motif. Because Motif itself is relatively expensive, not many Linux users own it. However, binaries statically linked with Motif routines can be freely distributed. If you write a program using Motif, you may provide a binary so users without the Motif libraries can use the program.

A major caveat to using the X Window System is its hardware requirements. A 80386-based CPU with 4 megabytes of RAM is capable of running X, but 16 megabytes or more of physical RAM is needed for comfortable use. A faster processor is nice to have as well, but having enough physical RAM is much more important. In addition, to achieve really slick video performance, we recommend getting an accelerated video card, like a VESA Local Bus (VLB) S3 chipset card. Performance ratings in excess of 300,000 xstones have been achieved with Linux and XFree86. Using adequate hardware, you'll find that running X and Linux is as fast, or faster, than running X on other UNIX workstations.

Networking

Would you like to communicate with the world? Linux supports two primary UNIX networking protocols: TCP/IP and UUCP. TCP/IP (Transmission Control Protocol/Internet Protocol) is the networking paradigm which allows systems all over the world to communicate on a single network, the Internet. With Linux, TCP/IP, and a connection to the Internet, you can communicate with users and machines via electronic mail, Usenet news, and FTP file transfer.

Most TCP/IP networks use Ethernet as the physical network transport. Linux supports many popular Ethernet cards and interfaces for personal computers, including pocket and PCMCIA Ethernet adaptors.

However, because not everyone has an Ethernet connection at home, Linux also supports SLIP (Serial Line Internet Protocol) and PPP (Point-to-Point Protocol), which provide Internet access via modem. Many businesses and universities provide SLIP and PPP servers. In fact, if your Linux system has an Ethernet connection to the Internet and a modem, your system can become a SLIP or PPP server for other hosts.

NFS (Network File System) lets your system seamlessly share file systems with other machines on the network. FTP (File Transfer Protocol) lets you transfer files with other machines. sendmail sends and receives electronic mail via the SMTP protocol; C-News and INN are NNTP based new systems; and telnet,rlogin, and rsh let you log in and execute commands on other machines on the network. finger lets you get information about other Internet users.

The full range of mail and news readers is available for Linux, including elm, pine, rn, nn, and tin. Whatever your preference, you can configure a Linux system to send and receive electronic mail and news from all over the world. The system provides a standard UNIX socket programming interface. Virtually any program that uses TCP/IP can be ported to Linux.

The Linux X server also supports TCP/IP, and applications running on other systems may use the display of your local system. UUCP (UNIX-to-UNIX Copy) is an older mechanism to transfer files, electronic mail, and electronic news between UNIX machines. Historically, UUCP machines are connected over telephone lines via modem, but UUCP is able to transfer data over a TCP/IP network as well. If you do not have access to a TCP/IP network or a SLIP or PPP server, you can configure your system to send and receive files and electronic mail using UUCP.

Telecommunications and BBS Software

If you have a modem, you'll be able to communicate with other machines via telecommunications packages available for Linux.

Many people use telecommunications software to access bulletin board systems (BBS's) as well as commercial, online services like Prodigy, CompuServe, and America Online. People use modems to connect to UNIX systems at work or school. Modems can send and receive faxes.

A popular communications package for Linux is seyon, which provides a customizable, ergonomic interface undex X and has built-in support for the Kermit and ZModem file transfer protocols. Other telecommunications programs include C-Kermit, pcomm, and minicom. These are similar to communications programs found on other operating systems, and are quite easy to use. If you do not have access to a SLIP or PPP server, you can use term to multiplex your serial line. The term program allows you to open more than one login session over a modem connection. It lets you redirect X client connections to your local X server via a serial line. Another software package, KA9Q, implements a similar, SLIP-like interface.

Operating a Bulletin Board System (BBS) is a favourite hobby and means of income for many people. Linux supports a wide range of BBS software, most of which is more powerful than that available for other operating systems. With a phone line, modem, and Linux, you can turn your system into a BBS and provide dial-in access for users worldwide. BBS software for Linux includes XBBS and UniBoard BBS packages.

Most BBS software locks the user into a menu based system where only certain functions and applications are available. An alternative to BBS access is full UNIX access, which lets users dial into your system and log in normally. This requires a fair amount of maintenance by the system administrator, but providing public UNIX access is not difficult. In addition to TCP/IP networking, you can make electronic mail and news access available on your system.

If you do not have access to a TCP/IP network or UUCP feed, Linux lets you communicate with BBS networks like FidoNet, which let you exchange electronic news and mail over a telephone line.

World Wide Web

It is worth noting that Linux includes web server software as well as web browsers. Linux distributions include different web browsers, and other browsers can be downloaded from the Internet. Available browsers include Lynx, Mosaic, Netscape, Arena, and Amaya. Linux provides complete support for Java and CGI applets, and Perl is a standard tool in the Linux programming environment.

Interfacing and MS-DOS

Various utilities exist to interface with MS-DOS. The most well-known application is the Linux MS-DOS Emulator, which lets you run MS-DOS applications directly from Linux. Although Linux and MS-DOS are completely different operating systems, the 80386 protected-mode environment allows MS-DOS applications to behave as if they were running in their native 8086 environment.

The MS-DOS emulator is still under development, but many popular applications run under it. Understandably, MS-DOS applications that use bizarre or esoteric features of the system may never be supported, because of the limitations inherent in any emulator. For example, you shouldn't expect to run programs that use 80386 protected-mode features, like Microsoft Windows (in 386 enhanced mode, that is).

Standard MS-DOS commands and utilities like PKZIP.EXE work under the emulators, as do 4DOS, a COMMAND.COM replacement, FoxPro 2.0, Harvard Graphics, MathCad, Stacker 3.1, Turbo Assembler, Turbo C/C++, Turbo Pascal, Microsoft Windows 3.0 (in real mode), and WordPerfect 5.1.

The MS-DOS Emulator is meant mostly as an ad-hoc solution for those who need MS-DOS for only a few applications and use Linux for everything else. It's not meant to be a complete implementation of MS-DOS. Of course, if the Emulator doesn't satisfy your needs, you can always run MS-DOS as well as Linux on the same system. Using the LILO boot loader, you can specify at boot time which operating system to start. Linux can also coexist with other operating systems, like OS/2.

Linux provides a seamless interface to transfer files between Linux and MS-DOS. You can mount a MS-DOS partition or floppy under Linux, and directly access MS-DOS files as you would any file.

Currently under development is WINE--a Microsoft Windows emulator for the X Window System under Linux. Once WINE is complete, users will be able to run MS-Windows applications directly from Linux. This is similar to the commercial WABI Windows emulator from Sun Microsystems, which is also available for Linux.

Other Applications

A host of miscellaneous programs and utilities exist for Linux, as one would expect of such a hodgepodge operating system. Linux's primary focus is UNIX personal computing, but this is not the only field where it excels. The selection of business and scientific software is expanding, and commercial software vendors have begun to contribute to the growing pool Linux applications.

Several relational databases are available for Linux, including Postgres, Ingres, and Mbase. These are full-featured, professional, client/server database applications, similar to those found on other UNIX platforms. Many commercial database systems are available as well.

Scientific computing applications include FELT (finite element analysis); gnuplot (data plotting and analysis); Octave (a symbolic mathematics package similar to MATLAB); xspread (a spreadsheet calculator); xfractint (an X-based port of the popular Fractint fractal generator); and xlispstat (statistics). Other applications include SPICE (circuit design and analysis) and Khoros (image and digital signal processing and visualization). Commercial packages like Maple and MathLab are available.

Many more applications have been ported to Linux. If you absolutely cannot find what you need, you can attempt to port the application from another platform to Linux yourself. Whatever your field, porting standard UNIX applications to Linux is straightforward. Linux's complete UNIX programming environment is sufficient to serve as the base for any scientific application.

Linux also has its share of games. These include classic text based dungeon games like Nethack and Moria; MUDs (multi-user dungeons, which allow many users to interact in a text-based adventure) like DikuMUD and TinyMUD; and a slew of X games like xtetris, netrek, and xboard, the X11 version of gnuchess. The popular shoot-em-up, arcade-style game, Doom, has also been ported to Linux. For audiophiles, Linux supports various sound cards and related software, like CDplayer, which makes a CD-ROM drive into an audio CD player, MIDI sequencers and editors, which let you compose music for playback through a synthesizer or other MIDI controlled instrument, and sound editors for digitized sounds.

Can't find the application you're looking for? The Linux Software Map, described in Appendix A, lists software packages which have been written or ported to Linux. Another way to find Linux applications is to look at the INDEX files found on Linux FTP sites, if you have Internet access.

Most freely-distributable, UNIX based software will compile on Linux with little difficulty. If all else fails, you can write the application yourself. If you're looking for a commercial application, there may be a free ``clone'' available. Or, you can encourage the software company to consider releasing a binary version for Linux. Several individuals have contacted software companies and asked them to port their applications to Linux, with various degrees of success.

COPYRIGHT ISSUES

Linux is covered by what is known as the GNU General Public License, or GPL. The GPL was developed for the GNU project by the Free Software Foundation and specifies several provisions for the distribution and modification of free software. Free, in this sense, refers to distribution, not cost. The GPL has always been subject to misinterpretation. We hope that this summary will help you understand the extent and goals of the GPL and its effect on Linux. A complete copy of the GPL is printed in Appendix C.

Originally, Linus Torvalds released Linux under a license more restrictive than the GPL, which allowed the software to be freely distributed and modified, but prevented any money from changing hands for its distribution and use. On the other hand, the GPL allows people to sell and profit from free software, but does not allow them to restrict another's right to distribute the software in any way.

First, it should be explained that free software that is covered by the GPL is not in the public domain. Public domain software by definition is not copyrighted and is literally owned by the public. Software covered by the GPL, on the other hand, is copyrighted by the author. The software is protected by standard international copyright laws, and the author is legally defined. The GPL provides for software which may be freely distributed but is not in the public domain.

GPL-licensed software is also not shareware. Generally, shareware is owned and copyrighted by an author who requires users to send in money for its use. Software covered by the GPL may be distributed and used free of charge.

The GPL also lets people take, modify, and distribute their own versions of the software. However, any derived works of GPL software must also be covered by the GPL. In other words, a company may not take Linux, modify it, and sell it under a restrictive license. If the software is derived from Linux, that software must be covered under the GPL also.

The GPL allows free software to be distributed and used free of charge. It also lets a person or organization distribute GPL software for a fee, and even make a profit from its sale and distribution. However, a distributor of GPL software cannot take those rights away from a purchaser. If you purchase GPL software from a third-party source, you may distribute the software for free, and sell it yourself as well.

This may sound like a contradiction. Why sell software when the GPL allows you to get it for free? Let's say that a company decided to bundle a large amount of free software on a CD-ROM and distribute it. That company would need to charge for the overhead of producing and distributing the CD-ROM, and may even decide to profit from the sales of the software. This is allowed by the GPL.

Organizations that sell free software must follow certain restrictions set forth in the GPL. They cannot restrict the rights of users who purchase the software. If you buy a CD-ROM that contains GPL software, you can copy and distribute the

CD-ROM free of charge, or resell it yourself. Distributors must make obvious to users that the software is covered by the GPL. Distributors must also provide, free of charge, the complete source code to the software distributed. This permits anyone who purchases GPL software to make modifications to that software.

Allowing a company to distribute and sell free software is a good thing. Not everyone has access to the Internet and the ability to download software for free. Many organizations sell Linux on diskette, tape, or CD-ROM via mail order, and profit from the sales. Linux developers may never see any of this profit; that is the understanding reached between the developer and the distributor when software is licensed by the GPL. In other words, Linus Torvalds knew that companies may wish to sell Linux, and that he might not see a penny of the profits.

In the free software world, the important issue is not money. The goal of free software is always to develop and distribute fantastic software and allow anyone to obtain and use it. In the next section, we'll discuss how this applies to the development of Linux.

DESIGNING OF LINUX

New users often have a few misconceptions and false expectations about Linux. It is important to understand the philosophy and design of Linux in order to use it effectively. We'll start by describing how Linux is not designed.

In commercial UNIX development houses, the entire system is developed under a rigorous quality assurance policy that utilizes source and revision control systems, documentation, and procedures to report and resolve bugs. Developers may not add features or change key sections of code on a whim. They must validate the change as a response to a bug report and subsequently ``check in" all changes to the source control system, so that the changes may be reversed if necessary. Each developer is assigned one or more parts of the system code, and only that developer can alter those sections of the code while it is ``checked out" (that is, while the code is under his or her control). Organizationally, a quality assurance department runs rigorous tests on each new version of the operating system and reports any bugs. The developers fix these bugs as reported. A complex system of statistical analysis is used to ensure that a certain percentage of bugs are fixed before the next release, and that the operating system as a whole passes certain release criteria.

The software company, quite reasonably, must have quantitative proof that the next revision of the operating system is ready to be shipped; hence, the gathering and analysis of statistics about the performance of the operating system. It is a big job to develop a commercial UNIX system, often large enough to employ hundreds, if not thousands, of programmers, testers, documenters, and administrative personnel. Of course, no two commercial UNIX vendors are alike, but that is the general picture.

The Linux model of software development discards the entire concept of organized development, source code control systems, structured bug reporting, and statistical quality control. Linux is, and likely always will be, a hacker's operating system. (By hacker, I mean a feverishly dedicated programmer who enjoys exploiting computers and does interesting things with them. This is the original definition of the term, in contrast to the connotation of hacker as a computer wrongdoer, or outlaw.)

There is no single organization responsible for developing Linux. Anyone with enough know-how has the opportunity to help develop and debug the kernel, port new software, write documentation, and help new users. For the most part, the Linux community communicates via mailing lists and Usenet newsgroups. Several conventions have sprung up around the development effort. Anyone who wishes to have their code included in the ``official" kernel, mails it to Linus Torvalds. He will test and include the code in the kernel as long as it doesn't break things or go against the overall design of the system.

The system itself is designed using an open-ended, feature-minded approach. The number of new features and critical changes to the system has recently diminished, and the general rule is that a new version of the kernel will be released every few weeks. New release criteria include the number of bugs to be fixed, feedback from users testing pre-release versions of the code, and the amount of sleep Linus Torvalds has had this week.

Suffice it to say that not every bug is fixed, nor is every problem ironed out between releases. As long as the revision appears to be free of critical or recurring bugs, it is considered to be stable, and the new version is released. The thrust behind Linux development is not to release perfect, bug-free code: it is to develop a free UNIX implementation. Linux is for the developers, more than anyone else.

Anyone who has a new feature or software application generally makes it available in an alpha version--that is, a test version, for those brave users who want to hash out problems in the initial code. Because the Linux community is largely based on the Internet, alpha software is usually uploaded to one or more Linux FTP sites and a message is posted to one of the Linux Usenet newsgroups about how to obtain and test the code. Users who download and test alpha software can then mail results, bug fixes, and questions to the author.

After the initial bugs have been fixed, the code enters a beta test stage, in which it is usually considered stable but not complete. It works, but not all of the features may be present. The software may also go directly to a final stage, in which the software is considered complete and usable.

Keep in mind that these are only conventions--not rules. Some developers may feel so confident of their software that they decide it isn't necessary to release alpha or test versions. It is always up to the developer to make these decisions.

You might be amazed at how such an unstructured system of volunteers who program and debug a complete UNIX system gets anything done at all. As it turns out, this is one of the most efficient and motivated development efforts ever employed. The entire Linux kernel is written from scratch, without code from proprietary sources. It takes a huge amount of work to port all the free software under the sun to Linux. Libraries are written and ported, file systems are developed, and hardware drivers are written for many popular devices--all due to the work of volunteers.

Linux software is generally released as a distribution, a set of prepackaged software which comprises an entire system. It would be difficult for most users to build a complete system from the ground up, starting with the kernel, adding utilities, and installing all of the necessary software by hand. Instead, many software distributions are available which include everything necessary to install and run a complete system. There is no single, standard distribution--there are many, and each has its own advantages and disadvantages. We describe installation of the various Linux distributions starting on.

LINUX AND OTHER OPERATING SYSTEMS

It is important to understand the differences between Linux and other operating systems, like MS-DOS, OS/2, and the other implementations of UNIX for personal computers. First of all, Linux coexists happily with other operating systems on the same machine: you can run MS-DOS and OS/2 along with Linux on the same system without problems. There are even ways to interact between various operating systems, as we'll see.

Why use Linux

Why use Linux, instead of a well known, well tested, and well documented commercial operating system? We could give you a thousand reasons. One of the most important, however, is that Linux is an excellent choice for personal UNIX computing. If you're a UNIX software developer, why use MS-DOS at home? Linux allows you to develop and test UNIX software on your PC, including database and X Window System applications. If you're a student, chances are that your university computing systems run UNIX. You can run your own UNIX system and tailor it to your needs. Installing and running Linux is also an excellent way to learn

UNIX if you don't have access to other UNIX machines. But let's not lose sight. Linux isn't only for personal UNIX users. It is robust and complete enough to handle large tasks, as well as distributed computing needs. Many businesses--especially small ones--have moved their systems to Linux in lieu of other UNIX based, workstation environments. Universities have found that Linux is perfect for teaching courses in operating systems design. Large, commercial software vendors have started to realise the opportunities which a free operating system can provide.

Linux vs. MS-DOS

It's not uncommon to run both Linux and MS-DOS on the same system. Many Linux users rely on MS-DOS for applications like word processing. Linux provides its own analogs for these applications, but you might have a good reason to run MS-DOS as well as Linux. If your dissertation is written using WordPerfect for MS-DOS, you may not be able to convert it easily to TeX or some other format. Many commercial applications for MS-DOS aren't available for Linux yet, but there's no reason that you can't use both.

MS-DOS does not fully utilize the functionality of 80386 and 80486 processors. On the other hand, Linux runs completely in the processor's protected mode, and utilizes all of its features. You can directly access all of your available memory (and beyond, with virtual RAM). Linux provides a complete UNIX interface which is not available under MS-DOS. You can easily develop and port UNIX applications to Linux, but under MS-DOS you are limited to a subset of UNIX functionality.

Linux and MS-DOS are different entities. MS-DOS is inexpensive compared to other commercial operating systems and has a strong foothold in the personal computer world. No other operating system for the personal computer has reached the level of popularity of MS-DOS, because justifying spending $1,000 for other operating systems alone is unrealistic for many users. Linux, however, is free, and you may finally have the chance to decide for yourself.

You can judge Linux vs. MS-DOS based on your expectations and needs. Linux is not for everybody. If you always wanted to run a complete UNIX system at home, without the high cost of other UNIX implementations for personal computers, Linux may be what you're looking for.

Linux vs. The Other Guys

A number of other advanced operating systems have become popular in the PC world. Specifically, IBM's OS/2 and Microsoft Windows have become popular for users upgrading from MS-DOS. Both OS/2 and Windows NT are full featured multitasking operating systems, like Linux. OS/2, Windows NT, and Linux support roughly the same user interface, networking, and security features. However, the real difference between Linux and The Other Guys is the fact that Linux is a version of UNIX, and benefits from contributions of the UNIX community at large.

What makes UNIX so important? Not only is it the most popular operating system for multiuser machines, it is a foundation of the free software world. Much of the free software available on the Internet is written specifically for UNIX systems.

There are many implementations of UNIX from many vendors. No single organization is responsible for its distribution. There is a large push in the UNIX community for standardization in the form of open systems, but no single group controls this design. Any vendor (or, as it turns out, any hacker) may develop a standard implementation of UNIX. OS/2 and Microsoft operating systems, on the other hand, are proprietary. The interface and design are controlled by a single corporation, which develops the operating system code. In one sense, this kind of organization is beneficial because it sets strict standards for programming and user interface design, unlike those found even in the open systems community.

Several organizations have attempted the difficult task of standardizing the UNIX programming interface. Linux, in particular, is mostly compliant with the POSIX.1 standard.

As time goes by, it is expected that the Linux system will adhere to other standards, but standardization is not the primary goal of Linux development.

Linux vs. Other Implementations of UNIX

Several other implementations of UNIX exist for 80386 or better personal computers. The 80386 architecture lends itself to UNIX, and vendors have taken advantage of this.

Oher implementations of UNIX for the personal computer are similar to Linux. Almost all commercial versions of UNIX support roughly the same software, programming environment, and networking features. However, there are differences between Linux and commercial versions of UNIX.

Linux supports a different range of hardware than commercial implementations. In general, Linux supports most well-known hardware devices, but support is still limited to hardware which the developers own. Commercial UNIX vendors tend to support more hardware at the outset, but the list of hardware devices which Linux supports is expanding continuously. We'll cover the hardware requirements for Linux in Section.

Many users report that Linux is at least as stable as commercial UNIX systems. Linux is still under development, but the two-pronged release philosophy has made stable versions available without impeding development.

The most important factor for many users is price. Linux software is free if you can download it from the Internet or another computer network. If you do not have Internet access, you can still purchase Linux inexpensively via mail order on diskette, tape, or CD-ROM.

Of course, you may copy Linux from a friend who already has the software, or share the purchase cost with someone else. If you plan to install Linux on a large number of machines, you need only purchase a single copy of the software--Linux is not distributed with a ``single machine'' license.

The value of commercial UNIX implementations should not be demeaned. In addition to the price of the software itself, one often pays for documentation, support, and quality assurance. These are very important factors for large institutions, but personal computer users may not require these benefits. In any case, many businesses and universities have found that running Linux in a lab of inexpensive personal computers is preferable to running a commercial version of UNIX in a lab of workstations. Linux can provide workstation functionality on a personal computer at a fraction of the cost.

Linux systems have travelled the high seas of the North Pacific, and manage telecommunications and data analysis for an oceanographic research vessel. Linux systems are used at research stations in Antarctica. Several hospitals maintain patient records on Linux systems.

Other free or inexpensive implementations of UNIX are available for the 80386 and 80486. One of the best known is 386BSD, an implementation of BSD UNIX for the 80386. The 386BSD package is comparable to Linux in many ways, but which one is better depends on your needs and expectations. The only strong distinction we can make is that Linux is developed openly, and any volunteer can aid in the development process, while 386BSD is developed by a closed team of programmers. Because of this, serious philosophical and design differences exist between the two projects. The goal of Linux is to develop a complete UNIX system from scratch (and have a lot of fun in the process), and the goal of 386BSD is in part to modify the existing BSD code for use on the 80386.

NetBSD is another port of the BSD NET/2 distribution to several machines, including the 80386. NetBSD has a slightly more open development structure, and is comparable to 386BSD in many respects.

Another project of note is HURD, an effort by the Free Software Foundation to develop and distribute a free version of UNIX for many platforms. Contact the Free Software Foundation (the address is given in Appendix C) for more information about this project. At the time of this writing, HURD is still under development.

Other inexpensive versions of UNIX exist as well, like Minix, an academic but useful UNIX clone upon which early development of Linux was based. Some of these implementations are mostly of academic interest, while others are full fledged systems.

HARDWARE REQUIREMENTS

You must be convinced by now of how wonderful Linux is, and of all the great things it can do for you. However, before you rush out and install Linux, you need to be aware of its hardware requirements and limitations.

Keep in mind that Linux is developed by users. This means, for the most part, that the hardware supported by Linux is that which the users and developers have access to. As it turns out, most popular hardware and peripherals for personal computers are supported. Linux supports more hardware than some commercial implementations of UNIX. However, some obscure devices aren't supported yet.

Another drawback of hardware support under Linux is that many companies keep their hardware interfaces proprietary. Volunteer Linux developers can't write drivers for the devices because the manufacturer does not make the technical specifications public. Even if Linux developers could develop drivers for proprietary devices, they would be owned by the company which owns the device interface, which violates the GPL. Manufacturers that maintain proprietary interfaces write their own drivers for operating systems like MS-DOS and Microsoft Windows. Users and third-party developers never need to know the details of the interface.

In some cases, Linux programmers have attempted to write hackish device drivers based on assumptions about the interface. In other cases, developers work with the manufacturer and try to obtain information about the device interface, with varying degrees of success.

In the following sections, we attempt to summarize the hardware requirements for Linux. The Linux Hardware HOWTO contains a more complete listing of hardware supported by Linux.

Disclaimer: Much hardware support for Linux is in the development stage. Some distributions may or may not support experimental features. This section lists hardware which has been supported for some time and is known to be stable. When in doubt, consult the documentation of your Linux distribution. for more information about Linux distributions.

Linux is available for many platforms in addition to Intel 80x86 systems. These include Macintosh, Amiga, Sun SparcStation, and Digital Equipment Corporation Alpha based systems. In this book, however, we focus on garden-variety Intel 80386, 80486, and Pentium processors, and clones by manufacturers like AMD, Cyrix, and IBM.

Motherboard and CPU Requirements

Linux currently supports systems with the Intel 80386, 80486, or Pentium CPU, including all variations like the 80386SX, 80486SX, 80486DX, and 80486DX2. Non-Intel clones work with Linux as well. Linux has also been ported to the DEC Alpha and the Apple PowerMac.

If you have an 80386 or 80486SX, you may also wish to use a math coprocessor, although one isn't required. The Linux kernel can perform FPU emulation if the machine doesn't have a coprocessor. All standard FPU couplings are supported, including IIT, Cyrix FasMath, and Intel.

Most common PC motherboards are based on the PCI bus but also offer ISA slots. This configuration is supported by Linux, as are EISA and VESA-bus systems. IBM's MicroChannel (MCA) bus, found on most IBM PS/2 systems, is significantly different, and support has been recently added.

Memory Requirements

Linux requires very little memory, compared to other advanced operating systems. You should have 4 megabytes of RAM at the very least, and 16 megabytes is strongly recommended. The more memory you have, the faster the system will run. Some distributions require more RAM for installation.

Linux supports the full 32-bit address range of the processor. In other words, it uses all of your RAM automatically. Linux will run with only 4 megabytes of RAM, including bells and whistles like the X Window System and emacs. However, having more memory is almost as important as having a faster processor. For general use, 16 megabytes is enough, and 32 megabytes, or more, may be needed for systems with a heavy user load.

Most Linux users allocate a portion of their hard drive as swap space, which is used as virtual RAM. Even if your machine has more than 16 megabytes of physical RAM, you may wish to use swap space. It is no replacement for physical RAM, but it can let your system run larger applications by swapping inactive portions of code to disk. The amount of swap space that you should allocate depends on several factors;

Hard Drive Controller Requirements

It is possible to run Linux from a floppy diskette, or, for some distributions, a live file system on CD-ROM, but for good performance you need hard disk space. Linux can co-exist with other operating systems--it only needs one or more disk partitions. Linux supports all IDE and EIDE controllers as well as older MFM and RLL controllers. Most, but not all, ESDI controllers are supported. The general rule for non-SCSI hard drive and floppy controllers is that if you can access the drive from MS-DOS or another operating system, you should be able to access it from Linux. Linux also supports a number of popular SCSI drive controllers. This includes most Adaptec and Buslogic cards as well as cards based on the NCR chip sets.

Hard Drive Space Requirements

Of course, to install Linux, you need to have some amount of free space on your hard drive. Linux will support more than one hard drive on the same machine; you can allocate space for Linux across multiple drives if necessary.

How much hard drive space depends on your needs and the software you're installing. Linux is relatively small, as

UNIX implementations go. You could run a system in 20 megabytes of disk space. However, for expansion and larger packages like X, you need more space. If you plan to let more than one person use the machine, you need to allocate storage for their files. Realistic space requirements range from 200 megabytes to one gigabyte or more. Each Linux distribution comes with literature to help you gauge the precise amount of storage required for your software configuration. Look at the information which comes with your distribution or the appropriate installation section in.

Monitor and Video Adaptor Requirements

Linux supports standard Hercules, CGA, EGA, VGA, IBM monochrome, Super VGA, and many accelerated video cards, and monitors for the default, text-based interface. In general, if the video card and monitor work under an operating system like MS-DOS, the combination should work fine under Linux. However, original IBM CGA cards suffer from ``snow'' under Linux, which is not pleasant to view. Graphical environments like X have video hardware requirements of their own. Rather than list them here, we relegate that discussion to Section Popular video cards are supported and new card support is added regularly.

Miscellaneous Hardware

You may also have devices like a CD-ROM drive, mouse, or sound card, and may be interested in whether or not this hardware is supported by Linux.

Mice and Other Pointing Devices

Typically, a mouse is used only in graphical environments like X. However, several Linux applications that are not associated with a graphical environment also use mice. Linux supports standard serial mice like Logitech, MM series, Mouseman, Microsoft (2-button), and Mouse Systems (3-button). Linux also supports Microsoft, Logitech, and ATIXL bus mice, and the PS/2 mouse interface. Pointing devices that emulate mice, like trackballs and touchpads, should work also.

CD-ROM Drives

Many common CD-ROM drives attach to standard IDE controllers. Another common interface for CD-ROM is SCSI. SCSI support includes multiple logical units per device so you can use CD-ROM ``jukeboxes.'' Additionally, a few proprietary interfaces, like the NEC CDR-74, Sony CDU-541 and CDU-31a, Texel DM-3024, and Mitsumi are supported. Linux supports the standard ISO 9660 file system for CD-ROMs, and the High Sierra file system extensions.

Tape drives

Any SCSI tape drive, including quarter inch, DAT, and 8MM are supported, if the SCSI controller is supported. Devices that connect to the floppy controller like floppy tape drives are supported as well, as are some other interfaces, like QIC-02.

Printers

Linux supports the complete range of parallel printers. If MS-DOS or some other operating system can access your printer from the parallel port, Linux should be able to access it, too. Linux printer software includes the UNIX standard lp and lpr software. This software allows you to print remotely via a network, if you have one. Linux also includes software that allows most printers to handle PostScript files.

Modems

As with printer support, Linux supports the full range of serial modems, both internal and external. A great deal of telecommunications software is available for Linux, including Kermit, pcomm, minicom, and seyon. If your modem is accessible from another operating system on the same machine, you should be able to access it from Linux with no difficulty.

Ethernet Cards

Many popular Ethernet cards and LAN adaptors are supported by Linux. Linux also supports some FDDI, frame relay, and token ring cards, and all Arcnet cards. A list of supported network cards is included in the kernel source of your distribution.

SOURCES OF LINUX INFORMATION

Many other sources of information about Linux are available. In particular, a number of books about UNIX in general will be of use, especially for readers unfamiliar with UNIX. We suggest that you peruse one of these books before attempting to brave the jungles of Linux. Information is also available online in electronic form.

You must have access to an online network like the Internet, Usenet, or Fidonet to access the information. A good place to start is If you do not, you might be able to find someone who is kind enough to give you hard copies of the documents.

Online Documents

Many Linux documents are available via anonymous FTP from Internet archive sites around the world and networks like Fidonet and CompuServe. Linux CD-ROM distributions also contain the documents mentioned here. If you are can send mail to Internet sites, you may be able to retrieve these files using one of the FTP e-mail servers that mail you the documents or files from the FTP sites. for more information on using FTP e-mail servers.

Linux on World Wide Web

The Linux Documentation Project Home Page is on the World Wide Web at http://sunsite.unc.edu/LDP This web page lists many HOWTOs and other documents in HTML format, as well as pointers to other sites of interest to Linux users, like ssc.com, home of the Linux Journal, a monthly magazine.

WINDOWS

INTRODUCTION

Windows is the operating system sold by the Seattle-based company Microsoft. Microsoft, originally christened

"Traf-O-Data" in 1972, was renamed "Micro-soft" in November 1975, then "Microsoft" on November 26, 1976.

Microsoft entered the marketplace in August 1981 by releasing version 1.0 of the operating system Microsoft DOS (MS-DOS), a 16-bit command-line operating system

The first version of Microsoft Windows (Microsoft Windows 1.0) came out in November 1985. It had a graphical user interface, inspired by the user interface of the Apple computers of the time. Windows 1.0 was not succesful with the public, and Microsoft Windows 2.0, launched December 9, 1987, did not do much better.

After minor revisions of Microsoft Windows 95, named Windows 95A OSR1, Windows 95B OSR2, Windows 95B OSR2.1 and Windows 95C OSR2.5, Microsoft released the next version of Windows on June 25, 1998: Windows 98. Windows 98 natively supported features other than those of MS-DOS but was still based upon it. What's more, Windows 98 suffered from poor memory handling when multiple applications were running, which could cause system malfunctions. A second edition of Windows 98 came out on February 17, 2000; it was named Windows 98 SE (for "Second Edition").

On September 14, 2000, Microsoft released Windows Me (for Millennium Edition), also called Windows Millennium. Windows Millennium was based largely on Windows 98 (and therefore on MS-DOS), but added additional multimedia and software capabilities. Furthermore, Windows Millennium included a system-restore mechanism for returning to a previous state in the event of a crash.

Concurrent with these releases, Microsoft had been selling (since 1992) an entirely 32-bit operating system (which therefore was not based on MS-DOS) for professional use, at a time when business primarily used mainframes. It was Windows NT (for Windows "New Technology"). Windows NT was not a new version of Windows 95 or an improvement on it, but an entirely different operating system

On May 24, 1993, the first version of Windows NT was released. It was called Windows NT 3.1, and was followed by Windows NT 3.5 in September 1994 and Windows 3.51 in

June 1995. With Windows NT 4.0, launched for sale on August 24, 1996, Windows NT finally became a true success.

In July 1998, Microsoft released Windows NT 4.0 TSE (Terminal Server Emulation), the first Windows system that allowed terminals to be plugged into a server, *i.e.* use thin clients to open a session on the server.

8

Digital Numbers

SIGNED BINARY NUMBERS

Binary representations of positive can be understood in the same way as their decimal counterparts. *For example*:

$$86_{10} = 1 \times 64 + 0 \times 32 + 1 \times 16 + 0 \times 8 + 1 \times 4 + 1 \times 2 + 0 \times 1$$

or

$$86_{10} = 1 \times 2^6 + 0 \times 2^5 + 1 \times 2^4 + 0 \times 2^3 + 1 \times 2^2 + 1 \times 2^1 + 0 \times 2^0 \text{ or}$$

$$86_{10} = 1010110_2$$

The subscript 2 denotes a binary number. Each digit in a binary number is called a bit. The number 1010110 is represented by 7 bits. Any number can be broken down this way, by finding all of the powers of 2 that add up to the number in question (in this case 2^6, 2^4, 2^2 and 2^1). You can see this is exactly analagous to the decimal deconstruction of the number 125 that was done earlier.

Likewise we can make a similar set of observations:

- To multiply a number by 2 you can simply shift it to the left by one digit, and fill in the rightmost digit with a 0. To divide a number by 2, simply shift the number to the right by one digit.
- To see how many digits a number needs, you can simply take the logarithm (base 2) of the number, and add 1 to it. The integer part of the result is the number of digits. For instance, $\log_2(86)+1=7.426$. The integer part of that is 7, so 7 digits are needed.
- With n digits, 2^n unique numbers (from 0 to 2^n-1) can be represented. If n=8, 256 (=2^8) numbers can be represented 0-255.

It is often convenient to handle groups of bits, rather than individually. The most common grouping is 8 bits, which forms a byte. A single byte can represent 256 (2^8) numbers. Memory capacity is usually referred to in bytes. Two bytes is usually called a word, or short word (though word-length depends on the application). A two-byte word is also the size that is usually used to represent integers in programming languages. A long word is usually twice as long as a word. A less common unit is the nibble which is 4 bits, or half of a byte.

It is cumbersome for humans to deal with writing, reading and remembering individual bits, because it takes many of them to represent even fairly small numbers. A number of different ways have been developed to make the handling of binary data easier for us. The most common is hexadecimal. In hexadecimal notation, 4 bits (a nibble) are represented by a single digit.

There is obviously a problem with this since 4 bits gives 16 possible combinations, and there are only 10 unique decimal digits, 0 to 9. This is solved by using the first 6 letters (A..F) of the alphabet as numbers. The table shows the relationship between decimal, hexadecimal and binary.

Decimal	Hexadecimal	Binary
0	0	0000
1	1	0001
2	2	0010
3	3	0011
4	4	0100
5	5	0101
6	6	0110
7	7	0111
8	8	1000
9	9	1001
10	A	1010
11	B	1011
12	C	1100
13	D	1101
14	E	1110
15	F	1111

There are some significant advantages to using hexadecimal when dealing with electronic representations of numbers (if people had 16 fingers, we wouldn't be saddled with the awkward decimal system). Using hexadecimal makes it very easy to convert back and forth from binary because each hexadecimal digit corresponds to exactly 4 bits ($\log_2(16) = 4$) and each byte is two hexadecimal digit. In contrast, a decimal digit corresponds to $\log_2(10) = 3.322$ bits and a byte is 2.408 decimal digits. Clearly hexadecimal is better suited to the task of representing binary numbers than is decimal.

As an example, the number $CA3_{16} = 1100\ 1010\ 0011_2$ ($1100_2 = C_{16}$, $1010_2 = A_{16}$, $0011_2 = 3_{16}$). It is convenient to write the binary number with spaces after every fourth bit to make it easier to read. Converting back and forth to decimal is more difficult, but can be done in the same way as before.

$$3235_{10} = C_{16} \times 256 + A_{16} \times 16 + 3_{16} \times 1$$
$$= C_{16} \times 16^2 + A_{16} \times 16^1 + 3_{16} \times 16^0$$

or

$$3235_{10} = 12 \times 256 + 10 \times 16 + 3 \times 1 = 12 \times 16^2 + 10 \times 16^1 + 3 \times 16^0$$

Octal notation is yet another compact method for writing binary numbers. There are 8 octal characters, 0...7. Obviously this can be represented by exactly 3 bits. Two octal digits can represent numbers up to 64, and three octal digits up to 512. A byte requires 2.667 octal digits. Octal used to be quiete common, it was the primary way of doing low level I/O on some old DEC computers. It is much less common today but is still used occasionally (*e.g.*, to set read, write and execute permissions on Unix systems)

In summary:

- *Bit*: a single binary digit, either zero or one.
- *Byte*: 8 bits, can represent positive numbers from 0 to 255.
- *Hexadecimal*: A representation of 4 bits by a single digit 0..9,A..F. In this way a byte can be represented by two hexadecimal digits
- *Long word*: A long word is usually twice as long as a word.
- *Nibble*: 4 bits, half of a byte.

- *Octal*: A representation of 3 bits by a single digit 0..7. This is used much less commonly than it once was (early DEC computers used octal for much of their I/O)
- *Word*: Usually 16 bits, or two bytes. But a word can be almost any size, depending on the application being considered—32 and 64 bits are common sizes

SIGNED BINARY INTEGERS

It was noted previously that we will not be using a minus sign (-) to represent negative numbers. We would like to represent our binary numbers with only two symbols, 0 and 1. There are a few ways to represent negative binary numbers. The simplest of these methods is called ones complement, where the sign of a binary number is changed by simply toggling each bit (0's become 1's and vice-versa). This has some difficulties, among them the fact that zero can be represented in two different ways (for an eight bit number these would be 0000 0000 and 1111 1111)., we will use a method called two's complement notation which avoids the pitfalls of one's complement, but which is a bit more complicated.

To represent an n bit signed binary number the leftmost bit, has a special significance. The difference between a signed and an unsigned number is given in the table below for an 8 bit number.

The value of bits in signed and unsigned binary numbers:

	Bit 7	Bit 6	Bit 5	Bit 4	Bit 3	Bit 2	Bit 1	Bit 0
Unsigned	$2^7 = 128$	$2^6 = 64$	$2^5 = 32$	$2^4 = 16$	$2^3 = 8$	$2^2 = 4$	$2^1 = 2$	$2^0 = 1$
Signed	$-(2^7)$ = h128	$2^6 = 64$	$2^5 = 32$	$2^4 = 16$	$2^3 = 8$	$2^2 = 4$	$2^1 = 2$	$2^0 = 1$

Let's look at how this changes the value of some binary numbers

Binary	Unsigned	Signed
0010 0011	35	35
1010 0011	163	–93
1111 1111	255	–1
1000 0000	128	–128

If Bit 7 is not set (as in the first example) the representation of signed and unsigned numbers is the same.

However, when Bit 7 is set, the number is always negative. For this reason Bit 7 is sometimes called the sign bit. Signed numbers are added in the same way as unsigned numbers, the only difference is in the way they are interpreted. This is important for designers of arithmetic circuitry because it means that numbers can be added by the same circuitry regardless of whether or not they are signed.

To form a two's complement number that is negative you simply take the corresponding positive number, invert all the bits, and add 1.

The example below illustrated this by forming the number negative 35 as a two's complement integer:

$35_{10} = 0010\ 0011_2$

invert $\rightarrow 1101\ 1100_2$

add 1 $\rightarrow 1101\ 1101_2$

So 1101 1101 is our two's complement representation of -35.

We can check this by adding up the contributions from the individual bits:

$1101\ 1101_2 = -128 + 64 + 0 + 16 + 8 + 4 + 0 + 1 = -35.$

The same procedure (invert and add 1) is used to convert the negative number to its positive equivalent. If we want to know what what number is represented by 1111 1101, we apply the procedure again

$?=1111\ 1101_2$

invert $\rightarrow 0000\ 0010_2$

add 1 $\rightarrow 0000\ 0011_2$

Since 0000 0011 represents the number 3, we know that 1111 1101 represents the number –3.

POSITIVE BINARY FRACTIONS

The representation of unsigned binary fractions proceeds in exactly the same way as decimal fractions.

For example:

$$
\begin{aligned}
0.625_{10} &= 1 \times 0.5 + 0 \times 0.25 + 1 \times 0.125 \\
&= 1 \times 2^{-1} + 0 \times 2^{-2} + 1 \times 2^{-3} \\
&= 0.101_2
\end{aligned}
$$

Each place to the right of the decimal point represents a

negative power of 2, just as for decimals they represent a negative power of 10. Likewise, if there are m bits to the right of a decimal, the precision of the number is 2^{-m} (versus 10^{-m} for decimal). Though it is possible to represent numbers greater than one by having digits to the left of the decimal place we will restrict ourselves to numbers less than one. These are commonly used by Digital Signal Processors. The largest number that can be represented by such a representation is $1\text{-}2^{-m}$, the smallest number is 2^{-m}. For a fraction with 15 bits of resolution this gives a range of approximately 0.99997 to 3.05E-5.

Note that this representationis easily extended to represent all positive numbers by having the digits to the left of the decimal point represent the integer part, and the digits to the right representing the fractional part.

Thus,

$$6.625_{10} = 110.101_2$$

SIGNED BINARY FRACTIONS

Signed binary fractions are formed much like signed integers. We will work with a single digit to the left of the decimal point, and this will represent the number –1 (= $-(2^0)$). The rest of the representation of the fraction remains unchanged. Therefore this leftmost bit represents a sign bit just as with two's complement integers. If this bit is set, the number is negative, otherwise the number is positive. The largest positive number that can be represented is still $1\text{-}2^{-m}$ but the largest negative number is -1. The resolution is still $1\text{-}2^{-m}$. There is a terminology for naming the resolution of signed fractions. If there are m bits to the right of the decimal point, the number is said to be in Q*m*format. For a 16 bit number (15 bits to the right of the decimal point) this results in Q15 notation.

BINARY CODES

INTRODUCTION

It would be stretching our imagination to suggest that

Sir Francis had digital audio on his minde (sic) when he wrote the prophetic words. Nonetheless, this basic idea forms the basis of everything we do in digital computing, digital communications, and digital audio/video. In 1832, Samuel F. B. Morse used the very same idea to propose that telegram *words* be coded into *binary addresses* or *binary codes* that could be transmitted over telegraph lines and decoded at the receiving end to unravel the telegram.

Morse abandoned his scheme, illustrated in Figure, as too complicated and, in 1838, proposed his fabled Morse code for coding letters (instead of words) into objects (dots, dashes, spaces) capable of a threefold difference onely (sic).

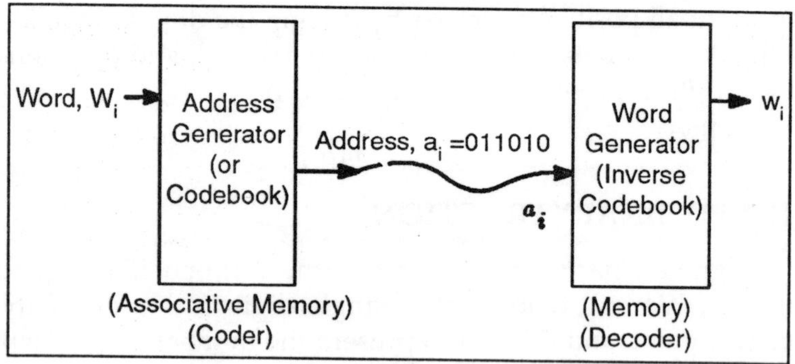

Fig: Generalized Coder-Decoder

The basic idea of Figure is used today in cryptographic systems, where the "address a_i" is an encyphered version of a messagew_i; in vector quantizers, where the "address a_i" is the address of a close approximation to data w_i; in coded satellite transmissions, where the "address a_i" is a data word w_i plus parity check bits for detecting and correcting errors; in digital audio systems, where the "address a_i" is a stretch of digitized and coded music; and in computer memories, where a_i is an address (a coded version of a word of memory) and w_i is a word in memory.

In this we study three fundamental questions in the construction of binary addresses or binary codes. First, what are plausible schemes for mapping symbols (such as words, letters, computer instructions, voltages, pressures, etc.) into binary codes? Second, what are plausible schemes for coding likely symbols with short binary words and unlikely symbols with long words in order to minimize the number of binary digits (bits) required to represent a message? Third, what are plausible schemes for "coding" binary words into longer binary words that contain "redundant bits" that may be used to detect and correct errors? These are not new questions. They have occupied the minds of many great thinkers. Sir Francis recognized that arbitrary messages had binary representations. Alan Turing, Alonzo Church, and Kurt Goedel studied binary codes for computations in their study of computable numbers and algorithms.

BASIC EXPLANATION

Did you know that everything a computer does is based on ones and zeroes? It's hard to imagine, because you hear people talking about the absolutely gargantuan (huge) numbers that computers "crunch".

But all those huge numbers-they're just made up of ones and zeros. It's kind of like the computer is made up of a bunch of lightswitches, and each lightswitch controls just one lightbulb. On or Off. One or Zero. But if you took *all* of those lightbulbs together, and said "Let's make each sequence of On-and-Off represent a different number!" Well then, you could get some pretty large numbers. What do I mean by sequence? Let's say you had two lightswitches.

There are four different ways we could flip those switches:

- Both Off
- First Off, Second On
- First On, Second Off
- Both On

Binary Code takes each of those combinations and assigns a num berto it, like this:

- BothOff= 0
- First Off, Second On = 1
- First On, Second Off = 2
- Both On = 3

Intermediate Explanation

Another way of thinking about it is this: let's give each lightbulb a point value. We'll say the first lightbulb is worth two points, and the second one is worth one point.

Now take a look at the combinations:

- Both Off = 0 + 0 = 0
- First Off, Second On = 0 + 1 = 1
- First On, Second Off = 2 + 0 = 2
- Both On = 2 + 1 = 3

If we added in another lightbulb, we would make it worth twice as many points as the 2 pointer. Then, if all the bulbs were on, the point value would be 4 + 2 + 1 = 7. And if we added in *another* bulb, we would make it worth 8 points (twice as much as four).

Now if they are all turned on, that's worth 8 + 4 + 2 + 1 = 15. As you can see, it's going to take a lot of lightbulbs to make a really big number!

Finally, even though we're giving point values to each of those lightbulbs, when we write them down we still only write them as ones and zeros. One means On, and Zero means Off.

So let's say we had 8 lightbulbs, and they were set up like this: Off Off On On Off On Off Off.

The point values of those eight bulbs are: 0 + 0 + 32 + 16 + 0 + 4 + 0 + 0 (remember-we only give points if they're turned on!) And that adds up to 52. So we would say the sequence of bulbs is worth 52. But how do we write it? We write it like this,

00110100

So now we can say $00110100_{binary} = 52$.

8421 BCD CODE

In the 8421 Binary Coded Decimal (BCD) representation each decimal digit is converted to its 4-bit pure binary equivalent.

For example: $57_{dec} = 0101\ 0111_{bcd}$

Addition is analogous to decimal addition with normal binary addition taking place from right to left.

For example,

6	0110	BCD for 6	42	0100 0010	BCD for 42
+3	0011	BCD for 3	+27	0010 0111	BCD for 27
	1001	BCD for 9		0110 1001	BCD for 69

Where the result of any addition exceeds 9(1001) then six (0110) must be added to the sum to account for the six invalid BCD codes that are available with a 4-bit number. This is illustrated in the example below

8	1001	BCD for 8
+7	0111	BCD for 7
	1111	exceeds 9 (1001) so
	0110	add six (0110)
	0001 0101	BCD for 15

Note that in the last example the 1 that carried forward from the first group of 4 bits has made a new 4-bit number and so represents the "1" in "15". In the examples above the BCD numbers are split at every 4-bit boundary to make reading them easier. This is not necessary when writing a BCD number down. This coding is an example of a binary coded (each decimal number maps to four bits) weighted (each bit represents a number, 1, 2, 4, etc.) code.

4221 BCD CODE

The 4221 BCD code is another binary coded decimal code where each bit is weighted by 4, 2, 2 and 1 respectively. Unlike BCD coding there are no invalid representations. The decimal numbers 0 to 9 have the following 4221 equivalents

Decimal	4221	1's complement
0	0000	1111
1	0001	1110
2	0010	1101
3	0011	1100
4	1000	0111
5	0111	1000
6	1100	0011
7	1101	0010
8	1110	0001
9	1111	0000

the 1's complement of a 4221 representation is important in decimal arithmetic.

In forming the code remember the following rules:

- Below decimal 5 use the right-most bit representing 2 first
- Above decimal 5 use the left-most bit representing 2 first
- Decimal 5 = 2+2+1 and not 4+1

GRAY CODE

Gray coding is an important code and is used for its speed, it is also relatively free from errors. In pure binary coding or 8421 BCD then counting from 7 (0111) to 8 (1000) requires 4 bits to be changed simultaneously. If this does not happen then various numbers could be momentarily generated during the transition so creating spurious numbers which could be read.

Gray coding avoids this since only one bit changes between subsequent numbers. To construct the code there are two simple rules. First start with all 0s and then proceed by changing the least significant bit (lsb) which will bring about a new state.

The first 16 Gray coded numbers are indicated below.

Decimal	Gray Code	Decimal	Gray Code
0	0000	1	0001
2	0011	3	0010
4	0110	5	0111
6	0101	7	0100
8	1100	9	1101
10	1111	11	1110
12	1010	13	1011
14	1001	15	1000

To convert a Gray-coded number to binary then follow this method:

- The binary number and the Gray-coded number will have the same number of bits
- The binary MSB (left-hand bit) and Gray code MSB will always be the same

- To get the binary next-to-MSB (*i.e.* next digit to the right) add the binary MSB and the gray code next-to-MSB. Record the sum, ignoring any carry.
- Continue in this manner right through to the end. Gray coding is a non-BCD, non-weighted reflected binary code.

ERROR DETECTING AND CORRECTING CODES

ERROR-CORRECTING CODES

Introduction

The theory of error detecting and correcting codes is that branch of engineering and mathematics which deals with the reliable transmission and storage of data. Information media are not 100% reliable in practice, in the sense that noise (any form of interference) frequently causes data to be distorted. To deal with this undesirable but inevitable situation, some form of redundancy is incorporated in the original data. With this redundancy, even if errors are introduced (up to some tolerance level), the original information can be recovered, or at least the presence of errors can be detected.

We saw in class how adding to the original message the parity bit or the arithmetic sum allows the detection of a (certain type of) error. However, that kind of redundancy doesn't allow for the correction of the error. Error-correcting codes do exactly this: they add redundancy to the original message in such a way that it is possible for the receiver to detect the error and correct it, recovering the original message. This is crucial for certain applications where the re-sending of the message is not possible (for example, for interplanetary communications and storage of data). The crucial problem to be resolved then is how to add this redundancy in order to detect and correct as many errors as possible in the most efficient way.

This document starts with an overview of the applications of the error-correcting codes, followed by a session describing the fundamental concepts. It then addresses some of the issues involved in the design of the codes. The last session is a brief introduction of the very last discovery in the theory of error-correcting codes: the turbo codes. Most of us have used error-correcting codes, perhaps without knowing it. The International Standard Book Number (ISBN) system identifies every book with a ten-digit number, such as 0-226-53420-0. The first nine digits are the actual number but the tenth is added according to a mathematical formula based on the first nine. If a single one of the digits is changed, as in a misprint when ordering a book, a simple check verifies that something is wrong.

Other common numbers with check digits include the Chemical Abstracts Service (CAS) method of identifying chemical compounds and the United States Postal Service (USPS) nine-digit "zip+four" code, which when it is bar-coded includes a tenth check digit hidden to the human eye but visible to the bar code reader.

Some high-end computer memory chips, "ECC RAM," use extended nine-bit bytes. The ninth bit, or "check bit," is always set so that the total number of ones in the extended byte is even. (This rule is called a "checksum." Specifically, if the sum of the nine bits is not even, an error has been detected.) This ninth bit is not used or even seen by your software, but the computer hardware itself will signal an error if it ever reads an extended byte that contains an odd number of ones.

All these processes can *detect* a single error within a very short message: nine decimal digits for the ISBN and USPS codes, a varying number of decimal digits for the CAS numbers, eight binary digits for ECC RAM. However, they cannot *correct* any error that is detected. Furthermore, some combinations of two or more errors occurring within the message will not be detected.

Coding Theory

Coding theory deals with ways of extending the check-bit and checksum ideas to enable detection and even correction of large numbers of errors within messages. It builds on some beautiful mathematical ideas that we can hint at here. Let's focus on binary messages, the stuff of which computer communications is built. The first thing is to break up the message into "words" of fixed size. We will focus on how to correct errors occurring within individual words.

If the words are n bits long, then there are 2^n possible messages each word can carry. The set of all such words has an interesting geometry based on the *Hamming distance*. The distance between two words is just the number of places in which they differ.

For example, let's consider the case n=7. The distance between 0100111 and 1100101 is two, because these words differ in the first and sixth places.Words can also be added to each other. This is done by the usual odd-even rules of addition, performed bit by bit. Specifically, 0+0=0, 0+1 = 1, 1+0 = 1, and 1+1 = 0. Thus 0100111 + 1100101 = 1000010.

Suppose you want to send a message in the form of a binary string, *i.e.*, a string of 0's and 1's. Due to noise in the medium over which you are transmitting the message, be it a telephone line, a radio link or the Internet, it is possible that some of the 0's will be received as 1's and vice versa. Let us denote the probability that any one bit is garbled in transmission by *p*.

Typically, *p* will be small, say about one in a million, but that may still be too large for our purposes. If we are transferring a file that has 10 million bits, the chance that the file is incorrectly received is nearly 90%. How can we improve the reliability of the transmission? The simplest method is to repeat ourselves three times. For example, if we want to send the string 010, we transmit 000111000. If a single error occurs in transmission, this may be received for instance as 001111000.

At the receiver, we use what is called majority decoding. We look at each set of 3 bits and decode it as the bit which occurs most often. Thus, the received message above is correctly decoded as 010 even though an error occured in transmission. In the above example, it could have happened that two errors occured and we received the string 101111000. This would be decoded as 110, which is different from the original message. This shows that we cannot eliminate errors altogether, we can only make them less likely. To see how much less likely, let us work out the probability that a single bit is incorrectly received. Since each bit is transmitted three times, it has to be incorrectly received at least twice in order for the decoder to get it wrong. The probability of this is $3p^2+p^3$, which, for p equal to one in a million works out to about one in 330 billion.

Thus, using the repetition code, a 10 Mbit file can be sent correctly with probability 99.997%. While this coding scheme dramatically reduces the likelihood of errors, it is rather inefficient. Can we do better?

Here's one way, using the famous (7,4) Hamming code. This works with a block of 4 bits at a time rather than with a single bit. Suppose we want to transmit the block 0011. Look at the picture below. We write these bits in the intersections of the circles. Next, we fill in the part of each circle lying outside the intersection using the rule that the total number of 1's contained in each circle should be even. The extra bits are called parity bits—they ensure even parity for the number of 1's in each circle. The message we transmit will consist of all seven bits, in a pre-arranged order so that the receiver can reconstruct the diagram. Suppose now that a single error occurs, so that the receiver gets a 1 in the intersection of the top two circles.

The receiver proceeds to work out the parity for each of the circles, and finds that the top two circles both have odd parity (odd number of 1's), while the bottom circle has even parity. This enables her to conclude that an error has occurred, and that the error is in the bit position common to the top two circles. Therefore, the intended message can be decoded correctly. It is not hard to see that a similar approach works if the error is in some other bit position. However, if there are two errors, then the decoding procedure fails in that it yields a message different from the intended one.

Applications of Error Correcting Codes

The increasing reliance on digital communication and the emergence of the digital computer as an essential tool in a technological society have placed error-correcting codes in a most prominent position. We cite here a few specific applications, in an attempt to indicate their practicality and importance.

Many computers now have error-correcting capabilities built into their random access memories; it is less expensive to compensate for errors through the use of error-correcting codes than to build integrated circuits that are 100% reliable. The single error-correcting Hamming codes, and linear codes in general, are of use here. Disk storage is another area of computing where error-coding is employed. Storage capacity has been greatly increased through the use of disks of higher and higher density. With this increase in density, error probability also increases, and therefore information is now stored on many disks using error-correcting codes.

In 1972, the *Mariner* space probe flew past Mars and transmitted pictures back to earth. The channel for such transmissions is space and the earth's atmosphere. Solar activity and atmospheric conditions can introduce errors into weak signals coming from the spacecraft. In order that most of the pictures sent could be correctly recovered here on earth, the following coding scheme was used. The source alphabet consisted of 64 shades of gray. The source encoder encoded each of these into binary 6-tuples and the channel encoder produced binary 32-tuples. The source decoder could correct up to 7 errors in any 32-tuple. This was done with the Reed-Muller codes.

In 1979, the *Voyager* probes began transmitting Colour pictures of Jupiter. For Colour pictures the source alphabet needed to be much larger and was chosen to have 4096 Colour shades. The source encoder produced binary 12-tuples for each Colour shade and the channel encoder produced 24-tuples (*i.e.* 24 dimensional vectors). This code would correct up to 3 errors in any 24-tuple, and is the Golay code.

The increasing popularity of digital audio is due in part to the powerful error-correcting codes that the digitization process facilitates. Information is typically stored on a small aluminized disk as a series of microscopic pits and smooth areas, the pattern representing a sequence of 0's and 1's. A laser beam is used as the playback mechanism to retrieve stored data. Because the data is digital, error correction schemes can be easily incorporated into such a system. Given an error-coded digital recording, a digital audio system can on playback, correct errors introduced by fingerprints, scratches, or even imperfections originally present in the storage medium. The compact disc system pioneered by Philips Corporation of the Netherlands in cooperation with Sony Corporation of Japan, allowing playback of pre-recorded digital audio disks, is an excellent example of the application of error-correcting codes to digital communication; *crossinterleaved Reed-Solomon* codes are used for error correction in this system. Digital audio tape (DAT) systems have also been developed, allowing digital recording as well as playback.

Error-correcting codes are particularly suited when the transmission channel is noisy. This is the case of wireless communication. Nowadays, all digital wireless communications use error-correcting codes.

Fundamental Concepts

We begin with a few definitions, in order to develop a working vocabulary. Let A be an alphabet of q symbols. For example, A = {a,b,c...,z) is the standard lower case alphabet for the English language, and A = (0,1) is the binary alphabet.

Definition: A block code of length n containing M codewords over the alphabet A is a set of M n-tuples where each n-tuple takes its components from A. We refer to such a block code as an [n,M]-code over A. In practice, we most frequently take A to be the binary alphabet.

Given a code C of block length n over an alphabet A, those specific n-tuples over A which are in C are referred to as codewords.

Note that while the channel encoder transmits codewords, the n-tuples received by the channel decoder may or may not be codewords, due to the possible occurrence of errors during transmission.

Example: Suppose the information we are to transmit comes from the set of symbols {A, B, C, D}. For practical considerations we associate sequences of 0's and l's with each of these symbols.

A → 00
B → 01
C → 10
D → 11

This is the source encoding. Now we want to add some redundancy (channel encoding).

A → 00 → 00000
B → 01 → 10110
C → 10 → 01011
D → 11 → 11101

We have just constructed a [5,4]-code over a binary alphabet. That is, we constructed a code with 4 codewords, each being a 5-tuple (block length 5), with each component of the 5-tuple being O or 1. The code is the set of n-tuples produced by the channel encoder (as opposed to the source encoder).

The source encoder transforms messages into k-tuples (k=2 in the example above) over the code alphabet A, and the channel encoder assigns to each of these information k-tuples a codeword of length n (n=5 in the example). Since the channel encoder is adding redundancy, we have n > k and hence we have message expansion. While the added redundancy is desirable from the point of view of error control, it decreases the efficiency of the communication channel by reducing its effective capacity. The ratio k to n is a measure of the fraction of information in the channel which is non-redundant.

Definition: The rate of an [n,M]-code which encodes information k-tuples is,

$$R = K/n$$

The rate of the simple code given in example 1 is 2/5. The quantity r = n-k is sometimes called the redundancy of the code. A fundamental parameter associated with an [n,M]-code C is the Hamming distance for C. Before we can define the Hamming distance for a code, we must define the Hamming distance between two codewords.

Definition: The Hamming distance d(x,y) between two codewords x and y is the number of coordinate positions in which they differ.

Example: Over the alphabet A = (0,1}, the codewords x and y x=(10110) y=(11O11) have Hamming distance d(x,y) =3.

Example: The codewords u and v over the alphabet A = (0,1,2), given by u = (21002) v=(12001) have Hamming distance d(u,v) =3.

Definition Let C be an [n,M]-code. The Hamming distance d of the code C is d= min {d(x,y): x,y belong to C, x != y}. In other words, the Hamming distance of a code is the minimum distance between two distinct codewords, over all pairs of codewords.

Example: Consider C = (c0,c1,c2,c3} where c0=(00000) c1 =(10110) c2= (01011) c3= (11101) This code has distance d = 3. It is the [5,4] code constructed earlier. Suppose we have an [n,M]-code C with distance d.

We need to adopt a strategy for the channel decoder (or just decoder). When the decoder receives an n-tuple r it must make some decision.

This decision may be one of:

- No errors have occurred; accept r as a codeword.
- Errors have occurred; correct r to a codeword c.
- Errors have occurred; no correction is possible.

In general, the decoder will not always make the correct decision; for example, consider the possibility of an error pattern occurring which changes a transmitted codeword into another codeword. The goal is that the decoder take the course of action which has the greatest probability of being correct. One usually makes the assumption that errors are introduced by the channel at random, and that the probability of an error in one coordinate is independent of errors in adjacent coordinates.

The decoding strategy we shall adopt, called nearest neighbour decoding, can then be specified as follows.

Nearest Neighbour Decoding: If an n-tuple r is received, and there is a unique codeword c that belongs to C such that d(r,c) is a minimun, then correct r to the c. If no such c exists, report that errors have been detected, but no correction is possible. By nearest neighbour decoding, a received vector is decoded to the codewords"closest" to it, with respect to Hamming distance.

The figure below illustrates the concept. The red dots are the codewords, the green ones are the received words that can be corrected to the closest codewords and the blue dot is a received word that is equidistant from 2 codewords and therefore cannot be corrected.

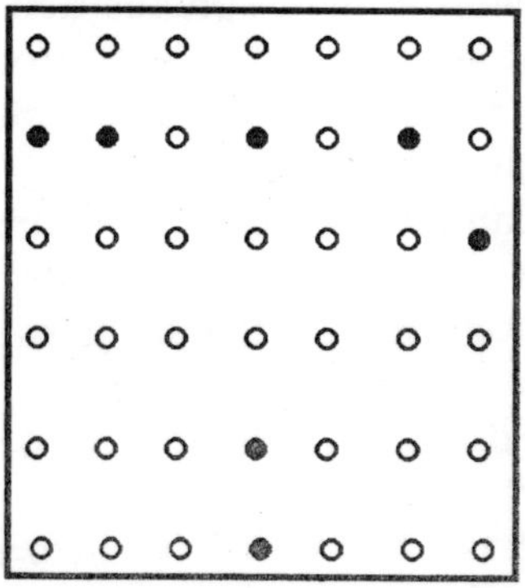

A code is said to correct e errors if a decoder using the above scheme is capable of correcting any pattern of e or fewer errors introduced by the channel. In this case, the decoder can correct any transmitted codeword which has been altered in e or fewer coordinate positions.

Theorem: Let C be an [n,M]-code having distance d = 2e+1. Then C can correct e errors. If used for error detection only, C can detect 2e errors.

Let c be one codeword of C and S be the set of all n-tuples over the alphabet of C and define

$$S(c) = \{x \text{ belongs to } S: d(x,c) \Leftarrow e).$$

S(c) is called the sphere of radius e about the codeword c. It consists of all n-tuples within distance e of the codeword c, which we think of as being at the Centre of the sphere. In the figure below, the"spheres" arount the codewords of the previous figure. The radius is in this case is 1.

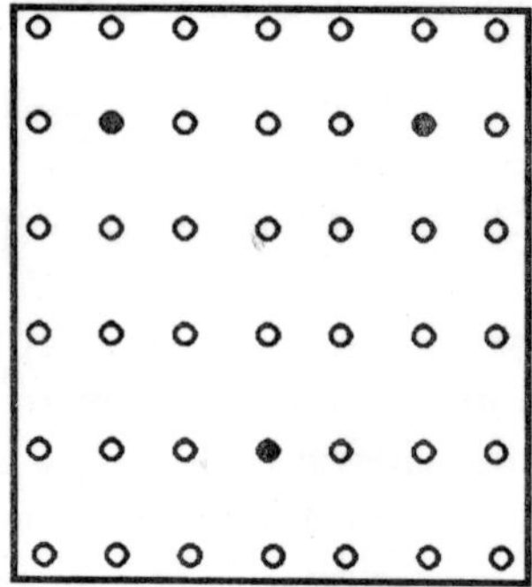

Given 2 codewords, their spheres don't intersect, hence if codeword c is transmitted and t<= e errors are introduced, the received word r is an n-tuple in the sphere S(c) and thus c is the unique codeword closest to r.

The decoder can always correct any error pattern of this type. If we use the code only for error detection, then at least 2e+1 errors must occur in a codeword to carry it into another codeword. If at least 1 and at most 2e errors are introduced, the received word will never be a codeword and error detection is always possible.

The spheres have to be disjoint in order to be able to correct errors. But if a received word happens to be in the space between the spheres, correction is not possible: that space doesn't belong to any sphere, *i.e.* to any codeword: the error is detected but not corrected. Therefore, we want to find codes such that the the spheres around the codewords are disjoint (to correctly correct the errors) but as close as possible to each other, to correct ALL the errors. If all the space is taken by the sphere, all the words received will fall into the sphere of a codeword and therefore can be corrected to that codeword. These are the perfect codes. Lets give the formal definition of perfect codes.

Definition: A perfect code is an e-error-correcting [n, M]-code over an alphabet A such that every n-tuple over A is in the sphere of radius e about some codework.

In a perfect code of block length n, the sphere of radius e about codeworks are not only disjoint (since the code is e-error-correcting) but exhaust the entire space of n-tuples.

Issues in the Design of Error-correcting Codes

Designing a good code is a very hard problem. Also, lots of factors need to be taken in account. For instance, in practice the code should be designed appropriately depending on the expected rate of errors for the particular channel being employed. If it is known that the probability that the channel will introduce 2 errors into any transmitted codeword is extremely small, then it is likely not necessary to construct a code that will correct all 2-bit error patterns.

A single error correcting code will likely suffice. Conversely, if double errors are frequent and a single error correcting code is being used, then decoding errors will be frequent. From this brief introduction, a number of questions arise.

- Given n, M and d, can we determine if an [n Al] code with distance d exists?
- Assuming such a code does exist, how would one be constructed in practice?
- How should information k-tuples be associated with codeword n-tuples to facilitate efficient channel encoding?
- How should channel decoding be performed?

Lets examine the issue of channel decoding in greater detail. When a word is received and it's not a codeword, finding the closest codeword involves computing the distance from the received word to each codeword, requiring M comparisons. While this might be acceptable for small M, in practice we usually find M quite large.

Suppose a code C is used with M = 2^50 codewords, which is not unrealistic. If we could carry out 1 million distance computations per second, it would take around 20 years to make a single correction. Clearly, this is not tolerable and more efficient techniques are required. Wishing to retain the nearest neighbour decoding strategy, we seek more efficient techniques for its implementation. The theory of error-correcting code is concerned with constructing codes for various values of n, M and d, and the consideration of appropriate encoding and decoding techniques. Most of the best known codes are algebraic in nature like the linear codes. Linear codes are an important and general class of error-correcting codes.

For example, theBCH codes used for CDs are linear codes. They are heavily mathematical and an appropriate description here is not possible. The next session describes instead the last"discovery" in the theory of error correcting codes, the Turbo codes.

Turbo Codes

In session 3, when we introduced the Nearest Neighbour Decoding, we didn't mention the fact that what the decoding actually does is maximizing the probability P(r|c) that r is received, given that c is sent. *i.e.* choosing the nearest codeword is equivalent to choosing the most likely input message c given the received tuple r. This decoding strategy is known as maximum likelihood decoding. We can then state the decoding problem in the following manner.

Let U be the original message, X the encoded message and Y the message received after the noisy channel. This is schematized in the following figure.

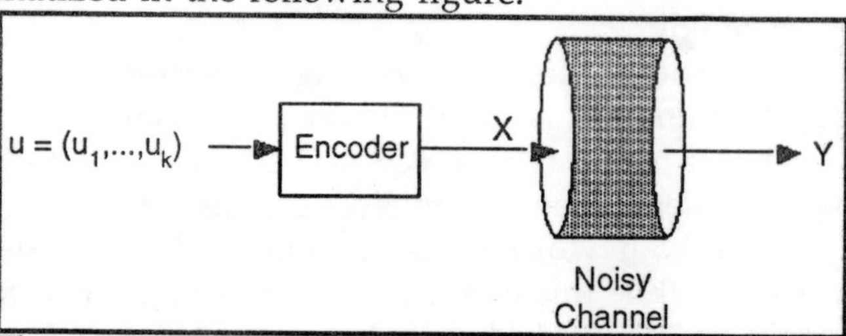

The receiver knows Y and the model of the encoder, *i.e.* is has a knowledge of how the original message was originally encoded.

The problem now is finding the U that maximizes the probability that U was sent given that Y was received, *i.e.* the probability P(U|Y).

Having stated the decoding problem in probabilistic terms, we can take advantage of various methods that deal with probability estimations. A class of such methods is the class of graphical models.

The simplest graphical model:

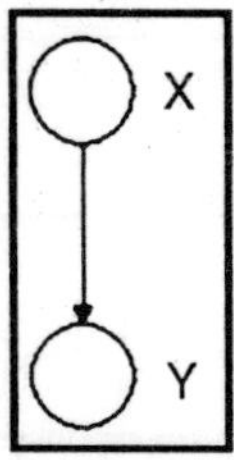

A classical problem of probability estimation is finding the probability distribution P(X|Y) where X and Y are 2 random variables. The graphical model framework allows for such probability estimations to be calculated in an efficient way. Note that the calculation of P(X|Y) from P(Y|X) and P(X) is just Bayes rule-P(X|Y) = P(Y|X)P(X)/P(Y)-and that graphical model inference algorithms can be viewed as generalizations of Bayes rule to arbitrary graphs. Lets now see how we can view error correcting codes as graphical models. In the figure below, a convolution code as a graphical model.Let U be the original message, X the encoded message and Y the message received after the noisy channel.

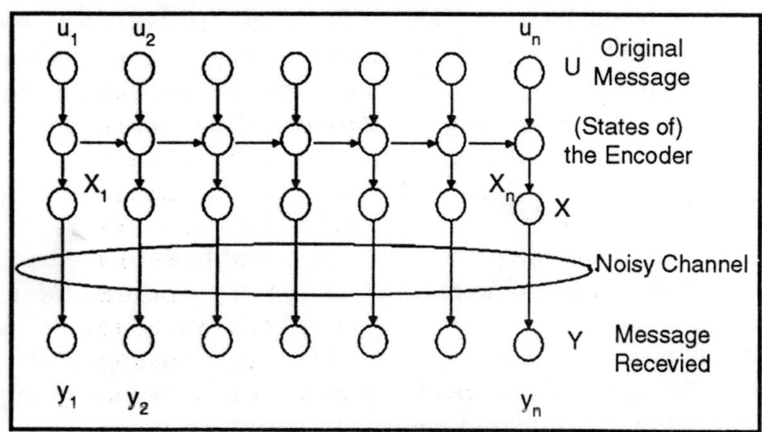

Now, the decoding problem of finding U that maximizes p(U|Y) can be tackled within the framework of graphical models. We have introduced the convolutional codes mainly because the Turbo codes are two convolutional codes put together. The following figure illustrate the graphical representation of a turbo code.

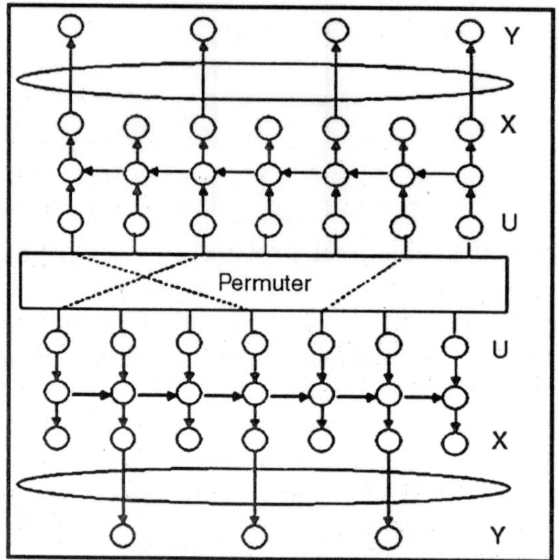

It should be mentioned that general inference in graphical models is NP-hard, and, in particular, exact inference, calculating P(U I Y), for turbo codes is infeasible and therefore an approximate inference algorithm is used. Turbo codes were discovered very recently. There is much excitement about them. They outperform all other kinds of error-correcting codes in the case of long block lengths, although the reason why they do so is not yet clear.

ERROR DETECTING

R. W. Hamming wrote the paper that both opened and closed this field in 1950. His interest was in providing a means of self-checking in computers, which were just being developed at the time he wrote this. the paper appeared in the Bell System Technical Journal, April, 1950. Definitely worth tracking down in the library and reading.

Bit Strings as Addresses in Binary Hypercubes

The best starting point for understanding ECC codes is to consider bit strings as addresses in a binary hypercube. A hypercube is a generalization of a cube to various dimensions; we're probably most familiar with the notion of a four-dimensional hypercube. Here's a picture of binary hypercubes for several different dimensionalities:

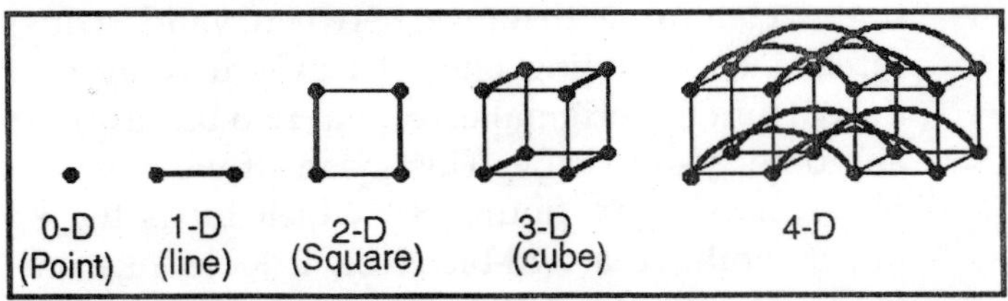

Each of them was created by copying the one to the left twice, and connecting corresponding vertices. We can assign each vertex in a hypercube a location in a coordinate space determined by the dimensionality of the hypercube.

- A zero-dimensional hypercube requires no coordinates to know where you are
- A one-dimensional hypercube can use one bit to tell whether you're at the bottom or the top of the line segment.
- A two-dimensional hypercube can use two bits: first bit is left vs. right, second is inherited from the line.
- A three-dimensional hypercube can use a bit to tell front square from back, and inherit two bits from the square.
- A four-dimensional hypercube can use a bit to tell left cube from right, and inherits three bits from cube.

This can continue through as many dimensions as you want. The Hamming distance between two bit strings is the number of bits you have to change to convert one to the other: this is the same as the number of edges you have to traverse in a binary hypercube to get from one of the vertices to the other. The basic idea of an error correcting code is to use extra bits to increase the dimensionality of the hypercube, and make sure the Hamming distance between any two valid points is greater than one.

- If the Hamming distance between valid strings is only one, a single-bit error results in another valid string. This means we can't detect an error.
- If it's two, then changing one bit results in an invalid

string, and can be detected as an error. Unfortunately, changing just one more bit can result in another valid string, which means we can't know which bit was wrong: so we can detect an error but not correct it.

- If the Hamming distance between valid strings is three, then changing one bit leaves us only one bit away from the original error, but two bits away from any other valid string. This means if we have a one-bit error, we can figure out which bit is the error; but if we have a two-bit error, it looks like one bit from the other direction. So we can have single bit correction, but that's all.
- Finally, if the Hamming distance is four, then we can correct a single-bit error and detect a double-bit error. This is frequently referred to as a SECDED (Single Error Correct, Double Error Detect) scheme.

Parity

The simplest case is by adding a parity bit. Suppose we have a three-bit word (so the bit strings define points in a cube). If we add a fourth bit, we can decree that any time we want to switch a bit in the original three-bit string, we also have to switch the parity bit. If we start with 000 in the left cube, so the full string is 0000, changing any one of the original three bits requires us to change to the other cube: 1001, 1010, and 1100. Now if we change a second bit, we have to move back to the left cube: 0011, 0101, 0110. And if we change the third bit, we move back to the right cube: 0111. So, there is a Hamming distance of two between any two valid strings. If we get a one-bit error, we know it is an error because it's on one of the invalid vertices. This can be computed by counting the number of 1's, and making sure it's always even (so this is called even parity). We could have selected exactly the opposite set of vertices as the valid ones, which would have given us odd parity. We picked even parity because we'll be using it in the next step.

DATA MODEL

We will first assume that the set of resources to be locked

is organized in a hierarchy. Note that this hierarchy is used in the context of a collection of resources and has nothing to do with the data model used in a data base system. The hierarchy of the following figure may be suggestive. We adopt the notation that each level of the hierarchy is given a node type that is a generic name for all the node instances of that type. For example, the database has nodes of type area as its immediate descendants, each area in turn has nodes of type file as its immediate descendants and each file has nodes of type record as its immediate descendants in the hierarchy. Since it is a hierarchy, each node has a unique parent.

DATA BASE
|
AREAS
|
FILES
|
RECORDS

A sample lock hierarchy: Each node of the hierarchy can be locked. If one requests exclusive access (X) to a particular node, then when the request is granted, the requestor has exclusive access to that node and implicitly to each of its descendants. If one requests shared access (S) to a particular node, then when the request is granted, the requestor has shared access to that node and implicitly to each descendant of that node. These two access modes lock an entire sub-tree rooted at the requested node.

Our goal is to find some technique for implicitly locking an entire sub-tree. In order to lock a sub-tree rooted at node R in share or exclusive mode it is important to prevent locks on the ancestors of R that might implicitly lock R and its descendants in an incompatible mode. Hence a new access mode, intention mode (I), is introduced. Intention mode is used to "tag" (lock) all ancestors of a node to be locked in share or exclusive mode. These tags signal the fact that locking is being done at a "finer" level and thereby prevents implicit or explicit exclusive or share locks on the ancestors.

The protocol to lock a sub-tree rooted at node R in

exclusive or share. The protocol to lock a sub-tree rooted at node R in exclusive or share mode is to first lock all ancestors of R in intention mode, and then to lock node R in exclusive or share made. For example, using the figure above, to lock a particular file one should obtain intention access to the database, to the area containing the file, and then request exclusive (or share) access to the file itself. This implicitly locks all records of the file in exclusive (or share) mode.

ACCESS MODES AND COMPATIBILITY

We say that two lock requests for the same node by two different transactions are compatible if they can be granted concurrently. The mode of the request determines its compatibility with requests made by other transactions.. The three modes X, S, and I are incompatible with one another, but distinct S requests may be granted together and distinct I requests may be granted together,.

The compatibilities among modes derive from their semantics. Share mode allows reading but not modification of the corresponding resource by the requestor and by other transactions. The semantics of exclusive mode is that the grantee may read and modify the resource, but no other transaction may read or modify the resource while the exclusive lock is set. The reason for dichotomizing share and exclusive access is that several share requests can be granted concurrently (are compatible) whereas an exclusive request is not compatible with any other request. Intention mode was introduced to be incompatible with share and exclusive mode (to prevent share and exclusive locks).

However, intention mode is compatible with itself since two transactions having intention access to a node will explicitly lock descendants of the node in X, S or I mode and thereby will either be compatible with one another or will be scheduled on the basis of their requests at the finer level. For example, two transactions can simultaneously be granted the database and some area and some file in intention mode. In this case their explicit locks on particular records in the file will resolve any conflicts among them.

The notion of intention mode is refined to intention share mode (IS) and intention exclusive (IX) for two reasons: intention share mode only requests share or intention share locks at the lower nodes of the tree (i.e. never requests an exclusive lock below the intention share node.) Hence IS mode is compatible with S mode. Since read only is a common form of access it will be profitable to distinguish this for greater concurrency.

Secondly, if a transaction has an intention share lock on a node it can convert this to a share lock at a later time, but one cannot convert an intention exclusive lock to a share lock on a node, Rather to get the combined rights of share node and intention exclusive mode one must obtain an X or SIX mode lock. We recognize one further refinement of modes, namely share and intention exclusive mode (SIX). Suppose one transaction wants to read an entire sub-tree and to update particular nodes of that sub-tree.

Using the modes provided so far it would have the options of:

- Requesting exclusive access to the root of the sub-tree and doing no further locking or
- Requesting intention exclusive access to the root of the sub-tree and explicitly locking the lover nodes in intention; share or exclusive mode.

Alternative:

- Has low concurrency. If only a small fraction of the read nodes are updated then alternative
- Has nigh locking overhead,

RULES FOR REQUESTING NODES

The implicit locking of nodes will not work if transactions are allowed to leap into the middle of the tree and begin locking nodes at random.

The implicit locking implied by the S and X modes depends on all transactions obeying the following protocol:

- Before requesting an S or IS lock on a node, all ancestor nodes of the requested node must be held in IX or IS mode by the requestor.
- Before requesting an X, SIX or IX lock on a node, all

ancestor nodes of the requested node must be held in SIX or IX mode by the requestor.

- Locks should be released either at the end of the transaction (in any order) or in leaf to root order. In particular, if locks are not held to end of transaction, one should not hold a lock after releasing its ancestors.

To paraphrase this, locks are requested root to leaf, and released leaf to root. Notice that leaf nodes are never requested in intention mode since they have no descendants, and that once a node is acquired in S or X mode, no further explicit locking is required at lover levels.

SEVERAL EXAMPLES

To lock record R for read:

```
Lock database                with mode = IS
Lock area containing R       with mode = IS
Lock file containing R       with mode = IS
Lock record R                with mode = IS
```

Don't panic, the transaction probably already has the database, area and file lock.

To lock record R for write-exclusive access:

```
Lock database                with mode = IX
Lock area containing R       with mode = IX
Lock file containing R       with mode = IX
Lock record R                with mode = X
```

Note that if the records of this and the previous example are distinct, each request can be granted simultaneously to different transactions even though both refer to the same file.

To lock a file F for read and write access:

```
Lock database                with mode   = IX
Lock area containing         F with mode = IX
Lock file P                  with mode   = X
```

Since this reserves exclusive access to the file, if this request uses the same file as the previous two examples it or the other transactions will have to wait. Unlike examples 1, 2 and 4, no additional locking need be done (at the record level).

To lock a file F for complete scan and occasional update:

```
Lock database            with node      = IX
Lock area containing     F with mode    = IX
Lock file F              with mode      = SIX
```

Thereafter, particular records in F can be locked for update by locking the desired records in X mode. Notice that (unlike the previous example) this transaction is compatible with the first example. This is the reason for introducing SIX mode.

To quiesce the data base:

```
Lock data base           with mode      = X.
```

Note that this locks everyone else out.

DIRECTED ACYCLIC GRAPHS OF LOCKS

The notions so far introduced can be generalized to work for directed acyclic graphs (DAGs) of resources rather than simply hierarchies of resources. A tree is a simple DAG. The key observation is that to implicitly or explicitly lock a node, one should lock all the parents of the node in the DAG, and so by induction lock all ancestors of the node. In particular, to lock a subgraph one must implicitly or explicitly lock all ancestors of the subgraph in the appropriate mode (for a tree there is only one parent). To give an example of a non-hierarchical structure, imagine the locks are organized as:

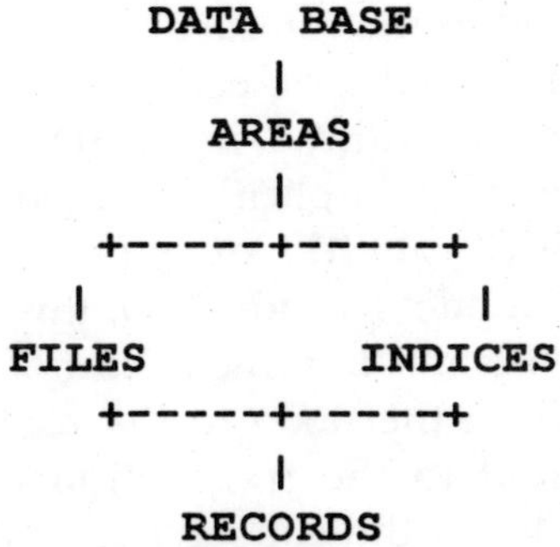

A non-hierarchical lock graph: We postulate that areas are "physical" notions and that files, indices and records are logical notions. The database is a collection of areas. Each area is a collection of files and indices. Each file has a few corresponding indices in the same area. Each record belongs to some file and to its corresponding indices. A record is comprised of field values and some field is indexed by the index associated with the file containing the record. The file gives a sequential access path to the records and the index gives an associative access path to the records based on field values. Since individual fields are never locked, they do not appear in the lock graph.

To write a record A in file P with index I:

```
lock data base                  with mode =IX
lock area containing F          with mode =IX
lock file F                     with mode =IX
lock index I                    with mode =IX
lock record R                   with mode = X
```

Note that all paths to record R are locked. Alternatively, one could lock F and I in exclusive mode thereby implicitly locking R in exclusive mode. To give a more complete explanation we observe that a node can be locked explicitly (by requesting it) or implicitly (by appropriate explicit locks on the ancestors of the node) in one of five modes: IS, IX. S, SIX, X. However, the definition of implicit locks and the protocols for setting explicit locks have to be extended for DAG's as follows: A node is implicitly granted in S mode to a transaction if at least one of its parents is (implicitly or explicitly) granted to the transaction in S, SIX or X mode. By induction, that means that at least one of the node's ancestors must be explicitly granted in S, SIX, or X mode to the transaction. A node is implicitly granted in X mode if all of its parents are (implicitly or explicitly) granted to the transaction in X mode. By induction, this is equivalent to the condition that all nodes in some cut set of the collection of all paths leading from the node to the roots of the graph are explicitly granted to the transaction in X mode and all ancestors of nodes in the cut set are explicitly granted in IX or SIX mode. By examination of the partial order of modes, a node is implicitly granted in IS mode if it is implicitly granted in S mode, and a node is implicitly granted in IS, IX, S and SIX mode if it is implicitly granted in X mode.

PROTOCOL FOR REQUESTING LOCKS ON A DAG

- Before requesting an S or IS lock on a node, one should request at least one parent (and by induction a path to a root) in IS (or greater) mode. As a consequence none of the ancestors along this path can be granted to another transaction in a mode incompatible with IS.
- Before requesting IX, SIX or x mode access to a node, one should request all parents of the node in IX (or greater) mode. As a consequence all ancestors will be held in IX (or greater mode) and cannot be held by other transactions in a mode incompatible with IX (i.e. S, SIX, X).
- Locks should be released either at the end of the transaction (in any order) or in leaf to root order. In particular, if locks are not held to the end of transaction, one should not hold a lower lock after releasing its ancestors.

To give an example using the non-hierarchical lock graph in the figure above, a sequential scan of all records in file F need not use an index so one can get an implicit share lock on each record in the file by:

```
lock data base              with mode =IS
lock area containing F with mode =IS
lock file F                 with mode = S
```

This gives implicit S mode access to all records in P. Conversely, to read a record in a file via the index I for file P, one need not get an implicit or explicit lock on file F:

```
lock data base              wi+h mode =IS
lock area containing R with mode =IS
lock index I                with mode = S
```

This again gives implicit S mode access to all records in index I (in file F). In both these cases, only one path was locked for reading. But to insert, delete or update a record R in file F with index I one must get an implicit or explicit lock on all ancestors of R. The first example of this section showed how an explicit X lock on a record is obtained. To get an implicit X lock on all records in a file one can simply lock the index and file in X mode, or lock the area in X mode. The latter examples allow bulk load or update of a file without further locking since all records in the file are implicitly granted in X mode.

PROOF OF EQUIVALENCE OF THE LOCK PROTOCOL

We will now prove that the described lock protocol is equivalent to a conventional one which uses only two modes (S and X), and which explicitly locks atomic resources (the leaves of a tree or sinks of a DAG).

Let G =(N, A) be a finite (directed acyclic) graph where N is the set of nodes and A is the set of arcs. G is assumed to be without circuits (i.e. there is no non-null path leading from a node n to itself).

A node p is a parent of a node n, and n is a child of p if there is an arc from p to n. A node n is a source (sink), if n has no parents (no children). An ancestor of node n is any node (including n) in a path from a source to n. A node-slice of a sink n is a collection of nodes such that each path from a source to n contains at least one node of the slice. Let Q be the set of all sinks of G.

Theorem: If two lock-graphs L1 and L2 are compatible, then their projections P1 and P2 are compatible. In other words if the explicit locks set by two transactions do not conflict then also the three-state locks implicitly acquired do not conflict.

Proof: Assume that L1 and L2 are incompatible. We want to prove that P1 and P2 are incompatible. By definition of compatibility there must exist a sink n such that L1(n)=X and L2(n) is in {S, X} (or vice versa). By definition of projection, there must exist a node-slice {n1,..., ns} of N such that L1(n1)=...=L1(ns)=X. Also there must exist an ancestor na of n such that L2(na) is in {S, SIX, X}. From the definition of lock-graph there is a path Path1 from a source to na on which L2 does not take the value NL. If Path1 intersects the node-slice at ni then L1 and L2 are incompatible since L1(ni)=X which is incompatible with the non-null value of L2(ni). Hence the theorem is proved.

LOCK MANAGEMENT PRAGMATICS

Thus far we have discussed when to lock (lock before access and hold locks to commit point) and why to lock (to guarantee consistency and to make recovery possible without cascading transaction backup,) and what to lock (lock at a granularity that balances concurrency against instruction overhead in setting locks.) The remainder of= this section will discuss issues associated with how to implement a lock manager.

Locks Names

The association between lock names and objects is purely a convention. Lock manager associates no semantics with names. Generally the first byte is reserved for the subsystem (component) identifier and the remaining seven bytes name the object. For example, data manager might use bytes (2... 4) for the file name and bytes (5... 7) for the record name in constructing names for record locks.

Since there are so many locks, one only allocates those with non-null queue headers. (i.e. free locks occupy no space.) Setting 1 lock consists of hashing the lock name into a table. If the header already exists, the request enqueues on it, otherwise the request allocates the lock header and places it in the hash table. When the queue of a lock becomes empty, the header is deallocated (by the unlock operation).

Locks Classes

Many operations acquire a set of locks. If the operation is successful, the locks should be retained. If the operation is unsuccessful, or when the operation commits, the locks should be released. In order to avoid double bookkeeping, the lock manager allows users to name sets of locks (in the new DBTG proposal these are called keep lists, in IMS program isolation these are called *Q class locks). For each lock held by each process, lock manager keeps a list of <class, count> pairs. Each lock request for a class increments the count for that class. Each unlock request decrements the count. When all counts for all the lock's classes are zero then the lock is not held by the process.

Latches

Lock manager needs a serialization mechanism to perform its function (e.g. inserting elements in a queue or hash chain). It does this by implementing a lower level primitive called a latch. Latches are semaphores. They provide a cheap serialization mechanism without providing the expensive features like deadlock detection, class tracking, and modes of sharing (beyond S or X). They are used by lock manager and by other performance critical managers (notably buffer manager and log manager).

Performance of Lock Manager

Lock manager is about 3300 lines of (PL/l like) source code. It depends critically on the Compare and Swap logic provided by the multiprocessor feature of System 370. It comprises three percent of the code and about ten percent of the instruction execution of a program in System R (this may vary a great deal.) A lock-unlock pair currently costs 350 instructions but if these notes are ever finished, this will be reduced to 120 instructions (this should reduce its slice of the execution pie.) A latch-unlatch pair requires 10 instructions (they expand in-line). (Initially they required 120 instructions but a careful redesign improved this dramatically.)

DEADLOCK

DEADLOCK DETECTION

One issue the lock manager must deal with is deadlock. Deadlock consists of each member of a set of transactions waiting for some other member of the set to give up a lock. Standard lore has it that one can have timeout, or deadlock-prevention, or deadlock detection.

Timeout causes waits to be denied after some specified interval. It has the property that as the system becomes more congested, more and more transactions time out (because time runs slower and because more resources are in use so that one waits more). Also timeout puts an upper limit on the duration of a transaction. 1n general the dynamic properties of timeout make it acceptable for a lightly loaded system but inappropriate for a congested system.

Deadlock prevention is achieved by: requesting all locks at once, or requesting locks in a specified order, or never waiting for a lock, or . . . In general deadlock prevention is a bad deal because one rarely knows what locks are needed in advance (consider looking something up in an index,) and consequently, one locks too much in advance.

Although some situations allow deadlock prevention, general systems tend to require deadlock detection. IMS, for example, started with a deadlock prevention scheme (intent scheduling) but was forced to introduce a deadlock detection scheme to increase concurrency (Program Isolation).

Deadlock detection and resolution is no big deal in a data management system environment. The system already has lots of facilities for transaction backup so that it can deal with other sorts of errors. Deadlock simply becomes another (hopefully infrequent) source of backup. As will be seen, the algorithms for detecting and resolving deadlock are not complicated or time consuming.

The deadlock detection-resolution scenario is:

- Detect a deadlock.
- Pick a victim (a lock to preempt from a process.)
- Back out a victim that will release lock.
- Grant a waiter.
- (optionally) Restart victim.

Lock manager is only responsible for deadlock detection and victim selection, Recovery management implements transaction backup and controls restart logic.

HOW TO DETECT DEADLOCK

There are many heuristic ways of detecting deadlock (e. g. linearly order resources or processes and declare deadlock if ordering is violated by a wait request.)

Here we restrict ourselves to algorithmic solutions. The detection of deadlock may be cast in graph-theoretic terms.

We introduce the notion of the wait-for graph:

- The nodes of the graph are transactions and locks.

- The edges of the graph are directed and are constructed as follows:
- If lock L is granted to transaction T then draw an edge from L to T.
- If transaction T is waiting for transaction L then draw an edge from T to L.

At any instant, there is a deadlock if and only if the wait-for graph has a cycle. Hence deadlock detection becomes an issue of building the wait-for graph and searching it for cycles.

Often this "transaction waits for lock waits for transaction" graph can be reduced to a smaller "transaction waits for transaction" graph. The larger graph need be maintained only if the identities of the locks in the cycle are relevant. I know of no case where this is required.

WHEN TO LOOK FOR DEADLOCK

One could opt to look for deadlock:

- Whenever anyone waits.
- Periodically.
- Never.

One could look for deadlock continuously. Releasing a lock or being granted a lock never creates a deadlock. So one should never look for deadlock more frequently than when a wait occurs.

The cost of looking for deadlock every time anyone waits is:

- Continual maintenance of the wait-for graph.
- Almost certain failure since deadlock is (should be) rare (i.e. wasted instructions).

WHAT TO DO WHEN DEADLOCK IS DETECTED

All transactions in a deadlock are waiting. The only way to get things going again is to grant some waiter. But, this can only be achieved after a lock is preempted from some holder. Since the victim is waiting, he will get the 'deadlock' response from lock manager rather than the 'granted' response. In breaking the deadlock some set of victims will be preempted. We want to minimize the amount of work lost by these preemptions. Therefore, deadlock resolution wants to pick a minimum cost set of victims to break deadlocks. Transaction management must associate a cost with each transaction. In the absence of policy decisions: the cost of a victim is the cost of undoing his work and then redoing it. The length of the transaction log is a crude estimate of this cost. At any rate, transaction management must provide lock management with an estimate of the cost of each transaction.

Lock manager may implement either of the following two protocols:

- For each cycle, choose the minimum cost victim in that cycle.
- Choose the minimum cost cut-set of the deadlock graph.

The difference between these two options is best visualized by the picture:

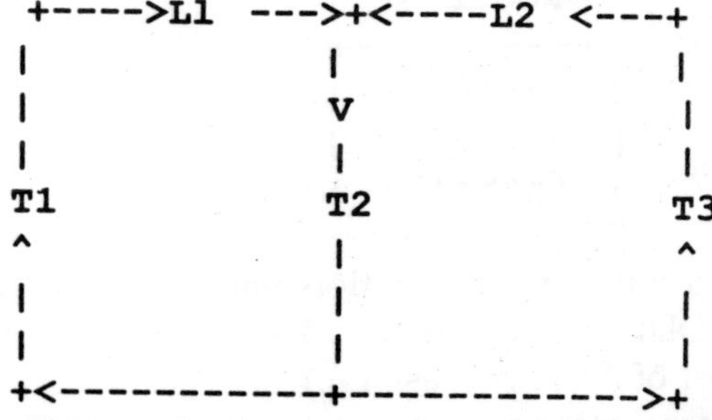

If T1 and T3 have a cost of 2 and T2 has a cost of 3 then a cycle-at-a-time algorithm will choose T1 and T3 as victims; whereas, a minimal cut set algorithm will choose T2 as a victim.

The cost of finding a minimal cut set is considerably greater than the cycle-at-a-time scheme. If there are N common cycles, the cycle-at-a-tine scheme is at most N times worse than the minimal cut set scheme. So it seems that the cycle-at-a-time scheme is better.

LOCK MANAGEMENT IN A DISTRIBUTED SYSTEM

To repeat the discussion in the section OIL distributed transaction management, if a transaction wants to do work at a new node, some process of the transaction must request that the node construct a cohort and that the cohort go into session with the requesting process. The picture below shows this.

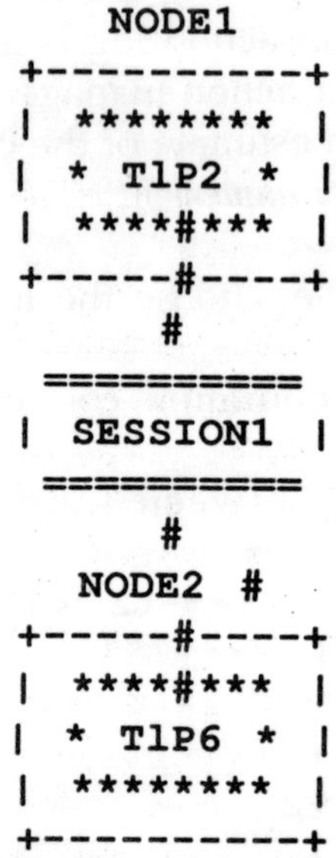

A cohort carries both the transaction name T1 and the process name (in NODE1 the cohort of T1 is process P2 and in NODE2 the cohort of T1 is process P6.)

The two processes can nor converse and carry out the work of the transaction. If one process aborts, they should both abort, and if one process commits they should both commit.

The lock manager of each node can keep its lock tables in any form it desires. Further, deadlock detectors running in each node may use any technique they like to detect deadlocks among transactions that run exclusively in that node. We call such deadlocks local deadlocks. However, just because there are no cycles in the local wait-for graph, does not mean that there are no cycles. Gluing acyclic local graphs together might produce a graph with cycles. So, the deadlock detectors of each node will have to agree on a common protocol in order to handle deadlocks involving distributed transactions. We call such deadlocks global deadlocks.

FINDING GLOBAL DEADLOCKS

The finding of local deadlocks has already been described. To find global deadlocks, a distinguish task, called the global deadlock detector is started in some distinguished node. This task is in session with all local deadlock detectors and coordinates the activities of the local deadlock detectors. This global deadlock detector can run in any node, but probably should be located to minimize its communication distance to the lock managers.

Each local deadlock Detector needs to find all potential global deadlock paths in his node. In the previous section it was shown that a global deadlock cycle has the form:

lockwait ->... -> sessionwait ->lockwait ->...->
sessionwait ->

So each local deadlock detector periodically
enumerates all

session -> lockwait ->...-> sessionwait

paths in his node by working backwards from processes that are in sessionwait (as opposed to console wait, disk wait, processor wait,...) Starting at such a process it sees if some local process is lock waiting for this process. If so the deadlock detector searches backwards looking for some process which has a session in progress.

When such a path is found, the following information is sent to the global deadlock detector:

- Sessions and transactions at endpoints of the path and their local preemption costs.
- The minimum cost transaction in the path and his local pre-emption cost.

(It may make sense to batch this information to the global detector.)

Periodically, the global deadlock detector:

- Collects these messages,
- Glues all these paths together by matching up sessions, and
- Enumerates cycles and selects victims just as in the local deadlock detector case.

One tricky point is that the cost of a distributed

transaction is the sum of the costs of its cohorts. The global deadlock detector approximates this cost by summing the costs of the cohorts of the transaction known to it (not all cohorts of a deadlocked transaction will be in known to the global deadlock detector.)

When a victim is selected, the lock manager of the node the victim is waiting in is informed of the deadlock. The local lock manager in turn informs the victim with a deadlock return. The use of periodic deadlock detection (as opposed to detection every time anyone waits)is even more important for a distributed system than for a centralized system, The cost of detection is much higher in a distributed system. This will alter the intersection of the cost of detection and cost of detecting late curves.

If the network is really large the deadlock detector can be staged. That is, we can look for deadlock among four nodes, then among sixteen nodes, and so on. If one node crashes, then its partition of the system is unavailable.

In this case, its cohorts in other nodes can wait for it to recover or they can abort. If the down node happens to house the global lock manager then no global deadlocks will be detected until the node recovers. If this is uncool, then the lock managers can nominate a new global lock manager whenever the current one crashes. The new manager can run in any node that can be in session with all other nodes. The new global lock manager collects the local graphs and goes about gluing them together, finding cycles, and picking victims.

RELATIONSHIP A OPERATING SYSTEM LOCK MANAGER

Most operating systems provide a lock manager to regulate access to files and other system resources. This lock manager usually supports a limited set of lock names, the modes: share, exclusive and beware, and has some form of deadlock detection. These lock managers are usually net prepared for the demands of a data management system (fast calls, lots of locks, many modes, lock classes,.,.)The basic lock manager could be extended and refined and in time that is what will happen. There is a big problem about having two lock managers in the same host. Each may think it has no deadlock but if their graphs are glued together a "global" deadlock exists. This makes it very difficult to build on top of the basic lock manager.

THE CONVOY PHENOMENON: PREEMPTIVE SCHEDULING IS BAD

Lock manager has strong interactions with the scheduler. Suppose that there are certain high traffic shared system resources. Operating on these resources consists of locking them, altering them and then unlocking them (the buffer pool and log are examples of this.) These operations are designed to be very fast so that the resource is almost always free. In particular the resource is never held during an I/O operation, For example, the buffer manager latch is acquired every 1000 instructions and is held for about 50 instructions.

If the system has no preemptive scheduling then on a uni-processor, then when a process begins the resource is free and when he completes the resource is free (because he does not hold it when he does I/O or yields the processor.) On a multi-processor, if the resource is busy, the process can sit in a busy wait until the resource is free because the resource is known to be held by others for only a short time.

If the basic system has a preemptive scheduler, and if that scheduler preempts a process holding a critical resource (e. g. the log latch) then terrible things happen: All other processes waiting for the latch will dispatched before this process is dispatched, and because the resource is high traffic each of these processes requests and waits for the resource. Ultimately the holder of the resource is re-dispatched and he almost immediately grants the latch to the next waiter.

But because it is high traffic, the process almost immediately rerequests the latch (i.e. about 1000 instructions later.) Fair scheduling requires that he wait, so he goes on the end of the queue waiting for those ahead of him. This queue of waiters is called a convoy. It is a stable phenomenon:

once a convoy is established it persists for a very long time. We (System R) have found several solutions to this problem. The obvious solution is to eliminate such resources. That is a good idea, and can be achieved to some degree by refining the granularity of the lockable unit (e-g, twenty buffer manager latches rather than just one.) However, if a convoy ever forms on any of these latches it will be stable so that is not a solution. I leave it as an exercise for the reader to find a better solution to the problem.

RECOVERY MANAGEMENT

MODEL OF ERRORS

In order to design a recovery system, it is important to have a clear notion of what kinds of errors can be expected and what their probabilities are. The model of errors below is inspired by the presentation by Lampson and Sturgis in "Crash Recovery in a Distributed Data Storage System", which may someday appear in the CACM.

MODEL OF STORAGE ERRORS

Storage comes in three flavors with independent failure modes and increasing reliability:

- Volatile storage: paging space and main memory,
- On-Line Non-volatile Storage: disks, usually survive crashes. Is more reliable than volatile storage.
- Off-Line Non-volatile Storage: Tape archive. Even more reliable than disks.

To repeat, we assume that these three kinds of storage have independent failure modes. The storage is blocked into fixed length units called pages that are the unit of allocation and transfer.

Any page transfer can have one of three outcomes:

1. Success (target gets new value)
2. Partial failure (target is a ness)
3. Total failure (target is unchanged)

Any page may spontaneously fail. That is a spec of dust may settle on it or a black hole may pass through it so that it no longer retains its original information, One can always detect whether a transfer failed or a page spontaneously failed by reading the target page at a later time. (This can be made more and more certain by adding redundancy to the page.) Lastly, The probability that N "independent" archive pages fail is negligible. Here we choose N=2, (This can be made more and more certain by choosing larger and larger N.)

MODEL OF DATA COMMUNICATIONS ERRORS

Communication traffic is broken into units called messages via sessions.

The transmission of a message has one of three possible outcomes:

1. Successfully received.
2. Incorrectly received.
3. Not received.

The receiver of the message can detect whether he has received a particular message and whether it gas correctly received.

RECOVERY MANAGEMENT

A transaction is begun explicitly when a process is allocated or when an existing process issues BEGIN _TRANSACTION. When a transaction is initiated, recovery manager is invoked to allocate the recovery structure necessary to recover the transaction. This process places a capability for the COMMIT, SAVE, and BACKUP calls of recovery manager in the transaction's capability list.

Thereafter, all actions by the transaction on recoverable data are recorded in the recovery log, using log manager. In general, each action performing an update operation should write an undo-log record and a redo-log record in the transaction's log. The undo log record gives the old value of the object and the redo log record gives the new value.

At a transaction save point, recovery manager records the save point identifier, and enough information so that each component of the system could be backed up to this point. In the event of a minor error, the transaction may be undone to a save point in which case the application (on its next or pending call) is given feedback indicating that the data base system has amnesia about all recoverable actions since that save point. If the transaction is completely backed-up (aborted), it may or may not be restarted depending on the attributes of the transaction and of its initiating message.

If the transaction completes successfully (commits), then (logically) it is always redone in case of a crash. On the other hand, if it is in-progress at the time of the local or system failure, then the transaction is logically undone (aborted).

Recovery manager must also respond to the following kinds of failures:

- *Action failure*: A particular call cannot complete due to a foreseen condition. In general the action undoes itself (cleans up its component)and then returns to the caller. Examples of this are bad parameters, resource limits, and data not found.
- *Transaction failure*: A particular transaction cannot proceed and so is aborted. The transaction may be reinitiated in some cases. Examples of such errors are deadlock, timeout, protection violation, and transaction-local system errors.
- *System failure*: A serious error is detected below the action interface. The system is stopped and restarted. Errors in critical tables, wild branches by trusted processes, operating system failures and hardware failures are sources of system failure. Most nonvolatile storage is presumed to survive a system failure.
- *Media failure*: A non-recoverable error is detected on some usually reliable (nonvolatile) storage device. The recovery of recoverable data from a media failure is the responsibility of the component that implements it. If the device contained recoverable data the manager must reconstruct the data from an archive copy using the log and then place the result on an alternate device. Media failures do not generally force system failure. Parity error, head

crash, dust on magnetic media, and lost tapes are typical media failures. Software errors that make the media unreadable are also regarded as media errors, as are catastrophes such as fire, flood, insurrection, and operator error.

The system periodically makes copies of each recoverable object and keeps these copies in a safe place (archive). In case the object suffers a media error, all transactions with locks outstanding against the object are aborted. A special transaction (a utility) acquires the object in exclusive mode. (This takes the object "off-line".)

This transaction merges an accumulation of changes to the object since the object copy was made and a recent archive version of the object to produce the most recent committed version. This accumulation of changes may take two forms: it may be the REDO-log portion of the system log, or it may be a change accumulation log that was constructed from the REDO-log portion of the system log when the system log is compressed. After media recovery, the data is unlocked and made public again.

The process of making an archive copy of an object has many varieties. Certain objects, notably IMS queue space, are recovered from scratch using an infinite redo log. Other objects, notably databases, get copied to some external media that can be used to restore the object to a consistent state if a failure occurs. (The resource may or may not be off-line while the cozy is being made.) Recovery manager also periodically performs system checkpoint by recording critical parts of the system state in a safe spot in nonvolatile storage (sometimes called the warm start file.)

Recovery manager coordinates the process of system restart system shutdown.

In performing system restart, it chooses among:

- Warm start: system shut down in controlled manner. Recovery need only locate last checkpoint record and rebuild its control structures.
- Emergency restart: system failed in uncontrolled manner. Non-volatile storage contains recent state

consistent with the log. However, some transactions were in progress at time of failure and must be redone or undone to obtain most recent consistent state.

- Cold start: the system is being brought up with amnesia about prior incarnations. The log is not examined to determine previous state.

RECOVERY PROTOCOLS

All participants in a transaction, including all components understand and obey the following protocols when operating on recoverable objects:

- Consistency lock protocol.
- Write-Ahead-Log protocol (WAL).
- Two-phase commit protocol.

The consistency lock protocol was discussed in the section on lock management. The remaining protocols are discussed below. Perhaps the simplest and easiest to implement recovery technique is based on the old-master new-master dichotomy common to most batch data processing systems: If the run fails, one goes back to the old-master and tries again. Unhappily, this technique does not seem to generalize to concurrent transactions. If several transactions concurrently access an object, then making a new-master object or returning to the old master may be inappropriate because it commits or backs up all updates to the object by all transactions.

It is desirable to be able to commit or undo updates on a per-transaction basis. Given an action consistent state and a collection of in-progress transactions (i.e., commit not yet executed) one wants to be able to selectively undo a subset of the transactions without affecting the others. Such a facility is called in-progress transaction backup.

A second shortcoming of versions is that in the event of a media error, one must reconstruct the most recent consistent state. For example, if a page or collection of pages is lost from non-volatile storage, then they must be reconstructed from some redundant information. Doubly-recording the versions on independent devices is quite expensive for large objects.

However, this is the technique used for some small objects such as the warm start file.

Lastly, writing a new version of a large database often consumes large amounts of storage and bandwidth. Having abandoned the notion of versions, we adopt the approach of updating in place, and of keeping an incremental log of changes to the system state. (Logs are sometimes called audit trails or journals.)

Each action that modifies a recoverable object writes a log record giving the old and new value of the updated object. Read operations need generate no log records, but update operations must record enough information in the log so that, given the record at a later time, the operation can be completely undone or redone. These records will be aggregated by transaction, and collected in a common system log that resides in nonvolatile storage. The system log is duplexed and has independent failure modes. In what follows we assume that the log never fails. By duplexing, triplexing, ..., one can make this assumption less false.

Every recoverable operation must have:

- A DO entry that does the action and also records a log record sufficient to undo and to redo the operation,
- An UNDO entry that undoes the action given the log record written by the DO action,
- A REDO entry that redoes the action given the log record written by the DO action, and
- Optionally, a DISPLAY entry that translates the log into a human-readable format.

To give an example of an action and the log record it must write, consider the database record update operator.

This action must record in the iog the:

- Record name
- The old record value (used for UNDO)
- The new record value. (used for REDO)

The log subsystem augments this with the additional fields:

- Transaction identifier
- Action identifier

- Length of log record
- Pointer to previous log record of this transaction

The log itself is recorded on a dedicated media (disk, tape,...). Once a log record is recorded, it cannot be updated. However, the log component provides a facility to open read cursors on the log that will traverse the system log or will traverse the log of a particular transaction in either direction.

The UNDO operation must face a rather difficult problem at restart: The undo operation may be performed more than once if restart itself is redone several times (i.e. if the system fails during restart.) Also one may be called upon to undo operations that were never reflected in nonvolatile storage (i.e. log write occurred but object write did not.) Similar problems exist for REDO. One may have to REDO an already done action if the updated object was recorded in non-volatile storage before the crash or if restart is restarted. The write-ahead-log-protocol and high-water-marks solve these problems.

Bibliography

Alexander, K.: *Systems Engineering: Principles and Practice*, London: Free Press, 1992.

Anderson, T.: *Computing Systems Reliability*, New York: Addison-Wesley Press, 2003.

Anna, L.: *Linguistics: A Guide to the Reference Literature*, UK : Addison-Wesley Press, 1995.

Dhamdhere, D. M.: *Operating Systems: A Concept-based Approach*, New York: Addison Wesley Press, 2003.

Gordon, B.: *The Blackwell Encyclopedic Dictionary of Management Information*, New York: John Wiley & Sons Publication, 2001.

Greg, G.: *Operating System Concepts*, London: Prentice Hall, 1996.

Greg, L.: *The Complete Free BSD: Documentation from the Source*, London: Free Press, 1992.

James, L.: *Operating System Concepts*, Berkeley, CA: Apress LP, 2001.

John, E.: *Design and Operating Guide for Aquaculture Seawater Systems*, New York : Prentice Hall PTR, 2002.

Lorna, M.: *Business Information*, PA: Idea Group Publishing 2005.

Marthe, A.: *Protection Errors in Operating Systems: A Selected Annotated*, MA: Addison-Wesley, 1999.

Michael, H.: *Genealogy on CD-ROM*, London: Free Press, 1992.

Michael, J.: *Smartphone Operating System Concepts with Symbian OS: A Tutorial Guide*, Berkeley, CA: Apress LP, 2002.

Morton, A.: *Direct Digital Control of Building Systems: Theory and Practice*, New York: Van Nostrand Reinhold, 1988.

Peter, B.: *Operating System*, Birmingham, UK: Wrox Press, 2002.

Qusay, H.: An Introduction to Database Systems, US: Yourdon Press, 2000.

Randell, M.: *Middleware for Communications*, New York: McGraw-Hill Osborne Media, 2005.

Randy, C.: *Distributed Operating Systems and Algorithms*, New York: John Wiley & Sons Publication, 2001.

Richard, C.: *A Practitioner's Handbook for Real-time Analysis: Guide*, London: Academic Press, 2005.

Silberschatz, A.: *Advanced Concepts in Operating Systems*, London: Prentice-Hall, 2006.

Tarkoma, S.: *Mobile Middleware: Architecture, Patterns and Practice*, New York: Application Development Advisor Company, 2001.

William, N.: *Structured Concurrent Programming with Operating Systems Applications*, New York: O'Reilly Media, 2003.

Index

I

M

P

R

S

T

V